"Kristin Kellen exemplifies the best of a biblically centered, clinically informed model in this volume. Those from a robust theological background will learn much to enhance their counseling skill, and those from a skilled clinical background will learn much to grow their theological depth. The end result? Read this volume, and no matter where you're starting from, you'll emerge better equipped to care for God's people."

—**Nate Brooks**, assistant professor of Christian counseling,
Reformed Theological Seminary–Charlotte

"Counseling takes place in many settings and between many different combinations of people. Dr. Kellen helps us think through counseling from one woman to another in a ministry context. There is great power in these caring relationships within a redemptive community. Dr. Kellen helps us ensure that this power is used for healing. I am grateful for and commend her work. I hope it will be read not only by women who want to be equipped to counsel, but also by pastors who want to be more effective shepherds for their entire congregation."

—**Brad Hambrick**, pastor of counseling,
The Summit Church, Durham, NC

"Time and time again I have been asked by women's ministry leaders if there is a resource to help them minister to women in crisis. I'm thankful I can now recommend this book. Not only does Kristin Kellen provide a biblical framework for counseling, but she has also given the reader practical helps for specific issues common to women. This is a must-have resource for the library of any leader who wants to be better equipped for meeting with women who are wrestling with difficult situations."

—**Kelly D. King**, women's ministry specialist,
Lifeway Christian Resources

"Kristin Kellen starts with a theology of womanhood as the basis of understanding counseling topics related to women. I appreciate Kristin's desire to help women think biblically about their problems and circumstances. Displaying years of counseling experience, Kristin shows an awareness of sensitive issues for women that strengthens the practical suggestions at the end of each chapter."

—**Lilly Park**, associate professor of biblical counseling,
Southwestern Baptist Theological Seminary

"Providing valuable foundational principles, Counseling Women is accessible, helpful, and profoundly practical. Kristin gives us a researched overview of each counseling issue. Yet, she wisely reminds us to seek to know each person and [her] unique struggles. A particular strength is the theological perspectives Kristin offers for each issue, helping orient counselors to understand the problems biblically while assisting them in setting a trajectory for counseling."

—**Darby A Strickland**, faculty and counselor,
Christian Counseling and Educational Foundation

COUNSELING WOMEN

COUNSELING WOMEN

Biblical Wisdom for Life's Battles

KRISTIN L. KELLEN

B&H
ACADEMIC
NASHVILLE, TENNESSEE

To my mom, my first counselor and teacher

CONTENTS

Acknowledgments

I am grateful to my husband and family for their patience during the writing of this book. As I write these acknowledgments, my three-week-old baby girl is snuggled up beside me. My husband and children have been gracious in this endeavor. I am also grateful for each woman I have counseled over the last decade or more. I have learned more from them than I ever would in a classroom, and many of the conversations we had were playing in my mind as I wrote. I am indebted to them.

I am also grateful to my colleagues for their continual support of my teaching and writing. I could not ask for a better institution to work for—Southeastern Baptist Theological Seminary is top-notch, with scholars that I dream of being like one day. Beyond Southeastern, I am thankful for my larger pool of colleagues within biblical counseling, particularly men like Robert Jones and Rob Green, with whom I just finished another biblical-counseling text manuscript. Conversations with them have made me a better counselor and teacher. I am grateful for those who provided feedback on this manuscript, especially Lauren Lanier. Last, I am thankful for the team at B&H Academic, who edit, correct, and challenge me to think and write more clearly. Each of these groups has sharpened me in ways I could not do on my own.

Preface

As a professor of biblical counseling at a large Southern Baptist seminary, and one of very few female counseling professors among our sister seminaries, I am often asked to speak to the unique needs of women in counseling. The task is both exciting and gives some pause. I am excited because people recognize there are unique needs, but it gives me pause because I am a firm believer that women and men are more alike than they are different. We are both image bearers of God, sinners in need of grace, and called to follow Christ and his Word. And yet, we as women have unique roles and functions, ones that complement our brothers so together we can more beautifully image God.

The aim of this text, then, is threefold: first, it presents a counseling approach that considers women as the unique beings they are. The counseling issues addressed are nuanced specifically for women and the counselor is assumed to be a woman as well. And yet, the principles included are not exclusive; they are certainly useful for either men counseling women or for counseling men. The aim is to be widely applicable while still considering how women are unique in how God made them.

Second, the aim of this text is to provide a basic understanding of counseling issues that are common for women. No text can be exhaustive, so the aim of this book is to help readers get a foundational understanding of both counseling proper and a handful of common issues. It provides a list of additional resources for the reader to explore for more information or further study on any topic of interest.

Finally, it is the aim of this text to provide a healthy balance between biblical counseling (as it has traditionally been done) and clinical practice. The reality is that many in clinical settings simply cannot have overt spiritual conversations as they might in ministry settings. The goal here is to provide both sides of the equation, a clinical understanding that may be necessary in those sorts of settings, but also clear biblical teaching from a biblical-counseling perspective to establish a solid framework for Christians who find themselves in secular clinical settings.

This book is arranged in two main parts. The first section, chapters 1 through 6, provides foundational teaching for counseling from a biblical perspective. Chapter 1 explores who we are as humans and, more specifically, who women are as we walk through Genesis 1–2. Chapter 2 focuses on the reality of sin, exploring Genesis 3. Chapter 3 discusses a woman's context, those voices that speak to her life and influence the decisions she makes. Chapter 4 establishes the necessity of God's Word speaking in the lives of our counselees and how the Bible provides a framework for counseling. Chapter 5 proposes a simple methodology of counseling, and chapter 6 concludes this section with an exploration of a woman's life stages. The second section of the book systematically walks through various topics that tend to present in a woman's life. This section cannot cover everything, but it provides a foundation for the reader to get started.

Writing this book has been a journey, and in many ways I stand on the shoulders of other women and men who have written about these same life struggles. As one who teaches courses on counseling women, I am very much aware of resources that are specific to this topic. Many other women have written solid texts that I have used in my own education and as I've written this book. I hope this book provides up-to-date guidance for counseling women and balances the biblical teaching well with formal counseling practice.

It is my hope that each reader walks away from this text more prepared to serve our sisters and encourage them in ways that honor the Lord. But it is also my hope that each reader worships the Lord for his provision through trials and that each reader is challenged to apply God's Word to their own life when they encounter these struggles. God's Word is rich with wisdom, we need only apply it rightly.

SECTION ONE

✤∽∽✤

A Framework for Understanding Women

1

Woman as God Made Her: A Theology of Womanhood

Before we can hope to counsel a woman, we must understand her well. A significant part of understanding women is knowing who God created her to be: her uniqueness as an image bearer of a perfect and holy God. We must know both universals (what is true about all women) and specifics (her unique situation). And we must have a proper point of reference as we seek to understand her as sinner, sufferer, and saint.

This chapter walks through Genesis 1 and 2, drawing out key components of who each woman was created to be. Much will be drawn from universal truths about both men and women. Men and women have a lot in common. But women are also unique: they have different roles and different tendencies. We will explore these areas of overlap and distinction in our discussion below, weaving through some connections to counseling practice.

GENESIS 1:26–31; 2:7, 20, 23–25

Then God said, "Let us make man in our image,[1] according to our likeness. They will rule the fish of the sea, the birds of the sky, the livestock, the whole earth, and the creatures that crawl on the earth." So God created man in his own image; he created him in the image of God; he created them male and female. God blessed them, and God said to them, "Be fruitful, multiply, fill the earth, and subdue it. Rule the fish of the sea, the birds of the sky, and every creature that crawls on the earth." God also said, "Look, I have given you every seed-bearing plant on the surface of the entire earth and every tree whose fruit contains seed. This will be food for you, for all the wildlife of the earth, for every bird of the sky, and for every creature that crawls on the earth—everything having the breath of life in it—I have given every green plant for food." And it was so. God saw all that he had made, and it was very good indeed. Evening came and then morning: the sixth day. . . . Then the LORD God formed the man out of the dust from the ground and breathed the breath of life into his nostrils, and the man became a living being. . . . The man gave names to all the livestock, to the birds of the sky, and to every wild animal; but for the man no helper was found corresponding to him. . . . [After the creation of Eve] And the man said: This one, at last, is bone of my bone and flesh of my flesh; this one will be called "woman," for she was taken from man. This is why a man leaves his father and mother and bonds with his wife, and they become one flesh. Both the man and his wife were naked, yet felt no shame.

Woman as God Made Her

Women as Created Beings (Gen 1:26)

After God created the earth and all the other creatures, on the sixth day he created man and woman. This is a point we must not miss: we are created beings. We did not create ourselves; it was our Creator God who intentionally set out to make us. From this reality come two important truths.

First, the creation of man and woman was planned. It was intentional. God was not responding to some lack in his creation, rather he determined it would be good that there would be those like him (more to come below). We aren't some afterthought to God, but planned and purposed.

Second, as created beings we are dependent on God. He defines our purpose, roles, and functions and he retains authority as our Creator over each of these things. All of Scripture points to humans' need of God for everything: food, work, propagation of the species, deliverance from sin and death, and, ultimately, re-creation back into what God had originally established. Man, and all of creation, is fully dependent on God for continued life (1 Tim 6:13).

This reality was true in the garden even before the fall; it is not the result of sin. God's first five days of creation work demonstrate what humans needed to survive, all of which came from God. Even in the garden, God provided food, companionship, opportunities to exercise dominion, and the capacity to bear children and continue the growth of the community.

Psalm 139 is a helpful commentary that teaches an important lesson related to humans as created beings: we are intimately connected to and known by God. By the very act of being created by him, we are also *known* by him. He knit us together in our mother's womb (Ps 139:13) and he knew us as we were being formed in secret (v. 15). He knows everything about us precisely because he created us.

As counselors, we see it is imperative that we recognize counseling cannot be done independently of the Creator. We must acknowledge human persons as dependent beings, rather than independent and self-directive, lest we risk believing we alone are able to discern the need for change and capable within ourselves to move toward that change. In recognizing our Creator, we establish that we are fully reliant on him to determine our need for change and for the strength to carry it out. We must recognize that we are intimately known by and connected to our Maker.

Women as Having Dominion (Gen 1:26, 28)

In both Gen 1:26 and 28, God says that people are to "rule" over his creation. The first example comes soon after, when Adam has the task of naming the animals. But it is essential to note that this is a *delegated* dominion; human beings do not have absolute rule over God's creation. Instead, we are stewards over what God has placed under us, with great responsibilities.

Further, men and women are to exercise care over God's creation. As the writer of Genesis notes in 2:15, we are to "work it and watch over it." All creation, from the tiniest ant to the most precious child, should matter to us. We are to protect and cultivate God's creation to help it function as it was created to function, rather than squander it or misuse it. It should flourish like it did for Adam and Eve.

In having dominion, we ought to treat creation as God would; we are to act as his representatives on earth. When we exercise power over creation, we are to reflect God's character. In Luke 12, we see a picture of how God cares for his creation: he feeds the birds of the air and clothes the grass, though they are temporal and soon to pass. He cares for even the smallest of his creation, the parts that we might dismiss without concern. As his representatives, we are to care for his creation as he does, working toward its flourishing. This comes with great reward but also great responsibility.

Women as Image Bearers (Gen 1:26–27)

Three times in these two verses, the Bible says God created mankind "in his image." There are myriad interpretations of what "image of God" means; one basic definition indicates that man and woman were intentionally created to be like God and represent him in creation. Genesis 1–3 indicates several ways Adam and Eve bore God's image:

> ❧ They were delegated to have dominion over God's creation (1:26), beginning with Adam naming the animals (2:19).

- ⚜ They were told to be fruitful and multiply (1:28; 4:1–2), just as God increased his family and community by creating a man and a woman.
- ⚜ They had a spirit (2:7).
- ⚜ They had choices to make (2:15–17; 3:6).
- ⚜ They were created in relationship with God and with one another (2:18–23; 3:8).
- ⚜ They had no shame because they were holy and sinless before the fall (2:25).

Only humans bear God's image. We are set apart from the rest of God's creation, intentionally made by God for a specific purpose. This means, first, that we are inescapably connected to God; any conversation about a person is insufficient if it fails to understand them in relation to their Maker. Therefore, the primary concern we should have about our counselee is the vitality of her relationship with God. Second, since each person bears the image of the Most High God, each person must be treated with dignity, honor, and respect. Regardless of race, age, gender, status, or capacity, we should highly value each person and speak to each person congruent with that value (Jas 3:9). Third, a violation against an image bearer is a violation against the Creator (Gen 9:6). As counselors, we will hear about tremendous violations against people; we will rightly grieve those offenses, in part because they are violations against the One who created the image bearers.

Women as Female (Gen 1:27)

This text in Genesis notes a few things that distinguish between male and female. First, God intended to create the distinction and did so out of his perfect wisdom. Gen 1:27 specifically says that God made them "male and female." Our observation of society affirms this reality. God established the differences in the genders. It was purposeful. As Creator, God exercised his authority over the organization of his creation to create a distinction between the image bearers he created.

The text notes that women were created to be both like men and, at the same time, different from them. Genesis 2:20 says that "no helper was found *corresponding to* him" (emphasis added). Unlike the animals, Adam was alone; there were no others like him. God then deemed (it was not Adam's assertion) it was "not good for the man to be alone" (Gen 2:18). Just as God existed in relationship with himself as the Trinity, so should man exist with others like him. So, God created someone else to "correspond" to Adam, and though they were quite similar, the reality that God created women as distinct from men should not be overlooked. Men and women have many similar purposes, like loving God and imaging him to his creation. They also have distinct roles and functions; for example, women as helpers, which we explore later in this chapter. These distinctions should be celebrated.

In our current western society, several distortions of the male-female distinction have taken place. While men and women were created as equal before God (Gal 3:28; 1 Cor 12:13), their roles are distinct.[2] There is no need for competition between male and female; there should be cooperation between them. And we must uphold the God-given distinctions, even down to biological distinctions, because it was the authoritative, wise God who established them.

Women as Blessed (Gen 1:28)

Right before God gave man and woman their first command, Gen 1:28 simply says, "God blessed them." What does that mean? The idea of "blessing" is repeated several times in Genesis alone (for instance, to Noah and to Abraham). We often associate blessing with the idea of prosperity; this is somewhat correct, but incomplete.

We find clues in the Genesis text to what being blessed by God means; immediately following the statement that he blessed them, God commands: "Be fruitful, multiply, fill the earth, and subdue it." God's blessing is that man and woman can live out their God-given purposes and flourish within God's creation. First, he commands them to be fruitful; this isn't simply biological reproduction, it is a command to mature, to bear fruit. They are to grow as human beings in relation to God, one another, and his creation, producing fruit in each of those arenas. Second, he commands them to "multiply, fill the earth." While a simple understanding of this command is that it refers to a biological process (i.e., have children), most scholars would contend there is a spiritual meaning as well. In his Great Commission (Matt 28:19–20), Jesus instructed his disciples to multiply spiritually, bringing others into fruitfulness with God. Last, God commands man and woman to subdue the earth, to have dominion over it.

By doing all these things, humans will be blessed with the fullness of what they need in the presence of God and in his creation. Women participate in this blessing, even after the fall. As we fulfill God's purposes for our lives—to be fruitful, multiply, and subdue the earth—we flourish and are blessed.

Women as Multipliers (Gen 1:28)

There is often confusion or misunderstanding about the idea of women as multipliers. There is a biological reality that we must multiply to sustain humanity, but the concept of multiplication means much more than that. Women (alongside men), biologically, bear children and physically can multiply. A woman pours a great deal into the multiplication of humanity: it is quite a task to bear and raise children.

And yet, we see an important shift happen in Scripture from the Old to New Testaments that expounds on this idea of multiplication. In the Old Testament, the concept of "family" was primarily biological or cultural (i.e., belonging to Israel and therefore to God). But in the New Testament, terms like "brother," "sister," "father," and "mother" come to primarily represent one's spiritual family. After Christ, the focus becomes the family of God rather than the family of man. This is not to say the biological family is no longer important—there are numerous commands to care for one's own family—but the picture of the early church, particularly in Acts and Paul's teachings, gives us a different idea of multiplication. Pair this with the command in Matt 28:19 to "go and make disciples," and our idea of multiplication is expanded.

While the responsibility to multiply certainly falls on both male and female, in practice this looks a little different for women. For instance, women and men have different roles as mother and father. But roles look different within the church as well. Women can certainly minister to and share the gospel with men, but there are clear instructions that women are at least to minister to other women (Titus 2:3–5). Their connection by gender, which includes their roles and common struggles, is significant.

Women as (Created) Very Good (Gen 1:31)

In Gen 1:31, we're told "God saw all that he had made [including woman], and it was very good indeed." God's creation, in that moment, was perfect and complete. Everything was as it should be; everything, including woman, was at peace with God and living in a way that aligned with his purposes. There was no sin.

This verse stands in slight contrast to the parallel verses before it (vv. 4, 12, 21, and 25), in which God declared what he had created "good." Here, it is described as "very good indeed." The creation of man and woman went above and beyond the rest of his creation, because man and woman bore his image. They were reflective of their Creator in a unique way.

Creation was good because the Creator was good. God created, perfectly, what he desired to create to reflect his own goodness. And at the end of those six days, upon creating man and woman, everything was flawless. Like God, it was without error. Woman, with the rest of what God had made, was beautiful, functioned flawlessly, had purpose, and had potential. It was as it ought to be: very good.

Women as Both Physical and Nonphysical Beings (Gen 2:7)

Genesis 2 tells more about Adam and Eve and how they were created: "Then the Lord God formed the man out of the dust from the ground and breathed the breath of life into his nostrils, and the man became a living being"

(Gen 2:7). Here, God physically forms Adam's body from a physical sub-stance (the earth) and breaths life (spirit) into his formed body. The Hebrew term used here for breath, *ruach*, is the same word used for spirit in other places in Genesis (like Gen 1:2). In other words, once God formed Adam's body, he "spirited" life into him. Adam had life that was both body (physical) and soul/spirit (nonphysical), and Eve was made to be like Adam.

There is abundant biblical teaching to demonstrate this duality,[3] and the implications are significant. As women, and especially as counselors, we must acknowledge the dual nature of the women around us. Each woman has a physical body that impacts her reality: she is physically bound, perhaps with physical limitations, and her body can be used as an instrument of either righteousness or unrighteousness (Rom 6:12–13).

However, each woman we encounter also has a soul/spirit. This defines much of who she is, and Scripture tells us her soul/spirit drives what she does: her heart, her mind, her emotions, her thoughts, and her choices. These nonphysical aspects of who she is are vital for us as counselors to understand.

Further, we know the heart and body are intricately connected: each one affects the other. For instance, a physical ailment or developmental limitation has the potential to impact (and yet not cause) choices that are made. At the same time, internal struggles like anxiety may have physical manifestations like pain or an increased heart rate. Furthermore, our behaviors (physical) come out of what is in our hearts (nonphysical).[4]

The women we care for are holistic beings, and we must treat them as such. We must not neglect either their body or soul. In considering many of the struggles discussed later in this text, we'll see that care for women must be holistic in nature, addressing sin and the effects of sin on the whole person and not just one part of her.

Women as Helpers (Gen 2:18–23)

Genesis 2 gives us a picture of God's creation of woman after man, in particu-lar his reasons for doing so. Gen 2:20 tells us, "The man gave names to all the livestock, to the birds of the sky, and to every wild animal; but for the man no helper was found corresponding to him." Subsequently, God causes Adam to fall asleep, takes one of his ribs, and forms Eve to be that helper. She was created, in large part, to fill a role alongside her husband.

Eve was created to be like Adam in many ways (image bearer, relational, having dominion, etc.) but was created differently and fulfilled a different role. Adam was commanded to work the ground and watch over it (Gen 2:15). But in v. 18, it is God who says, "I will make a helper corresponding to him." This new creation, Eve, corresponded to Adam, in that she was like him, but God calls out that she is the helper. She is to come alongside him and assist him in fulfilling the command God gave him. This is a slight nuance, perhaps, but significant. Being a helper is an important part of who women were created to be, but not all of it. Further, becoming a helper teaches us something very important: we are to be both hearers and doers. We do not simply hear God's Word and do nothing; we were created to respond in obedience, to do what he has instructed us to do.

Women in the Context of Relationships (Gen 2:23–24)

As image bearers of God, we were also created to be in relationship. We were created in vertical relationship with God, but we also exist in horizontal relationship with others. A woman's relationships, both in marriage and with others, are meant to mirror the relationship that has always existed between the Father, Son, and Spirit. If she is a believing woman, her marriage relationship is also meant to mirror Christ and the church (Eph 5:30–32) and her family to be a picture of her own adoption into the family of God (Eph 1:3–6).

In his creation of man and woman, God saw that just as he existed in horizontal relationship with himself, so should people. Therefore, God created Eve to form community among his image bearers.

How does this relational aspect direct our counseling? First, we were created to express love within both our vertical and horizontal relationships. Primarily, we are to love God, but we are also to love our neighbor (Matt 22:35–40)—the two greatest commandments. Not only are we created to exist in relationship, as image bearers we should reflect our Maker within our relationships. Second, we should understand the importance of the relationships our counselees have with others. No person exists as an island; our counselees' relationships have real impact on them. We must seek to understand the relational context of the counselee, both with God and others (marriage, family, community, etc.). Third, we should pay attention to our relationship with our counselees inside the counseling room. How we relate to them and they relate to us are vital dynamics in the counseling process.

Women without Sin or Shame (Gen 2:25)

Genesis 2:25 tells us something of utmost importance about God's creation of men and women: "Both the man and his wife were naked, yet felt no shame." Adam and Eve were created perfect, complete and at peace with the rest of God's creation. Though the capacity for sin was present, and would soon be realized, sin had not yet entered the world. There was no embarrassment, no shame, and no fear. All was as it should be.

This perfection was short-lived. Adam and Eve did not remain sinless for long. When their disobedience led to the realization that they were naked, they ran from God and covered themselves (Gen 3:7–8). Their relationship with God was forever changed, to their detriment. (Chapter 2 will explore sin in more depth.)

And yet, we also know that one day restoration is coming. He will make all things new (Rev 21:5). We long for the day when that restoration comes. For today, we and our counselees live under the reality of sin and shame. We are faced with the real consequences of sin as we await redemption, hence our need for counsel from the Word of God, just as Adam and Eve needed and received counsel from God.

Women as Individuals

Genesis 1 and 2 give us a picture of God's creation of only one man and one woman. Another key aspect of womanhood must be considered: she is an individual. No two women are alike, just as Adam and Eve were not alike. Though all women share the characteristics listed above, beyond that there is great diversity. Every woman has her own family and relationships, her own cultural realities, and her own experiences in life. She is unique.

As counselors of women, we must recognize the uniqueness of each counselee. We must love, listen to, learn about, and labor alongside *her* (more to come in chapter 5), rather than leading based on her struggle alone. Just as Jesus sought to know and respond to each person he encountered, we must acknowledge the unique needs of each woman we see. She is unique and we must treat her as such.

As counselors, we counsel *people*: women uniquely made in the image of God, created to have dominion over God's creation, made of body and soul, and having multiple roles (helper, multiplier, and in the context of relationships). Each of these matters significantly for counseling and we must not consider a woman as *just* her problems or struggles. We must first consider her as who she was created to be. Only once we understand who she is, can we rightly understand her struggle and how God's Word speaks to those struggles.

2

What's Been Broken: The Impact of Sin

In chapter 1, we explored how women were created: unique individuals made in the image of God, perfect and without sin. In his own evaluation of his creation, God called what he had made "good," and called his creation of humankind "very good." All was as it should be. Everything that God created functioned well, lived at peace with every other part of creation, and brought glory to their Maker.

And yet, this perfect creation was short-lived. By the third chapter of Genesis, everything had changed. Adam and Eve, by their own choice, rejected God and separated themselves from him. Sin entered the world, and sin changed everything; until creation is restored, we find ourselves still living under the curse of sin. Our counselees feel those effects day in and day out, as do we.

This chapter explores the impact of sin on women, particularly what that means for counseling. Sin is inescapable and the underlying reason counseling is needed. If sin had not entered the world, counselors would not exist. Sin permeates the life of every woman we see. Therefore, it is a pivotal topic in our understanding of the women we counsel.

Where Things Went Wrong: A Brief Discussion of Genesis 3

Chapter 1 walked through God's creation in Genesis 1 and 2. When we get to Genesis 3, everything changes. The chapter opens by telling the reader of the serpent's, or Satan's, cunning, setting the stage for what is to come. The woman found herself with the serpent, who went on the attack. He asked her, "Did God really say, 'You can't eat from any tree in the garden'?" (v. 1). He immediately questioned her Creator and his counsel.

Eve responded, "We may eat the fruit from the trees in the garden. But about the fruit of the tree in the middle of the garden, God said, 'You must not eat it or touch it, or you will die'" (v. 2). Interestingly, this isn't quite what God said to Adam, which was to be shared with Eve. In Gen 2:16–17, God said, "You are free to eat from any tree of the garden, but you must not eat from the tree of the knowledge of good and evil, for on the day you eat from it, you will certainly die." In Eve's response, she minimized God's gift, his blessing. She altered God's words, leaving out the "free to eat" and "any tree," ever so slightly reducing the goodness of what God provided. She also added the prohibition of touching the fruit, which God had not given. And she left out what type of tree it was: the tree of the knowledge of good and evil. This wasn't just any tree; it had special significance. While these may not sound like important details, they contributed to her deception.

Satan then responded to Eve, "No! You will certainly not die. . . . In fact, God knows that when you eat it your eyes will be opened and you will be like God, knowing good and evil" (3:4–5). Satan outright lied to Eve, challenging the truthfulness of God's word. He set God up as fearful of others being like him, which questions his goodness and his power. Eve, seeing "that the tree was good for food and delightful to look at, and that it was desirable for obtaining wisdom" (v. 6), took the fruit and ate it. She then gave some to

Adam, who was presumably with her the entire time, and he ate as well. In a moment, she believed that fruit was better than her God. Motivated by a desire to self-satisfy (visually, physically, and mentally), she rejected the God who had already provided full satisfaction.

Immediately, Adam and Eve realized they had sinned. Genesis 3:7 tells us they realized they were naked, so they sewed fig leaves together to cover themselves. They were ashamed in front of one another, and soon ran from God in shame as well. They tried to cover themselves, but realizing it was insufficient, they hid when they heard God walking in the garden to meet them. Their eyes had indeed been opened, but not in the way the serpent promised.

Genesis 3:8–13 shows us the second consequence of sin, after shame: blame shifting. When God asked Adam if he had eaten the fruit, Adam responded to God, "The woman you gave to be with me—she gave me some fruit from the tree, and I ate." Adam blamed God for giving Eve to be with him, as if God was the one at fault. Then God turned to Eve and asked her what she had done. Just like Adam, Eve failed to take responsibility for her actions, blaming the serpent. Both knew they had done wrong, but neither owned it.

The rest of Genesis 3 recounts how God cursed the serpent, then Eve, then Adam. Conflict would come between the serpent and mankind (though God foreshadowed the coming Savior in Gen 3:15); Eve was cursed with pain in childbirth and conflict with her husband (cursed in both of her roles: mother and wife); and Adam was cursed with hard, painful work and physical death. Adam and Eve lived in perfect peace with God, one another, and the rest of creation until that point, but that changed in an instant.

Nevertheless, God displayed undeserved grace in those moments. Despite the curse, Adam and Eve did not immediately die (physically). They were removed from the garden and allowed to continue living, with additional hardship. We also see God's grace displayed in Gen 3:21: "The LORD God made clothing from skins for the man and his wife, and he clothed them." God covered their shame, and he did so through a blood sacrifice, foretelling the coming sacrifice of Jesus. God, Creator of all things, intervened to cover their disgrace.

Why is this exposition of Genesis 3 so important? Because not much has changed. Sin originates in the heart when something is elevated above God. Most often, sin stems from seeing something that appears to satisfy ("good for food"), is beautiful ("delightful to look at"), or brings an elevation of self ("desirable for obtaining wisdom"). Sin also comes when we question the goodness of God ("Did God *really* say . . . ?"). And the result of sin is shame and disgrace, a need for our Creator to cover us. This is our ultimate need, and it is why Jesus came. We continue to live under the same curse as Adam and Eve and it impacts every part of our world.

The Categories of Sin and Their Impact on Us

Genesis 3 gives us a picture of original sin, and it also allows us a glimpse into what sin is. Sin is more than just wrong choices; it is the condition under which we live. Sin is pervasive and perpetual: it impacts every part of creation at every moment of every day. Not only are we sinners, we are also broken and enslaved to sin, apart from Christ. Without him, we cannot *not* sin. Our sin has consequences—spiritually, relationally, and physically. Let's briefly explore each of the presentations of sin.

Personal, Volitional Sin

We all make choices. Every moment, each person makes a choice of what she is going to do. Sometimes our choices are conscious, evaluated internally then followed through. Other choices are habitual or automatic, made without much thought or evaluation. In either case, these choices—behaviors, thoughts, emotions, and so on—are volitional. I choose what to do and I am responsible for the sinfulness or righteousness of those choices. Volitional sin always flows out of what we worship, who or what occupies the throne of our heart.

Remember, those apart from Christ are enslaved to their sin (Rom 6:17), but believers have "been set free from sin" (v. 18). A believing counselee is able to choose a right response that honors God. An unbelieving counselee cannot make that choice (Ps 115:4–8). Even if her actual behavior is the exact same as a believing counselee, it is still sinful before a holy God, because it is done apart from his power and his grace. Apart from Christ, an unbelieving counselee ultimately can never honor God with her choices; she is perpetually at odds with him.

Furthermore, our choices have consequences: before God, for ourselves, and toward others. No woman exists independently of others and her sin will always impact someone, at the very least herself and God. Sin causes division, just like it did for Adam and Eve, between each other and between us and God. In this sense, our sin always has a vertical (between us and God) and a horizontal (between us and others) component.

As sin relates to counseling, sometimes women seek counsel because of their own sinful choices. The consequences cause pain or distress, driving them to seek help. Sin's consequences might be overt, like conflict with others or outright harm to another person, or it may be furthering wrong beliefs that impact future choices, causing even more pain or distress. As counselors, we must evaluate any potential volitional sin and how it might be impacting the life of the woman coming to see us. Only then can we move toward proper change.

The Sin of Others against Us

Just as our sin has consequences for others, the sin of others has consequences for us. That sin may be aimed directly at us (abuse, violence, conflict), or it may be a side effect of their choices (family member of an addict, caring for or providing for another person in the wake of their sin). The sin of others can have a tremendous impact on a woman, and quite often it is outside her control. We see examples of this type of sin in the Bible with the rape of Tamar, the selling of Joseph into slavery, and David's taking of Bathsheba. Not much has changed since biblical times.

Like with our own volitional sin, much pain and suffering can result from the sin of others. A woman may need counseling when she has suffered because others have sinned against her. She may feel defenseless and hopeless that change can happen. Or she may be at her wit's end, having called out to God for relief and found none. As counselors, we must acknowledge the impact of the sin of others on our counselees, including subsequent feelings of hopelessness, fear, or fatigue.

Brokenness of Creation, Including Our Bodies

Paul tells us in Rom 8:22 that "the whole creation has been groaning together with labor pains until now." In other words, things do not work the way they should; all of creation is "groaning" in anguish, awaiting the day of redemption. Part of this reality is our bodies are also awaiting that redemption. They do not function as they should; we experience disease, decay, and dysfunction. Sometimes suffering comes simply because our bodies are broken and fallen.

The effects of sin on our bodies can lead to temptation to volitional sin. Consider chronic pain: those afflicted will attest that it is easy to believe their condition will never change, that they will never find relief. Their pain lends itself to hopelessness.[1] Their pain is a source of temptation to frustration, bitterness, and even anger toward God.

As counselors, though we do not fully understand the body-soul dynamic, we do know that people are made of both. Both body and soul are fallen, leading us toward sin and suffering. Body and soul influence one another. The counselor, then, should recognize the potential role of the broken body in a counselee's struggles, though it might not always be clearly observable.

A Combination of Factors

Often, counseling issues encompass more than one type of sin. For example, we always have a choice of how to respond to the sin of others against us or our fallen bodies; this response (volitional choice) then has consequences. We may see this in a counselee who has been the victim of abuse (the sin of another person against her) but who chooses to respond with bitterness (volitional choice). Or, using the example above, a woman dealing with chronic pain (fallen body) chooses to be hopeless. We are entirely responsible for volitional sin, and the temptation to engage in it always enters the picture in some way if either the sin of others against us or the consequences of a fallen creation are present. We are to repent when we commit personal, volitional sin and we are to recognize how our sin affects others. It has ripple effects that we must not ignore. As counselors, we are responsible to sift through these sin categories and ensure that we are addressing each appropriately.

People as Sinners, Sufferers, and Saints

Several times in this chapter, we have referred to the fact that women are both sinners and sufferers. We suffer because of our own sin and the sin of others, both the result of Adam's original sin (Rom 5:12). And yet, we must balance how we view people relative to sin. If we see a woman solely as sinner, we fail to understand her pain, empathize with her struggle, and care for her properly. Should we regard her as sufferer only, she remains guilty before a holy God, ignorant of how to move toward true and proper change. She might be suffering more than she is sinning, or sinning more than she is suffering, but she is never solely sinner or solely sufferer.

Alongside her sin and suffering, if she is in Christ, she is also a saint. This truth permeates both her sin and her suffering; it is the good news of the gospel for restoration. Apart from Christ, a person will remain eternally as sufferer because of their sin. But in and through Christ, she is clean before God, perfectly brought back into right relationship with her Maker, as his chosen daughter.

Every woman's greatest need, regardless of the counseling issue at hand, is redemption in Christ. This does not necessitate that every counseling encounter is evangelistic, though some may be. Rather, the counselor must recognize as long as her counselee remains apart from Christ, relief from her suffering is only temporary and her standing before the Lord as sinner cannot change. We must keep first things first; we must aim to restore each woman we counsel to right relationship with her Father.

How Do We Respond to Sin?

The reality of sin demands a response; if we remain in sin, we remain separated from God like Adam and Eve. To restore a right relationship with God, when we sin, we must repent. We must demonstrate genuine sorrow over our sin, turn from it, and actively work to not repeat that sin. We are human, and continue to live with a sinful nature even as believers, but we now have the capacity to turn from our sin and choose to do right.

Understandably, when the conversation in counseling turns to sin and repentance, many counselees feel uncomfortable. All of us, in our pride and self-defensiveness, naturally (and sinfully) dislike conversations about personal sin. It is a reminder that we are not as we ought to be and for some, it makes us feel "less than." It is personal.

When done properly, even conversations about our own sinfulness can bring great hope. But here is the key component: grace. We cannot, should not, have a conversation about sin and fail to include grace in that conversation. That is the gospel message: "He made the one who did not know sin to be sin for us, so that in him we might become the righteousness of God" (2 Cor 5:21). By God's grace, we can turn to the One who became sin on our behalf so we could be made right before our Creator.

Because of grace, as counselors we can have direct conversations about sin. We can call our counselees to repentance. But we do so only because of the grace that is undeservedly shown to us. We can encourage our counselees through the process of acknowledging personal, volitional sin (behavior, choices, thoughts, emotions, etc.), recognizing that it is sinful before a holy God, expressing godly sorrow, repenting of the sin to God and anyone impacted, turning from that sin, accepting any consequences, and finding freedom from guilt or shame. Then, we celebrate and worship the God who enables us to do these things.

What does this look like in a clinical setting, perhaps one where discussions of "sin" are not prevalent and may even be frowned upon? We can certainly acknowledge the presentations of sin noted above, discussing what things the counselee is responsible for (volitional sin), things done against her (sin directed at her), and the brokenness of the world she lives in (living in a context of sin). This might be nuanced slightly if the counselee is a nonbeliever or a nominal believer who is not comfortable using "sin" terminology. As Mark McMinn outlines in his book *Sin and Grace*, even practitioners in secular settings should not neglect conversations about sin. Discussions of grace (or leniency as it relates to personal responsibility) are significantly cheapened when sin is left out of the equation. The grace of the gospel means little if it is not in response to sin.

A final note is warranted here: we might be tempted to "repent" beyond what is appropriate. We are to repent of our own personal sin, in any way that presents, but we are not responsible to repent of the sin of others or our fallen bodies. In our evaluation of sin, let us be sure when we do call out sin, it is in fact appropriate to do so, rather than placing an undue and undeserved burden on our counselees. Some counselees need gentle reminders of what is their responsibility and what is not, so we must be wise in our handling of such matters.

Conclusion

We live in a fallen world, which is a large part of why counseling exists. The women we counsel are simultaneously sinners and sufferers, and by God's grace through his Son, also saints. As counselors, we must recognize the true needs of our counselees. If she is apart from Christ, she needs Christ. She needs redemption. If she is suffering, she needs help and encouragement. When she is sinning, she needs change through repentance and right living. As her counselor, we address each of these needs for each woman in her particular situation (1 Thess 5:14; more to come in chapter 3). We work for the good of the woman in our counseling room; to that end, we must recognize what the Lord identifies as her needs and seek to meet them his way, through his Word and by the power of his Spirit (see chapter 4).

3

Living in a Fallen World: A Woman's Context

In chapter 2, we walked through the three different types of sin and how we properly respond to personal, volitional sin. This chapter focuses on the influence of others on us, whether that be sinful or not sinful. In other words, this chapter seeks to acknowledge a woman's context. She does not live as an island; there are many who are speaking into her life and influencing her choices.

The Bible teaches in Proverbs about the wisdom of many counselors/advisors (Prov 15:22), that as iron sharpens iron, so one person sharpens another (Prov 27:17), and that the wise man listens to advice (Prov 12:15). It argues that of the many voices in our lives competing for our attention, we should strive to listen to wise voices. As counselors, we must point women to the ones that speak truth and order in the midst of lies and chaos.

A helpful description is found in *The Gospel for Disordered Lives*:[1] we have a triad of enemies—the flesh, the world, and the devil. There is a true complexity in that all three are working all the time, but only our heart *causes* sin. Despite the influence of the world and spiritual powers, they are only that: an influence. They do not make us sin—only we can do that. And yet, they are very real. They have real effect on the choices we make. We must be aware of these factors and not ignorant of their influence on our counselees.

A Woman's Context

We all influence and are influenced by those around us. There are constant "voices" speaking into each of our lives. For some, the greatest influence is family, whether parents, siblings, spouse, or children. For others, their friends have the greatest influence in their lives, speaking loudly about matters of identity, preferences, or values. Still others are most influenced by their church or religious community, especially those in positions of leadership or preaching. Some find themselves valuing what is valued by their surrounding culture or the media.

Our past experiences and our evaluation of those experiences might hold significant weight. For example, if a woman's experiences with men have been negative and abusive, that carries weight for her interactions with other men. Or a woman who was neglected as a child might believe that is normal and good. We tend to continue in what we know and what we are used to. This is partly why some women move from one abusive relationship to another. It is simply all she knows, and the voice in her head tells her it is normal.

Further, beliefs about "the way things ought to be" might also influence a counselee's perception of her struggle. Perhaps a woman believes she is "the strong one in the family," so when hardship comes, she cannot express any sort of emotion because it will be interpreted, even by her, as weakness. Or, maybe a woman was taught as a child that it is not acceptable to cry. When strong emotions well up, she fights them instead of acknowledging they are present. These beliefs might also be cultural, such as "it is my responsibility to care for my aging parents because I'm the daughter" (prescribed gender roles). She might feel an obligation to do certain things because they are expected of her.

Or a woman comes to counseling with a prior diagnosis and is dissatisfied with her progress, feeling she should be farther along by now.

There are also "rules" that she must live by. Sometimes these are explicit, like the reality that she is married. But most often, these rules are implicit and not easily identified. They may be family roles/norms that are assumed and learned from experience; unspoken rules (norms) within her family of origin when she was growing up; what her culture or subculture affirms or rejects; or behaviors or actions that are considered normal or abnormal. For every woman, these rules are different, even within the same family. But most women operate within the rules of their given systems, whether good or bad.

Most of us have some combination of all these "voices," though we all give them different weights. The voices in a woman's life are formative for her worldview and her understanding of reality. She constantly evaluates what is going on around and within her, but that is not done in isolation. Every moment, her experiences, her values and beliefs, and the people she listens to play a role in what she will choose next and even how she responds in the present moment.

Why is this important? Because to understand a woman's circumstances well, we must understand the context in which she lives. We cannot fully understand, for example, the conflict in her marriage unless we understand how her family of origin handled conflict, her beliefs about her role in the marriage and how much she is valued, the couple's history of conflict resolution, and many other factors. Her relationships, hardships, family background, stressors, support system, and other factors matter tremendously, so we must seek to understand them. She lives in a constant state of influence, both positive and negative.

Negative Influences

When we think of negative influences, what often comes to mind is the teenage girl who gives in to peer pressure. She is highly influenced by her friends and her culture, which leads her to make poor decisions. But negative influences do not stop when a woman ceases to be a teenager; they continue throughout life. As counselors seeking to understand our counselees as best we can, it serves us well to bear in mind potential negative influences in a woman's life, including hardships she might face that impact her in negative ways.

Ungodly Culture

No matter where a woman lives or where she comes from, her culture has an influence on her. Often, particularly in the West, that influence is negative. It fosters greed and self-centeredness, pushing people to obtain more and more as an indicator of their value. There is strong pressure to conform; those who deviate from the norm are shunned, dismissed, or labeled negatively for their failure to be like the rest of society. In some cultures, there may even be laws and customs that go directly against God's Word. Each of these things influences a woman as she lives within that culture, hearing those counterbiblical messages daily.

A Dysfunctional or Abusive Family of Origin

A woman might also come from a dysfunctional childhood family where no one modeled God-honoring behavior like healthy communication or conflict resolution. There may have been a failure to teach God's ways as he directs in Deuteronomy 6. This woman may grow up without a firm sense of right and wrong because she is not grounded in God's Word. For some women, their family of origin might have been abusive, causing trauma with long-lasting impact. A woman with a history of negative influence might struggle to make proper sense of her current reality, because her experiences have taught her differently. And she might be tempted to respond in ways characteristic of her home life rather than how God directs.

An Unhealthy Marriage

Another negative influence in a woman's life may be an unhealthy marriage. A marriage relationship that is not thriving can bring significant strain and stress, which can lead to temptation to respond in ways that do not honor the Lord. A woman in an unhealthy marriage might also feel trapped or out of control and respond out of fear or desperation rather than trusting the Lord and acting in ways that honor both herself and her husband.

Poverty or a Lack of Access to Resources

Many women also experience poverty or a lack of access to things they need. She might be unable to get help that is needed, like counseling, so she struggles to make decisions on her own or tries to find wise counsel in her current circle. Women struggling in these ways might understandably be so focused on meeting basic needs that it is difficult to focus on other things; if she does not have food on the table for her family, how can she justify getting help for her emotional struggles? Women in these circumstances often do not know how to change their circumstances, and struggle to change even basic things about their lives (like homelessness, joblessness, or a lack of food). Her poverty proves to be a negative influence as well as a hardship.

Lack of a Support System

One of the most beneficial things a woman can have in her life is a strong support system. This might be family or friends, or a church family. Without a support system, a woman has no one to provide encouragement or to hold her accountable for her actions. Her lack of a support system contributes to feelings of isolation and loneliness, often tempting her to minimize her sin or think it isn't significant because others don't know about it. When facing tough life decisions, she also might struggle with indecision or second-guessing because there aren't other women in her life to give counsel.

Spiritual Warfare

Though this is an area we often minimize, we must remember that our enemy does exist and he hates us (Eph 6:12); he delights to see us in our sin and leading others toward sin. And he delights when negative influences are present in our lives because they tend to pull us from the Lord. As Chuck Lawless and William Cook write, "Satan, man's adversary, continues to deceive and divert people from finding salvation in Jesus Christ, and to harass and hinder Christians through enticement to sin and exploitation of weakness."[2] And yet, we must remember that though our enemy and his forces are a reality, they are not omnipotent.[3] Believers can resist his strong temptations because "the one who is in you is greater than the one who is in the world" (1 John 4:4).

No Saving Relationship with God

The strongest influence over a woman is sin, particularly enslavement to sin apart from Christ. In this state, she is unable to do what is right. She cannot not sin. She is separated from God for eternity, having no access to the throne of her Father and she does not have his Spirit to help her know and do what is right. She is also unable to understand the wisdom of God and his directives.

In such cases, though we may provide counsel, ultimately it will be insufficient. She is unable to fully change, rightly change, until she comes into right relationship with the Lord. The helps presented in the remainder of this text will do little to help her. Her symptoms might be reduced or relationships restored, but in the context of eternity, she will still end her days here on earth separated from her Maker. She will spend eternity apart from him. This is, therefore, the most significant negative influence in a woman's life.

Positive Influences

There are many positive influences that may be present in a woman's life. The list here starts with those that are most influential in her life.

A Saving Relationship with Jesus

The most important influence in a woman's life is her relationship with her Savior, Jesus. Apart from him, she is enslaved to her sin; but in Christ, she is a new creation, a daughter of God and a delight to him. She is no longer separated from him, but united with Christ. She is able to obey his commands and to understand wisdom from God and his Word. Her eternal state is secure through Christ, influencing her perspective on everything else in her life.

The Holy Spirit Living within Believers

Because of her saving relationship with Jesus, the Holy Spirit now lives in her and positively influences her toward right living. The Spirit empowers her to make choices that honor the Lord and helps her fight spiritual warfare. Women who are in Christ, indwelled by his Spirit, can resist their enemy because the battle is already won.[4] Because of the Spirit, she can put on the full armor of God and be prepared to handle any trial that comes her way. She is now able to live in right relationship with those around her, pursuing peace instead of division and living selflessly instead of selfishly.

Support System, Such as a Church Body

As noted previously, the absence of a support system means there is a tremendous need in a woman's life. With a support system—a strong family unit, a small group at church that does life together, or a group of friends that checks in often—in place, she is built up. Others are there to encourage her when things get hard. There are other women present to provide accountability for sin and correct her when it is needed. She has friendship and community to combat feelings of isolation and loneliness. When she is in need, she knows there are people she can call who support her.

Access to Resources and Help

When a woman's basic needs are met and she has access to the resources she needs, she can get support like counseling and discipleship. She can focus on deeper, spiritual matters and on relationships instead of expending all her energy to simply survive. Not only is she better able to identify where change is needed, she will have the support she needs to move toward change. This might be access to solid counseling, community resources, support groups, or other resources that support her and positively influence her toward meaningful change.

A Healthy Marriage

While an unhealthy marriage is a source of temptation toward despair, a healthy, God-honoring marriage has built-in support and encouragement. Husband and wife mutually build one another up, each picking up the slack when the other is struggling. A healthy marriage is a living image of a relationship with the Lord, a picture of how Christ leads his church. There are opportunities to love one another, deal with conflict, and communicate well, all of which are for her good. A healthy marriage also contributes to feelings of security and health. These are all positive influences toward right living.

A Healthy Family of Origin

Those who come from healthy families of origin have been positively influenced toward replicating them. There has been a proper modeling of God's ways and proper teaching of his Word. A woman takes these lessons into adulthood and they serve her well.[5] Even more, a godly family of origin provides a healthy base for understanding relationships, conflict, support, and love. She knows how to make good choices because they were demonstrated for her as she grew up. There is less temptation to deviate from these good choices because she has seen the positive outcomes they bring.

Godly Culture

Though an overarching godly culture is hard to find, a woman might be a part of a subculture that seeks to honor the Lord. For instance, maybe she lives in an area or community that is churched and most of those around her are believers. Such a culture fosters service to and elevation of others before self, rather than affirming the negative values of the larger culture. A godly culture encourages right living according to God's laws rather than the permissive laws of man. Its laws and customs align with biblical teaching instead of worldly "wisdom." When a woman lives in this context, where others are striving to live rightly before God, it encourages her to do the same. It is a positive influence on her.

Implications for Counseling

A woman who seeks counseling might be experiencing bits and pieces of any or all the influence categories discussed above. She might even feel conflicted as corresponding negative and positive influences are at play. And at any point, any one of these influences might pop up; a woman lives in an ever-changing environment with continually evolving experiences. We must be wise in identifying and evaluating which influences are at play and what effect they have on her.

This is a complex endeavor. There is a balance between knowing enough and knowing everything we could. We could spend session after session exploring her situation and the influences in her life, but we must distinguish between necessary information, useful information, and extraneous information. The wise counselor balances that well.

On a practical level, we cannot counsel as if the woman is an individual with no external voices. That woman simply does not exist. It is wise to identify the voices present in that particular woman's life and discuss them as needed, especially if they are out of balance. We should be able to identify when one person's voice holds more weight than it should or if God's Word holds less weight than a person. Many struggles come because there are competing voices in a woman's life. In this case, we can help her put external voices, as well as her own voice, in their proper place.

Counselors must acknowledge the weight of a woman's circumstances and their influence (though not causation) on her struggles. We can help her see that she still has choices, despite the reality of significant influencers on her. When a woman feels helpless, or believes she cannot make certain choices because of her circumstances, this is something to explorewith her. We want to affirm both a fallen world, which sometimes means intense negative influences, and that she is still enabled by the Lord to do what is right.[6]

Counselors should also focus on finding and strengthening the positive influences in a woman's life, affirming those that are present and seeking to establish those that are missing. Positive influences can be tremendously supportive in counseling and can significantly contribute to godly growth and change. We should especially seek to confirm and strengthen the woman's relationship with the Lord and establish a strong support system, including a mentor mature in the faith who can walk alongside her in her counseling journey. Most of the topic chapters later in this text include some guidance toward a support system and enlisting a care team, specifically because of the positive effect they can have on a counselee.

Conclusion

A woman's context matters. She will have a multitude of voices speaking into her life, and we should work together with her toward ensuring those voices build her up and point her toward God and his Word. She will also have both positive and negative influences affecting her and her choices. Despite outside influences, though, she is the one responsible for her choices and right living before God. As counselors, we can navigate these circumstances with her, providing godly counsel and encouraging her toward godliness.

4

❧ ❦ ❧

The Necessity of Scripture:
God's Solutions for Life's Problems

In the last chapter, we explored the voices in a woman's life, from her culture and the people around her. We also looked at both positive and negative influences on her as she makes choices. It is important to know what influences her as we seek to understand her and then give counsel. These voices and influences fall under a woman's epistemology, or her understanding of reality, knowledge, and authority. She employs this framework to make sense of the world around her and to make decisions on how she will feel, think, and act.

There are many sources of knowledge and even more potential sources of authority in a woman's life. Internal sources of knowledge and authority are vast: she might employ reason or logic, rely on her conscience, learn from past experience, or let her emotions drive her. Externally, she might listen to family or friends, those within her culture, trusted advisors like her pastor or her physician, or rely on a text like the Bible to be authoritative in her life. It is no wonder decisions are sometimes difficult to make.

The Need for Truthful, Authoritative Wisdom

In evaluating the sources of knowledge and authority listed above, it is imperative to recognize that all but the Bible are impacted by sin. We do not always use good logic, our conscience is tainted by sin, our past experiences are biased, and our emotions don't always point us the right direction. Those around us are influenced by sin as well: family, friends, pastors, and physicians are all sinners. At times, they all give poor counsel. God's Word is the only source of true, perfect knowledge all the time.

Proverbs 1:7 tells us, "The fear of the LORD is the beginning of knowledge." A proper understanding of God, and reverence toward him and his Word, is where true knowledge comes from. We must find truth from the source of truth, the Bible that God gives us to know him and know his desires for our lives. As the psalmist writes in Psalm 119, "How happy are those whose way is blameless, who walk according to the LORD's instruction! . . . Your command makes me wiser than my enemies, for it is always with me. I have more insight than all my teachers because your decrees are my meditation. I understand more than the elders because I obey your precepts. . . . You are righteous, LORD, and your judgments are just. The decrees you issue are righteous and altogether trustworthy" (Pss 119:1, 98–100, 137–38). God's Word is wise and leads us toward knowledge and righteousness.

Further, we know that God's Word is authoritative, primary, and comprehensive. It is authoritative because God is authoritative; it should hold higher authority in our lives over the other sources of knowledge/authority (i.e., it is primary). We should value the Word of God over the words of others. It is comprehensive in that it speaks to all of life in some way. Though it is not exhaustive, and does not claim to be, it provides everything we need to know from God on any topic. That might be direct teaching or instruction, or it may simply be how we think about a particular matter. Either way, God's Word speaks broadly and sufficiently on all that it speaks to.

The Scriptures are given to us from a God who is compassionate, wise, just, and holy. He is perfect; his ways are perfect and his directions to us are perfect. Therefore, they are trustworthy because he is trustworthy. Anything that we find in Scripture can be relied on unwaveringly, with no need for doubt or reservation. As counselors, we can trust that when we give counsel from God's Word, the authority and wisdom are the Lord's.

The Bible's Role in Speaking to Life's Struggles

Let's see how God's authoritative and trustworthy Word connects to counseling. How does the Bible speak to life's struggles? Sometimes, it speaks directly. In Phil 4:6, Paul tells us, "Don't worry about anything, but in everything, through prayer and petition with thanksgiving, present your requests to God." Here and in the surrounding verses, we are told not to worry and then how to combat our anxiety: praying and presenting the need to God (v. 6), resting in the peace of God (v. 7), and thinking on what is true, honorable, just—"anything praiseworthy" (v. 8).

Other times, the Bible speaks less directly, but still speaks clearly. For example, the Bible doesn't give us a verse clearly saying, "don't commit suicide," but there are principles prohibiting murder (Deut 5:17, which would include self-murder), stressing the value of human life as image bearers of God (Gen 9:6), and reminding that our bodies are temples of the Holy Spirit (1 Cor 6:19). From these truths, we can easily infer the sinfulness of suicide.

The Bible also gives us a framework of how to think about who we are, what is wrong with us, and what we need. These are the topics of various chapters of this book, purposefully drawn from the Bible's teaching. Because of the extensiveness of the Bible's teaching, we can develop an approach to counseling that is built on truth and the authority of God rather than falsehood and the "authority" of men.

The Bible helps us evaluate all other sources of knowledge, both internal and external. It helps us know whether counsel from a friend, teaching by a pastor, or our own logic or conscience is sinful or righteous. Specific to counseling, it helps us evaluate approaches like cognitive-behavioral therapy, EMDR therapy, emotion-focused therapy, or a host of other theories/interventions. We can determine what aligns with God's Word and what was given to us to use by his common grace, versus what is contrary to Scripture and should therefore be rejected.

In sum, the Bible gives direct counsel, but it also acts as both a framework and a filter for all other knowledge. We build a method for counseling from the Bible, and for any information that is not directly given, we can use principles from the Word to filter what might be useful. When the Bible is used for both these functions, it is fully sufficient for handling any of life's struggles that we might encounter in counseling.

Principles for Interpreting Scripture Properly

Though Scripture is wholly true and useful for teaching (2 Tim 3:16–17), our interpretation of Scripture has the potential to be impacted by sin. We all can likely recall an occasion when a verse or section was misinterpreted or used to say something it didn't mean. We must guard against that, particularly as we seek to give counsel to other women. Several principles for proper interpretation are useful to keep in mind.

First, all passages should be interpreted in context, including the author's original intent. The passage's context might include surrounding verses, the book as a whole, its setting in either the Old or New Testament, and its place in the overall canon. We must also recognize the genre of the passage; we would interpret a proverb differently than one of Paul's epistles. Context and setting determine the meaning of the verse or passage.

Additionally, we must consider the author's original intent. Jesus had lessons in mind when he taught in parables; those parables are not to be taken literally as actual occurrences, but as stories employed to convey a lesson.

Many of the prophets issued warnings to Israel that were specific for their time and context. We can apply principles to our lives today, but those warnings might not be directly applicable. In our setting as counselors, we must remember the Bible was not meant to be a counseling textbook, though much can be gleaned from its teachings. We must exercise caution to keep verses in their context and within the author's original intent.

Second, we should use Scripture to interpret Scripture. God's Word will never contradict itself; to do so would be reflective of a God of disorder and confusion, which he is not. Therefore, when we encounter a difficult passage, we should use other, clearer passages to make sense of it. Sometimes, Scripture is not to be taken literally, but interpreted in context or alongside other teachings. We may not be capable of understanding the entire canon completely (like the book of Revelation). Our understanding is limited; his is not (Isa 55:9).

Third, and particularly pertinent for counseling, we must distinguish between descriptive and prescriptive texts. Sometimes this is easy: the narratives in the Old Testament are clearly descriptive; Paul's letters are filled with prescriptive "do this" passages. But other passages are not so clear. For instance, Prov 22:6 gives the teaching, "Train up a child in the way he should go; even when he is old he will not depart from it" (ESV). This is an example of a text that might (wrongly) be taken as prescriptive, rather than descriptive. Generally, when we train up children correctly, they continue to live by the values they were taught, but this is not a promise. We must hold texts in their proper place within these categories.

Finally, interpretation of Scripture should always be done under the guidance of the Spirit, with much prayer. We should trust the Lord for guidance, not letting our own pride keep us from consulting him. The Holy Spirit is the Spirit of wisdom and understanding (Isa 11:2), the helper and teacher (John 14:26), and the Spirit of truth (John 16:13). It is foolishness to try to understand truth and reality apart from him. Given this, we must be quick to ask the Lord for wisdom and understanding as we search his Word, because he gives it freely to those who ask (Jas 1:5).

Evaluating External Sources of Knowledge, Particularly Secular Psychology

What are we to make of knowledge found outside of Scripture? How useful might it be in our care of women if our truth comes from the Lord and his Word? We noted above that the Bible acts as a foundation and a filter, but what does that mean for how much time and attention we give secular knowledge in our counseling? We should consider truth and comprehensiveness, priority, and attention in our evaluation and use of secular knowledge, particularly secular counseling theories.

A Matter of Truth and Comprehensiveness

The Scriptures teach us conclusively who we are, what is wrong with us, and what we need, but secular theories also address these questions. For instance, some would argue that we are solely bodies, the mind or soul only a function of a complex brain. For those in this category, disease is our problem, so a medical approach is most appropriate for healing life's ailments. Others believe human beings are complex and have a distinct soul, but morality is subjective and individualized. For those following these lines of thought, what we need is affirmation and our own sense of morality, whatever works best for the individual.

Other approaches seem to have a bit more overlap with biblical teaching. For example, cognitive behaviorists, particularly third-wave practitioners, recognize the role of one's thoughts in their behavior. Some focus strongly on personal values and the role they play in a person's life. This is similar to the Bible teaching that a man's "mouth speaks from the overflow of the heart" (Luke 6:45). The heart (one's desires, values, and motivations) drives everything else in life, and some secular theories acknowledge this reality.

Despite some areas of commonality, secular approaches often fall far short of true explanations of who we are as women. Other times, by God's grace, they come close to the Bible's teachings. In each scenario, the counselor should wisely evaluate the secular approach alongside Scripture, and in the areas where it agrees, it can be accepted and utilized. To use a concrete example, the counselor might use the cognitive-behavioral technique of reframing and incorporate a discussion of motivations and desires (heart matters) with it. Such approaches recognize the gap in the secular approach and seek to align it with biblical teaching.

A Matter of Priority

The second consideration when it comes to secular psychology is the issue of priority. Are we prioritizing biblical truth or are we prioritizing secular interventions and techniques? Each has its place, and each can be tremendously useful, but only biblical truth is *necessary*. At the very least, we must always speak in line with God's truth, and when it is helpful and appropriate, we may include secular approaches, techniques, or interventions, like the example of reframing mentioned above.

Scripture must always remain primary and authoritative over secular approaches/claims. The Bible speaks in several places about man's wisdom, most notably in Col 2:8 where Paul warns, "Be careful that no one takes you captive through philosophy and empty deceit based on human tradition, based on the elements of the world, rather than Christ." The Proverbs affirm Paul's teaching, saying, "There is a way that seems right to a person, but its end is the way to death" (Prov 14:12). In the context of this discussion, secular knowledge cannot compete with God's wisdom, so it should remain secondary in importance and use.

What might this look like in a clinical setting, specifically when a diagnosis or approach is required to be documented? Or what about when we seek to minister to unbelievers who are averse to quoting Scripture in a session? In these circumstances, we must be careful to discern what we are upholding as the priority in our counseling room: Is it relief for the sake of relief, or is it the use of a secular tool as a bridge to later gospel conversations? Are we using, let's say, mindfulness to simply bring about awareness of the counselee's thoughts and feelings, or can we use that technique to point at the heart (a biblical priority)? The use of diagnoses or techniques is not off limits; rather, we must hold them in their proper place secondary to the truth of God's Word and his counsel for living. This must be true in both theory and practice.

A Matter of Attention or Time Given

We must also consider the attention or time allotted to the inclusion of secular approaches. If Scripture is to be authoritative and primary, secular approaches must be secondary in time and attention. Theory drives practice, or put another way, theology drives practice. Therefore, our counsel must be clearly biblical, *derived from* and *driven by* the Bible rather than biblical teaching *tacked on* to other sources. This includes our understanding of people, their problems, and the solutions to those problems.

More time should be given to the priorities of God's Word (the gospel and sanctification) than to lesser priorities (happiness, relief of suffering for relief's sake). More attention given to the former does not negate the latter; happiness and relief from suffering are useful goals to pursue, but they should be done secondarily to becoming more like Christ. This order of focus places first things first and second things second.

It is helpful to consider here what this means for more formal, clinical practices. Since the counsel we give must be derived from and driven by Scripture, those counseling, even in licensed settings, must reject any single approach to therapy. It is, and will always be, insufficient for true change. The licensed biblical counselor will likely also reject any approach that is humanistic in nature, those that assert that the counselee has the capacity and the knowledge within themselves to change. The Bible tells us these assertions are not so. Instead, the capacity for change, the direction of change, and the authority over change lies with the Lord. Again, though secular techniques or even some theories need not be fully rejected, they also cannot be entirely accepted if our counseling is to remain in line with biblical teaching.

True Hope Versus False Hope

Ultimately, placing Scripture as primary and secular sources as secondary distinguishes between true, gospel hope and false, worldly "hope," which is no hope at all. It will ultimately fail. We rejoice over God's common grace working through secular approaches, but they can never bring salvation and restoration to right relationship with God. Without this restoration, the counselee might feel relief in the moment, and even long-term moving forward in life, but without Christ they will spend eternity apart from their Creator. To quote a colleague, when we focus only on symptom relief, failing to address real issues with the truth of God's Word, we only "air condition their train to hell."

As counselors who believe in the Word of God, we may use both Scripture and secular approaches to help our counselee. We have the freedom to do so, wisely and carefully. But the final goal must be the Lord's: salvation and sanctification, more than relief and happiness. It might be that we as counselors must help our counselees understand these biblically aligned priorities and our use of a biblically derived method of care. Though we may utilize information outside Scripture, it is insufficient on its own, and therefore must be kept in its proper place. We must give true, lasting hope rather than false, temporary hope.

Conclusion

There are many voices competing for a woman's attention: her own thoughts and feelings, friends and family, our culture, and others. Surrounded by all of these, a woman must be directed toward true wisdom, toward true knowledge. Because true wisdom is only found in God's Word, as counselors we must not shy away from pointing our counselees to the truths of Scripture. It must hold authority and primacy in our counseling room. Secular approaches may be useful and utilized, but only secondarily to God's teaching.

The following, topical chapters, provide biblical teaching on various topics related to counseling wisdom. At times, the teaching is clear and direct; other times, we draw principles from Scripture that must be brought to bear on a particular struggle. Each chapter includes input from secular sources, but we must continually remember that it is secondary to biblical principles.

5

Counseling One Another: How to Help

Now that we have laid our foundation for the rest of the text, we transition to discuss what we *do* in light of the truths we've explored and the problems of those we encounter. This chapter explores what counseling is, how it is done, where it takes place, and with whom.

What Is Counseling?

There is no shortage of definitions of counseling. A helpful, basic definition for us comes from Heath Lambert's text *A Theology of Biblical Counseling*: "Counseling is a conversation where one party with questions, problems, and trouble seeks assistance from someone they believe has answers, solutions, and help."[1] Inherent in this definition are a few key components:

1. People: both those seeking help and those they believe have answers
2. Problems: something has gone wrong

3.   A search for answers: active, intentional seeking to change
4.   Solutions for their struggles: some belief that help is available
5.   A conversation: a relational, intentional act of acquiring desired help

Counseling is more complex than we might realize. Let's narrow this a bit further: as believers, we are to be a specific *type* of counselor. The Word of God must be preeminent to us; it must inform all that we do, including our counseling. Terminology and debates abound about what this looks like in practice. Deepak Reju provides a helpful definition for counseling from a biblical perspective.

> As biblical counselors, we seek to build strong relationships and help people to apply the gospel in ways that are meaningful and direction-giving. Our counseling is shaped by a Christ-centered view of human life as found in the Christian Scriptures, which takes seriously the physical, social, and developmental nature of our difficulties. We believe that people can be healed, strengthened, and built up as they grow in their understanding of the gospel and in their relationship with Christ. However, this doesn't happen apart from our personal dependence on Him and seeking of His help.[2]

His definition sets some parameters for us as we seek to counsel in a way aligned with God's directives. First, counseling is intentional and targeted. Relationships are built intentionally. We point to the gospel and Christ *intentionally*.[3] And we must depend on God and his help to do what we do. Second, relationships significantly impact our counseling, relationships between us as counselor and our counselees, between our counselee and the Lord, and between our counselee and others around her. As stated previously, no woman lives on an island, a reality we must acknowledge in our direction. Third, counseling is multifaceted. Reju reminds us "a Christ-centered view of human life . . . takes seriously the physical, social, and developmental nature of our difficulties." Women are complex beings and we must see them and treat them as such. Fourth, our counsel must be ethical. We view people as the image bearers they were created to be, as

God has determined them. We work toward their good and hold appropriate goals based on God's directives.

Most important, our counsel must align with God's directives. This includes the use of his Word as our framework to speak to life and its problems and not just our filter. It also means we intentionally discuss topics like sin *and* suffering, not neglecting either one. We work toward sanctification, our counselee becoming more like Christ in her daily walk. And we focus on the heart, not just a woman's thoughts or her behaviors. Those things matter, but ultimately the state of one's heart is what flows out into those thoughts and behaviors (Luke 6:45). Finally, since true healing and change only comes from the Lord, we recognize both our and our counselee's desperate need for him to work in and through us.

What Does Counseling Look Like?

Counseling should always be tailored to the individual seeking help, addressing her problems and meeting her needs. Below is a helpful framework (note: not process) for how to do counseling with each woman.[4] An easy way to remember this framework is the six *L*s: love, listen, learn, labor alongside, lead, and leverage the local church.

Love

When Jesus was asked which commandment in the Scriptures was the greatest, he responded, "Love the Lord your God with all your heart, with all your soul, and with all your mind. This is the greatest and most important command. The second is like it: Love your neighbor as yourself" (Matt 22:37–39). Jesus then stated that all the Law and the Prophets (i.e., the rest of the Bible) depend on these two commands. In other words, we could summarize all of Scripture's directives by saying, "Love God and love others."

As counselors, this is our foundation. We counsel because we love God and want to obey his directives. We also counsel because it is a tangible expression of loving our neighbor. To come alongside a struggling woman with patience, endurance, and compassion is an act of love and a clear demonstration of God's love for her through us.

Love for God and neighbor demands that we view our counselee as an image bearer of God, worthy of dignity, honor, and respect. We speak with kindness and compassion even when correction is warranted. And we demonstrate love for her in pointing her to Christ and his solutions for her struggles.

We also recognize that love for our counselee means we point her to the gospel message, that Christ died on her behalf, paid the penalty for her sins, and empowers her by his Spirit to become more like him. This doesn't just apply to her salvation, though that is important. It applies to her everyday life and is pertinent to every moment of every day in every struggle. A counselor is not a savior: the role of the counselor, in loving her counselee, is to point her to *the* Savior.

As counselors, we also want to communicate love intentionally in our words and actions. This does not necessarily mean we tell our counselees we love them; rather, our disposition is one of genuine care and concern. We desire their good, we desire to see them relieved of their suffering, and we desire to see God work in them for their good and his glory. We act lovingly toward them in all things.

Listen

A major component of counseling, and counseling in a way that is loving, is listening well. Counseling is a conversation; conversations, by definition, can't be unidirectional. Counselors must listen intently to the counselee, seeking to understand her, her struggles, her desires, and her needs.[5]

James 1:19 reminds all believers that we are to be "quick to listen, slow to speak, and slow to anger." While this applies to more than counselors, a helpful reminder is given here: we should listen much more than we speak. Our words carry weight and we must be wise in their use. Proverbs 18:13 echoes, "The one who gives an answer before he listens—this is foolishness and disgrace for him." Our speech can be pertinent only after we have adequately listened.

What does this look like? Initially, this means that the counselor seeks to hear her counselee's story. While the depth of the story might be limited by time constraints in the first session or two, the woman should feel heard and understood. She should feel that the counselor understands her struggle well and values her perspective in the struggle.

Good listening skills are essential here. The counselor should use basic attending skills like maintaining proper eye contact, appearing engaged in the conversation, using both verbal and nonverbal affirmations of hearing her (like saying "mm-hm" or nodding). The counselor can also mirror body language (leaning in when the counselee leans in) and using appropriate emotional/facial expression mirroring (expressing sadness when the counselee expresses sadness). Each of these conveys to the counselee that the counselor is listening well and cares about what she has to say.

The counselor can also use reflective and/or clarifying statements to convey that she is listening and understanding. For instance, reflecting content might be a statement like, "Your boss seems to be putting a lot of pressure on you this week," in response to the counselee's description of a rough week at work. Or, when a counselee is describing a recent loss, a clarifying statement might be something like, "It seems like you're upset and deeply sad about losing your grandmother; is that right?" While the counselor may or may not choose to use some of the same words as the counselee, reflection statements convey that the counselor is listening and at the same time check for proper understanding.

Learn

Part of listening, yet in many ways distinct from it, is learning. In our counseling framework, learning is twofold. First, we must learn about our counselee: her unique context, her unique struggles, and her unique needs. Scripture informs us in part on each of these, but she is an individual who must be treated as such.

How can we best learn about our counselees? One way is through asking good questions. We can ask clarifying questions or questions that go deeper into her story. We can use open-ended questions to elicit more discussion or we can utilize closed-ended questions to get at concrete details quickly. We can also use things like scaling questions (rate on a scale of 1 to 10), relational questions ("Were you more or less upset about . . . ?"), or general reflection questions ("As you think back to when you were in that situation, what feeling was the strongest?") to garner information. Questions can also be used to guide a counselee to particular conclusions, such as asking how a specific text of Scripture relates to her struggle.

We can also use observation skills. What is her body language as she is talking about a struggle? Is she physically tense or relaxed? What are her facial expressions? Is she conveying anger or sadness? Observation of the counselee's outward appearance can tell us much about how she is feeling and her thoughts.

Questions and observations should not convey that she is being "interviewed." Counseling is a *conversation*, not an interrogation. That conversation should happen naturally and easily, just as if she were talking with a friend. It is targeted and intentional, yes, and most likely she is in a more vulnerable place than she would be with most other people, but both counselor and counselee should be comfortable and at ease.

The second aspect of "learn" in this model is learning what God's Word might say about her struggles. Is she conveying that she is depressed? Then where might we see the Bible directly deal with melancholy and despair? The remaining chapters of this text will help point you in the right direction here. Counselors should learn not only about the counselee, but also learn about potential helps and how to give wise counsel. Recall Prov 18:13: "The one who gives an answer before he listens—this is foolishness and disgrace for him." In this verse, the writer reminds his readers we are to listen and listen well before we speak; otherwise, we risk giving a foolish response. To speak wisely, we need to listen to know what to say.

Labor Alongside

A common theme in counseling is the idea of empathy—a term often misunderstood. Put briefly, empathy is the ability to understand and share the feelings of another person. Within the context of counseling, it is the ability of the counselor to listen and learn, then step into the world (feelings, thoughts, context) of the counselee without being consumed by it. Put into New Testament terms, Paul tells us to "carry one another's burdens" (Gal 6:2), and to "rejoice with those who rejoice; weep with those who weep" (Rom 12:15). This is empathy.

I like to imagine this as the counselee carrying a fifty-pound sack of rice. My role as the counselor is to come alongside her, take half that weight, and walk her path with her. That means I climb mountains with her (rather than standing at the top looking down) but also I point her toward the end of that path. She is not alone.

This requires much patience and perseverance. No one comes to counseling because things are going right in their life; they come to counseling burdened and weary. They come needing help. The counselor's role is to recognize the burden and weariness, be willing to step into it, yet retain such a perspective to be able to guide her to the way out.

Let us not forget that we do not labor alongside her alone. If she is a follower of Jesus, the Spirit of God dwells in her, and as believers, he dwells in us as we lead. There are three people carrying that burden, and the reality is that it is ultimately him carrying it for us. Part of laboring alongside a counselee is reminding her often of this reality and continually pointing her to the One who bears our burdens on our behalf.

The first four Ls are essential to develop the counseling relationship. Counseling is vulnerable; we are asking our counselees to share the best and the worst of themselves, their greatest triumphs and deepest struggles. Without any of these four components (loving, listening, learning, and laboring alongside), that therapeutic relationship is not as strong as it could be. Each part fosters trust, openness, and vulnerability in our counselees.

Lead

An essential component of counseling is leading. We can love the counselee, listen extensively, ask all the questions we want, and labor alongside her, but ultimately change comes because she is led toward something.[6] She must be led toward God, his directives, and his healing.

What does this look like in practice? While counselors will each have personal preferences about didactic teaching (leading a counselee through a Bible study or giving direct educational counsel) versus reflective guiding (asking intentional questions to help the counselee arrive at appropriate conclusions), some sort of leading must take place. The counselor and counselee might walk through a particular passage together, jointly applying it to her situation, exploring connections between heart, mind, and behavior (desires, thoughts, and actions). For instance, the counselor may choose to explore Phil 4:5–9 as it relates to a counselee's anxiety, drawing out implications for her unique struggle.

The counselor may also choose to model as a form of leading. For example, prayer can be used, in part, to demonstrate how the counselee might bring her struggles before the Lord, transparently and honestly but also expressing faith and trust in her God (see Psalm 86 for an example). Or the counselor may choose to role-play with the counselee to model conflict resolution. The counselor becomes the teacher/director, but is leading the counselee to draw counsel from the exercise rather than by direct teaching.

Last, the counselee might be directed to journal specific things throughout the week to lead her toward a particular end. This might be used with anxiety, depression, grief, and a host of other struggles, but the intention is to discern patterns of triggers, thoughts, feelings, and behaviors to then address them in the counseling session. Such exercises expose areas of need and lead to appropriate counsel.

Leverage the Local Church

This last *L* isn't one that is often cited in secular approaches to counseling, but it is necessary. This step seeks to connect a counselee with the support system available to her, ideally her spiritual family within the local church, but hopefully that will also include close friends and family.

We are relational beings. None of us exist in isolation, nor should we. Just as God lives in community (as the Trinity), so should we. Therefore, others should be included in a woman's care team.

Research consistently demonstrates that strong support systems are tied to positive counseling outcomes. The greater the support system the woman has, the more likely she is to successfully work through her struggles. Given the nature of the church and what it was created to be (see Acts 2:42–47), we would be foolish not to utilize this resource. God works and moves through his church; we should connect our counselees to that body.

One way to do this is through intentional connection with church leadership and small groups. We should encourage regular attendance, openness with those within the church who can lead and mentor her, and her willingness to be cared for by her brothers and sisters. We want to see ongoing discipleship and personal and corporate worship. As counselors, we can directly and actively encourage her involvement in her local church body.

Church involvement goes beyond support during counseling. Our aim is to transition her out of formal counseling to the care of her church/support system. We cannot counsel her forever. Instead, we want to set her up to have the resources in place so that when she has been led sufficiently by us, when she knows where to go and what to do in her struggles, her church can provide ongoing care for her. This might be a small group or a team approach to care, but it might also be a spiritually mature mentor who can walk alongside her during and after counseling, debriefing after sessions then reminding her of lessons learned once counseling is complete.

The Who and Where of Counseling

Who can and should counsel others? The simple answer is everyone. All believers are called to care for one another (love our neighbors) and bear one another's burdens. All Christians are equipped with the Spirit of God and the

Word of God and are in many ways both called and qualified to love, encourage, and lead others.

However, counseling is unique in that it often brings to light issues that require more training and knowledge than the average churchgoer has. Training in trauma and abuse is tremendously helpful before trying to lead a woman through the complexities of those experiences. More in-depth knowledge about life struggles and the Bible's application to them are warranted.

Many women need counselors who have been trained specifically in counseling as a whole or in particular life struggles. This training might be completed through formal degree programs or certifications in counseling; the level of training would then relate to the types of issues the counselor can and should address. Training may also, however, be direct observation or life experience. Let us not undervalue the role of life experience and appropriate modeling from others in learning how to address life struggles. Ideally, the well-trained counselor will have both formal (educational) and informal (observation and experience) training that leads to wisdom and insight.

God has established within the church a unique structure for leading and teaching. Titus 2:1–6 gives us a helpful model for leadership roles of men and women. The passage encourages older men to lead and teach younger men, while it directs older women to lead and teach younger women. This model is just that: a model. It does not exclude women counseling men or men counseling women. Instead, it is conveying that older women are to *at least* counsel or lead younger women, particularly in the areas noted (in their roles as wives and mothers, to be self-controlled and pure so as not to slander God's Word).

Where should counseling be done? Given that counseling is in obedience to God and essentially ministry to another, ideally this counseling happens within the church. Many churches have counseling available to members or those in the community; such ministries are gospel work and should be celebrated.

However, many churches/pastors/leaders do not have the capacity to counsel within their churches or they have not been formally trained to handle moderate to complex counseling issues. In this situation, parachurch ministries (those outside of a particular church, but intentionally connected to the larger church) might offer counseling services. For instance, a parachurch ministry may focus on those impacted by domestic violence or marital issues. They serve the church and its members, but are able to handle more complex struggles because they specialize in one area and have more extensive training.

Finally, there are situations where clinical practices may be most useful. I assert that biblically based counsel is *always* superior to counsel that is not, so the ideal clinical practice still functions in a way that points people to their greatest need (Jesus) and directs them to truths from God's Word. Given the complexities of state licensure boards and ethical guidelines, sometimes this is more feasible than others. The clinical counselor should remember that they function as a missionary to the culture; their aim is not simply to provide relief but to lead people to proper living in God's truth.

Conclusion

This chapter has covered a lot of ground: a definition and framework for counseling along with brief explorations of the "who" and "where" of counseling. The rest of this text will explore the "what": how we apply biblical truths to various life struggles. Together, they will prepare you to encounter much of what arises in counseling situations.

6

A Woman's Life Stages

It is important that counselors understand the context of a woman in each stage of life. We counsel a fifteen-year-old differently than we would a thirty-five-year-old, and we would counsel that thirty-five-year-old differently than a sixty-five-year-old. Her context matters.

Part of a woman's context is her age and stage of life. Various stages bring different struggles; we will explore some of those below. Not all women will go through all these struggles, and not all women's young adulthood, let's say, will look the same. There is an infinite number of directions a woman's life might take. We must understand the individual woman in her individual context.

However, there are significant commonalities between women in the same stage of life. Most young girls live in their parents' home under their authority, or at least under the care of an adult. Most young women need to figure out what they want to do with their lives and think through possibilities like career, marriage, and friendships. Most middle-aged women must consider their family in the decisions they make. While the particulars of each of these stages are unique to the individual woman, there are common-alities that are useful to keep in mind. This is part of knowing the woman well to lead her well.

This chapter will walk through the four major life stages of a woman, noting common characteristics within each. Each section will list several com-mon struggles experienced by women in these stages, as a point of reference for the counselor seeking to care for the women who desire her counsel. These stages provide some context for the following chapters and should be consid-ered alongside the direction given in the rest of this book.

Childhood and Adolescence

Childhood and adolescence, or the time up until a young person is eighteen, is a time of significant change. Children and teens are growing and changing almost constantly, physically, cognitively, spiritually, emotionally, and relation-ally. This time in a woman's life is marked by more change than any other stage; those changes often bring significant struggles as a young woman fig-ures out who she is and who she wants to be. A few common struggles are addressed below. This list is not comprehensive, only the most common that a counselor might encounter.

Because of the amount of change taking place, there are developmental stressors that come with that change. As a young woman's body changes and matures, she is encountering new things in her life that she has never experi-enced before: the introduction of hormones, physical changes to her body, and adjustments in simple things like gross and fine motor skills. There is a shift in how a young woman relates to those around her (increased independence) and the value she places on those relationships (e.g., the shift from family-based relationships to peer-based ones). Cognitively, she is understanding more and more, moving from concrete to abstract thought and learning how to plan ahead for consequences of actions. Spiritually, as she understands and observes more, she has to wrestle with things that she never has before, like the reality of pain, sin, and suffering.

The developmental stressors impact her struggles in many ways during this life stage. For instance, as a young woman grows, there is typically an increase in family or peer conflict. Much of this is related to the sinfulness of her heart, but it is also impacted at times by a desire for independence, a lack of understanding situations fully, or even the changing hormones that she is learning to control. Conflict is a normal part of life, but it begins early in this stage.

Further, young woman's self-image is formed significantly in this stage. She is figuring out who she is and who she wants to be in relation to those around her. The changing dynamics of family, friendships, and other peer relationships means this is not a static process; her understanding of herself is constantly changing. Depending on the health of these relationships, including her relationship with the Lord, her feelings of self-worth are being formed as well.

This stage also brings the potential for the beginnings of emotional struggles like anxiety and depression. Many women who report these struggles in adulthood can point to a time in their childhood when these feelings began. A young woman is introduced to stress for the first time in this stage, sometimes early in life. Her stress may come from academic demands, peer relationships, or from abusive or unhealthy life situations. A woman's body is built to handle some stress, but it was not meant to endure it constantly. A young woman's exposure to stress and how she copes with it early on in life influences how she handles stress in the future.

Later in this stage, a young woman is faced with important life decisions. In high school (sometimes earlier) a young woman must determine her future educational or vocational endeavors. At such a young age, these decisions can bring significant stress, or feelings of accomplishment or failure. She might also begin romantic relationships that influence future relationships, or she might even begin dating her future husband. Again, at such a young age, decisions like these are significant and impact her future, so they might carry with them a good amount of stress.

We must keep in mind the complexity of a young woman (see chapter 1). It is easy and common for adults, even counselors, to fail to understand teenage girls or children simply because they are viewed with limited capacities or abilities. Adolescents do not yet have all the abilities of adults, but they are capable of quite a bit. Young women should be viewed in light of what God teaches us in his Word, held to appropriate standards for those learning yet still accountable. The wise counselor balances her view of teenagers appropriately, not underestimating them but also not equating them to "little adults."

Young Adulthood

As a young woman transitions into adulthood, changes continue. Most often in this stage of life (ages eighteen to thirty-five), a young woman moves out of her parents' home, either to college and a subsequent job (which might or might not be near her family), straight out of her parents' home to take a job, or by getting married and starting a home with her husband. She might also become a new mother, married or unmarried, during this stage (the topic of motherhood is addressed later in this chapter). A young woman's shifts in relationships are significant during this stage and are likely a major point of conversation in counseling sessions.

There is a broad range of potential struggles that a young woman might face; we will explore some of the most common. First, there is a significant shift in relationships. She goes from being dependent on others (mainly her parents) in childhood to being self-sufficient. She now has to provide for herself financially, pay her own bills (and manage all that paying bills entails), take care of her own residence, and make weighty decisions that could change her life substantially. For instance, she might have to choose who to live with, where to go to school, what job to take, and who she will marry, all as she is coming out of childhood where major life decisions were made in conjunction with her parents. She is balancing independence and uncertainty.

Another struggle the young woman faces is establishing and working toward her goals for the future. She probably has some sense of where she wants to be in ten years' time. For most young women, this is likely to include graduating from college or graduate/professional school, finding a husband, establishing a career, and perhaps beginning a family. Sometimes these goals are unmet, and the young woman finds herself wrestling with a host of emotions (grief, frustration, disappointment) when her life goals don't pan out. She might seek counseling to process these emotions or to figure out how to alter her plans.

Tied with life goals is a sense of identity, much of which is formed in this stage of life. Though quite often identity struggles present themselves earlier on, it is during this stage that women follow through with establishing their identity. For instance, during this period of life many women "make their faith their own." The young woman is actively choosing whether or not to go to church, follow the Lord's directives for her life, or engage in a small group/discipleship group. She no longer has to attend at her parents' behest; for the first time in her life, it's her choice. But in this process of choosing, she might experience uncertainty, isolation, or a lack of support as she finds another community. Other aspects of identity, such as vocation, social circle, sexuality, and personality, also tend to emerge more clearly in this stage.

Another reason a young woman might come for counseling is the amplification of already-established emotional struggles, or the addition of stress in her life. Anxiety and depression that began as a teenager, with the addition of life stressors and independence, tend to magnify. The young woman might not have dealt with those struggles sufficiently as a teenager, perhaps because of lack of counsel, and they are growing as she ages. This stage of life, and the decisions that come with it, increases stress levels, which can contribute to problematic emotions, struggles sleeping or caring for herself, or uncertainty and the inability to make decisions. Such struggles are common counseling issues.

Finally, it is quite common for women toward the end of this stage who remain single (and do not desire to be single) to come to counseling to deal with those unmet expectations. She might have parents urging her to "find someone" because they "want grandkids" or are pushing her to be "less picky." Such conversations only increase dissatisfaction. Many young women in this category begin to question if something is wrong with them, or if they should just settle for a man who is "good enough." If that is the case, the counselor should encourage her and grieve with her, knowing this is a significant issue if it is being presented in counseling. Some women will go on to marry, but others will not; we must recognize that reality and be cognizant of the impact on her life if this is the case.

Middle Adulthood

Middle adulthood, roughly ages thirty-five to sixty-five, makes up a large part of a woman's life. Much happens during this stage. A woman might be single or married, a mother or childless, working or staying at home with children. This stage is quite broad, so the struggles encountered are broad as well.

In this stage, much of a woman's identity and life trajectory has been established. She is likely married, done with her education, starting to have children, and in the career she will stay in. While there are certainly exceptions (each of which is a potential reason to seek counseling), the major life decisions that were present in the earlier stages of life aren't as common in this stage.

When there are significant life decisions, they most often revolve around family matters rather than individual choices. Most likely, the woman in this stage (a married, working mother) has others to consider when making those decisions, whereas the young woman typically only has herself and perhaps one other person (like a new husband) to consider. For the middle-aged woman, a life decision like taking a new job becomes increasingly complex as she considers her husband's thoughts and leadership, her children (their schooling, friends, etc.), selling their home, proximity to her aging parents, and a host of other potential factors. In seeking counsel, quite often she needs help to figure out how to balance all these factors.

Another common counseling issue presented is struggles within her marriage. Perhaps she is experiencing a great deal of marital conflict or is overall dissatisfied in her marriage. She might have a sense of hopelessness that she is "stuck" and unhappy. In such cases, care must be taken to help her understand God's design for marriage and his aims for it—it is not primarily to make her happy, but to bring both spouses closer to him and toward becoming more like Christ. But often, our culture rejects that message, telling her she deserves to be happy. This mix of messages creates internal conflict in a woman, and sometimes she seeks counseling.

Along with struggles in marriage, a woman might come to counseling because of parenting-related issues. Perhaps she and her husband are struggling to start a family (fertility issues) or disagree on if/when to have children. These issues can create significant conflict between partners; if infertility is the issue, it might cause division or emotional pain.

Another parenting issue that might arise is a decision, or decisions, around how to parent. For instance, the woman might want to stay home with their children while the husband works outside the home, or vice versa. They might disagree on this because of value differences or financial concerns. The woman and her husband might also disagree on discipline or rule setting. Perhaps one partner is stricter than the other, creating dissension between them and increasing conflict. The pair might seek out counseling to resolve that conflict or get another opinion on how to parent a particularly difficult child (see chapter 19 on parenting struggles).

There is also the potential in this stage for postpartum depression, particularly when the couple already experiences stress or there is a lack of support from her husband. Postpartum depression is quite common, affecting around 10 percent of women. A woman may find herself struggling with the "baby blues," but can't seem to shake it, so she seeks out counseling. Postpartum depression can also go away for a season and return, or come up in a second, third, or fourth pregnancy when it did not with earlier ones. In such cases, the counselor should provide support and encouragement, but also help her connect with her physician to receive medical treatment.

Finally, just like young adulthood brought greater levels of stress, and therefore had the potential to exacerbate unresolved emotions from earlier in life, the same is true in middle adulthood. During this stage, women are typically juggling more than they ever have, and while many women succeed, that is not always the case. Sometimes, the stress and mental/emotional energy expended become overwhelming, and the emotional struggles that had been pushed aside earlier in life have to be dealt with.

Older Adulthood

As a woman enters the later stage of life, the empty-nest stage or older adulthood (sixty-five-plus), she has undergone significant changes in her life. She has moved from child to young adult and through her middle-adult years and has likely been married (or in a significant relationship) and had children. But now, by sixty-five, those children are adults and probably having children of their own.

The older woman in this stage might find herself single, either having been single throughout her life, now divorced, or because her spouse has passed away. Typically, women outlive men, so it is not uncommon to encounter women who are widowed, which brings new struggles. She might find herself unable to do the things she once could because of chronic pain or physical or health limitations. If her children have moved away, she may be missing her family tremendously.

Several challenges might present themselves in this stage of life. First, as her children move out and potentially after the loss of her husband (through death or divorce), she might struggle with her "new" identity. It is easy for women to view themselves as "so-and-so's wife," or "so-and-so's mom," so when these labels are removed, she struggles with who she is again. Every woman wants to feel valued and wanted; when children grow up and leave, some of this sense of value and necessity is taken away.

She might also struggle with her role as the mother of an adult child. Perhaps this includes her role as a mother-in-law or grandmother, a secondary family member rather than the matriarch. If she had a large role in providing counsel and guidance to her children, once that is no longer needed or sought out, she might struggle with feeling left out or no longer useful. She might even try to insert herself into these relationships, causing conflict.

For older adult women who are still married, there might be marriage adjustments as they move into retirement. She and/or her husband might now be retired and finding themselves at home together much more than they ever were before. This sometimes causes conflict as each has an idea of what retirement will be like; sometimes those expectations do not correspond to reality. Perhaps the woman and her husband disagree on life decisions like whether or not to move closer to children and grandchildren, how to spend money in retirement, or how to spend their time. While marriage in this stage can be sweet and comfortable, when children leave the home, it can also unmask conflict that had been avoided.

Toward the end of middle adulthood and into older adulthood, many women find themselves faced with caring for aging parents. Her own mortality becomes much more real, both as the woman herself ages and as her parents begin to pass away. She might find herself struggling to balance caring for her husband or children/grandchildren with ensuring her aging parents are taken care of. She might feel guilt over her own limitations in caring for them, or she and her husband (or her siblings) might disagree over her role in caring for them.

Finally, some older adults wrestle with their place in doing ministry during retirement. Most sixty-five-year-olds entering retirement are still more than capable of "working," but often do not want the expectation placed on them to do more than they would like to do. A counselor might be sought out to navigate what is realistic for them to consider, but also to encourage them toward a particular area of ministry.

Our Role as Counselor

Much more space could be spent on how to work through each of the potential areas of counseling mentioned above; the following chapters will address many of them. It is the responsibility of the counselor to consider the individual woman and where she is in life, as together they walk through the six stages of helping.

- *Love.* The counselor should love the counselee enough to care about where she is in her life, knowing that her life stage brings with it several potential struggles. The counselor must also, in loving her, point her to the gospel and how it relates to her personally. This certainly must connect to her individual struggle, but it should also relate to her stage of life. For instance, we see in the Scriptures that Jesus welcomed the little children; this is a picture of the gospel to young girls. Also, we see that Proverbs talks about the value of older adults, and that Job 12:12 calls them wise; we should affirm their wisdom and value their life experience.

❧ *Listen.* The counselor should also listen well to the counselee for particular struggles related to her stage of life. This is not to presume that all struggles are related to just her life stage, but quite often, they are nuanced in a way related to the woman's age. For example, parenting in young adulthood (e.g., parenting a two-year-old) looks different from parenting in older adulthood (e.g., parenting a thirty-two-year-old). The wisdom of parenting an adult is greater than that of parenting a child, simply because of life experience. The counselor should listen for those nuances, taking note and incorporating them into their counsel.

❧ *Learn.* In listening to the counselee's story, the counselor should consider the stage of life the woman is in. Her struggles are influenced by her age and her context. They are also influenced by her life experiences up until that point. The wise counselor listens to her story, seeking to learn about her unique struggles in her unique season of life and with her unique experiences. Over time, the seasoned counselor will be able to draw out commonalities with other women in that same stage, providing encouragement from what she has learned helping others in similar situations.

❧ *Labor alongside.* Regardless of the woman's stage of life, the counselor should labor alongside her, bearing her burden with her. This looks different for each woman. For example, a forty-year-old counselor will labor alongside a teenager differently than laboring alongside an older adult. For the teenager, she will encourage, direct, and build a relationship with her. For the older adult, the counselor will focus more on listening, reflecting, and supporting, rather than directing or correcting. Both are laboring alongside, but they differ according to the counselee's stage of life.

- *Lead.* Similarly, the counselor will lead women in different stages somewhat differently. In some ways, the counselor's style of leading will depend on that counselor's own stage of life. Leading young people tends to be more directive and include more teaching, whereas leading older people tends to be more gentle guidance and asking thought-provoking questions. Also, while both counselees are capable of reading God's Word, there is often a large gap in understanding, partly because of life experience. Each stage of life comes with its own challenges, but it is necessary to lead in each stage.

- *Leverage support.* Finally, leveraging support can look different with each stage of life. Support for a teenager might be other peers or young adults with whom the teen already has a relationship, while adult women are often more open to sharing their struggles with other women in a small group setting or with women who have experienced similar struggles. Support for a young woman might naturally be her family, whereas this might not be an option for an older woman. Again, women in each stage of life need the support of those around them, but the type of support might look different depending on the age and context of the woman.

Each stage of helping is necessary for all women, but the stage of life might influence what that helping looks like.

Conclusion

Now that we have explored a woman's various stages of life, we can better understand some of the most common struggles women face. The rest of this book addresses a number of those issues, and while no single chapter can be exhaustive, paired with this chapter, the counselor should feel equipped to love, listen, learn, labor alongside, lead, and leverage support for the women who seek her counsel.

SECTION TWO

✤⌁⌁✤

Common Counseling Issues

7

Depression

> *A young woman in her late twenties, Dawn, shares with you that she has not felt like herself in a long time. "It's like I'm walking through a cloud, but I don't care what's on the other side." She appears as if she hasn't showered in a few days; her hair is disheveled, and she barely makes eye contact. When you ask about her interactions with her family and friends, she just shrugs her shoulders and says, "I'm more of a burden than anything; they don't need all of this." She feels alone and hopeless, like she is fading away into nothing.*

Depression is one of the most common experiences in the mental health realm; the American Psychiatric Association's *Diagnostic and Statistical Manual of Mental Disorders*, 5th edition (hereafter cited as *DSM-5*) reports that it is one of the "most commonly diagnosed conditions in psychiatry."[1] Anyone who counsels regularly will encounter counselees with depression and must be equipped to provide adequate and competent care.

What Is Depression?

What distinguishes depression from general sadness or even grief? This
term is used frequently in our culture to indicate feelings of despair, hopelessness, or deep melancholy, and counselees may describe their experience
using common metaphors (like Dawn in the vignette above), but the term
"depression" must be understood correctly. The *DSM-5* provides a useful set
of criteria that we might consider,[2] but in providing them, it affirms what
we already know as Christian practitioners, a reality we explored in chapter 1: humans are holistic beings. Our experiences of even "mental illnesses"
affect both body and soul. Depression is no exception: the experience of this
condition is not just cognitive or affective (emotional); there is very likely a
physical aspect as well.

A brief look at the *DSM-5* criteria is helpful here. Below are the criteria
listed for Major Depressive Disorder;[3] at least five of the following nine criteria must be met within a two-week period:

a. Depressed mood or irritable most of the day nearly every day
b. Decreased interest or pleasure in most activities
c. Significant weight change
d. Change in sleep
e. Change in physical activity
f. Fatigue or loss of energy
g. Feelings of guilt or worthlessness, or excessive guilt
h. Diminished concentration
i. Feelings or thoughts of suicide

The text indicates alongside these criteria that they must not present proportionate to or "appropriate" for a recent life event, like the loss of a loved one.
Such responses are considered normal and expected. Of the criteria listed
above, at least four of them are physical expressions. While presumably a person could meet the five-of-nine requirement excluding those four and have
little if any physical symptoms, that certainly is not the norm.

This affirms to us as practitioners that we must understand both the complexity and the holistic experience of depression. It is insufficient to address *only* sadness or *only* despair; the whole person must be considered in any treatment approach.

Biblical and Theological Perspectives

Though the Scriptures do not use the term "depression" (that is modern terminology), the Bible has much to say about the experience. Many in biblical history experienced depressive episodes in response to a variety of situations. For instance, Elijah (1 Kgs 19:4) and Jeremiah (Jer 20:14–18) expressed feelings of deep sadness. However, there are two writers in the Bible who are worth more focused attention, to draw some principles for understanding and treating depression.

King David experienced bouts of deep sadness and despair in several situations. David reflects on the depth of his sin in Ps 38:4–8: "My iniquities have flooded over my head; they are a burden too heavy for me to bear. . . . I am bent over and brought very low; all day long I go around in mourning. For my insides are full of burning pain, and there is no soundness in my body. I am faint and severely crushed; I groan because of the anguish of my heart." Though David recognizes that his despair and even physical pain are because of his own sin, his heart is heavy and unbearable. Further, psalm after psalm is written by David in response to his troubles or trials. He acknowledges in Ps 143:4, "My spirit is weak within me; my heart is overcome with dismay," and in Ps 102:4, "My heart is struck down like grass and has withered; I forget to eat my bread" (ESV). These descriptors closely align with someone struggling with depression.

David writes of his own response to someone in that state, "The righteous cry out, and the LORD hears, and rescues them from all their troubles. The LORD is near the brokenhearted; he saves those crushed in spirit" (Ps 34:17–18). David knows, and reminds us, that the Lord hears and responds to those who call to him in their despair. Almost every psalm of lament or crying out to the Lord for help in trials includes some reminder of who God is. Each one urges the reader to look to him for help rather than relying on herself (see Psalms 13, 22, 34, 69, 102, and 143 as examples).

Like David, Job also experienced great depression (see chapter 3). Job's situation is one that is not often considered; his struggle was a direct result of Satan's affliction. Spiritual warfare was a present reality for Job. He lost almost everything he had, understandably resulting in deep sadness and despair. There are three quick lessons to learn from Job. First, note his response to the suffering from the very beginning: "The LORD gives, and the LORD takes away. Blessed be the name of the LORD" (Job 1:21). Job acknowledged the Lord as the source of all things, and blessed him. Second, note the initial response of his friends, even though they would go on to give some poor advice: when they saw him, they wept aloud with him, and then "they sat on the ground with him seven days and nights, but no one spoke a word to him because they saw that his suffering was very intense" (2:13). Job's friends sat and wept with him without saying a word. They observed and they listened before they spoke. Finally, remember the solution to his despair: God himself. Before restoring Job's family and possessions, God's answer to Job's struggle was an encounter with the living God, Creator of all things and Sustainer of all life. Job did not *need* his family or possessions restored; he *needed* God. In his grace, the Lord demonstrated this need to Job in a very direct and personal way.

Moving to the New Testament, James, the brother of Jesus, also offers an important perspective on depression, particularly when it presents as a trial in the life of a believer. He writes, "Consider it a great joy, my brothers and sisters, whenever you experience various trials, because you know that the testing of your faith produces endurance. And let endurance have its full effect, so that you may be mature and complete, lacking nothing" (Jas 1:2–4). He is speaking here to both one's attitude during trials and a proper understanding of the purpose throughout them, teachings certainly applicable to depression.

In a similar vein, Paul reminds us of how we should view struggles like depression. He writes in 2 Cor 4:17, "For our momentary light affliction is producing for us an absolutely incomparable eternal weight of glory." Similarly, the writer of Hebrews says in 12:1–3 that each of us is to run the race that is set before us, pushing forward to Christ as our prize. In both these passages, the focus is not primarily on the situation, but rather on what is coming at the end of the race. That does not diminish the struggle, but it gives it the proper perspective.

The Scriptures are clear that we are holistic beings and therefore our struggles in this world are often holistic as well. They involve the entire person. Many things identify us as individuals: gender, ethnicity, personality, experiences, and so forth, but each of us as women are both body and soul, physical and nonphysical beings. Further, Scripture makes clear the interaction between the nonphysical (heart, mind) and the physical (body, actions/behaviors). Luke 6:45 reminds us that it is from the overflow of the heart that the mouth speaks. Depression, like many struggles, ultimately flows from one's heart. Though there may be physical expressions and perhaps physiological contributing factors,[4] despair and hopelessness ultimately reflect attitudes of the heart. This is why, as James says, we can "count it all joy" when trials come, and why, as David records, we can put our hope in the Lord despite our circumstances. The presence of the Spirit in the heart of the believer is what reshapes those heart desires and beliefs.

Care for the Depressed Woman

Given the dynamics of the heart and mind as they play out in emotions and behaviors, but also the Bible's teachings, how then might we care for the woman struggling with depression? Let's start with the body and work our way back to thoughts and her heart. The aim is to understand the individual woman's depression as fully as possible, starting with the least complex to address and working up to the most complex.

First, we must recognize that there are legitimate physiological factors that might be at play. While the neurotransmitter imbalance theory has widely been rejected,[5] there are a myriad of other factors that might be present. One clear example is postpartum depression (PPD), which is clearly linked to hormonal changes in the pregnant and postpartum woman. In these cases, there are certainly thought processes and desires/motivations at play, but a significant factor is her body. In cases of PPD, or similar conditions like PCOS (which leads to hormonal imbalances) or hypo-/hyperthyroidism, it is wise to involve a physician early on and remember that these hormone imbalances likely can be managed or will resolve on their own.

Another basic, physiologically directed treatment intervention is to regulate the woman's body. In other words, encourage a regular pattern of uninterrupted sleep (if possible), healthy eating patterns, and regular exercise. Taking care of one's body, the temple of the Holy Spirit, is encouraged in Scripture (1 Cor 6:19–20); regulating sleeping, eating, and exercising is an easy approach to help control any potential physiological factors. If hormonal imbalances or other health conditions are suspected, a referral to a physician may be warranted as well.

Another key area of exploration is the counselee's thought patterns and belief systems. Most of the time, a woman's depression "says something": it has messages that play on repeat or pop up regularly. Sometimes these thoughts are easily rejected, but other times they become so ingrained that she struggles to separate truth from lie.

Remember the vignette at the beginning of this chapter? Dawn's response when asked about her support system was that she was a burden and essentially that she was not worth taking care of. Theologically, let's dig into this a bit. Might her care be a burden for someone else? Perhaps, but God tells us to "Carry one another's burdens; in this way you will fulfill the law of Christ." (Gal 6:2). Is she worth taking care of? Absolutely! As an image bearer of our Creator, she is of infinite worth to God and should be to her brothers and sisters. There is clear evidence that she is believing a lie, which is having a direct impact on her emotions and her behavior.

Some other commonly held beliefs or thoughts that flow into depression might be:

- I'm not good enough
- Everything is a failure and not worth working at

- I will never amount to anything
- Nothing in life has turned out the way I want it to, and it won't no matter how hard I try
- No one will ever love me
- It's just not worth fighting anymore

In each of these, thoughts are most likely directly flowing into emotions and resulting actions.

Each of those examples reveals underlying motivations and desires. Taking the above in order, they reveal:

- I desire to earn the affections or approval of others
- I desire control and right now, I don't have it
- I am worthless, yet I want to be worth something (by my standards or theirs)
- I deserve to choose my destiny
- I desire to be loved
- I desire life to be easy

These motivations and desires flow right into thought patterns, which then become emotions and behaviors, specifically depression in these cases. But each of them is also directly counter to what God says in his Word to be true.

What happens if we simply seek to treat the physical or even stop at treating a woman's thoughts? We never get at the underlying root. Timothy Lane and Paul Tripp shared a helpful "three trees model" drawn from Jeremiah 17 and Luke 6:43–45.[6] What these authors demonstrate is that the root drives the fruit; we do not expect apples from an orange tree. Luke writes in 6:43, "A good tree doesn't produce bad fruit; on the other hand, a bad tree doesn't produce good fruit." A tree is known by its fruit. What this means as we counsel women is that (1) we can identify the tree/root (motivation/desire) from the fruit (behavior/emotion/thoughts) on the outside, and (2) we must address the roots underneath to change the fruit. Stopping at behavior or thought patterns is insufficient for change.

Techniques for Change

This section shares some practical interventions or activities that may be used in the counseling room or as homework. Simple interventions such as regulating eating, sleeping, and exercise can be recommended from the first session. Along with those physical disciplines, the counselee should be encouraged to continue in her spiritual disciplines as well. Feeding on the Word of God regularly, presenting requests to the Lord in prayer, and regular individual and corporate worship are essential for healthy spiritual functioning. None of these are recommendations specific only to depression, but they are especially pertinent, given the physical expressions as well as the isolation that depression tends to bring.

The counselor can also seek to determine if there are situational or environmental triggers that are contributing to the counselee's struggles. When these arise, the counselor should aim to adjust them where possible. For example, if the counselee is struggling with stress from work, and feeling hopeless that things will get better, the counselor may help by exploring ways the situation might be changed, a different perspective on her job, or even stress-reduction techniques. While these approaches will not cure, they can aid in recovery.

It is helpful and necessary to explore what drives a woman's depression. What thought patterns are present that are problematic and are the mediators between her heart and her feelings and behavior? Explore with her those listed earlier, but she may also benefit from journaling throughout the week the messages she is hearing. When she feels depressed, what thoughts are going through her mind? Why are these troublesome to her? Which thoughts tend to be on repeat or pop up often and are there themes that can be identified?

The counselor, with this information in hand, can go two different directions, and should go both. Together, they can explore how the counselee's thought patterns are influencing behavior and feelings, demonstrating the connection between them. Then, and more importantly, the counselor can walk with the counselee through identifying underlying beliefs, desires, or motivations that are sinful and counter to God's teaching in his Word. For instance, if a woman is struggling with the thought, "I'm not good enough," the counselor might help her see how that is playing out behaviorally (lack of effort at work or in relationships) and emotionally (feelings of worthlessness or despair), but also the underlying wrong belief and desire to earn affection or approval from others.

Continuing with the example of "I'm not good enough," the counselor must also demonstrate to the counselee the *truth* of God's Word in response. For this counselee, it is helpful to walk through a passage such as Eph 2:8–9 ("For you are saved by grace through faith, and this is not from yourselves; it is God's gift—not from works, so that no one can boast.") or working through Paul's story of conversion despite his opposition to the church (Acts 9). The counselor might help the counselee better understand that she would never be able to earn God's love, and ultimately, his love is the only love that matters. Finally, the counselor can help the counselee put these truths into action as they begin to take root in her heart. Action reflects belief, so the counselee should be challenged to act rightly in response to knowing and believing rightly.

Once the counselor demonstrates this approach, the counselee can begin doing her own exercises as problematic thoughts or feelings come up through the week. Her journal may look something like this:

Thoughts and emotions journal entry:

Problematic thought/behavior: _____

Resulting emotion: _____

Potential underlying motivation or trigger: _____

Biblical truth related to motivation/thought/behavior/emotion: _____

Result if biblical truth is applied (how do I change?): _____

Example:
Problematic thought/behavior: **Felt hopeless about my future**

Resulting emotion: **Sadness, fear, despair**

Potential underlying motivation or trigger: **I want to know the future is secure; I don't like unknowns**

Biblical truth related to motivation/thought/behavior/emotion: **My future is secure in Christ (Jer 29:11; Matt 6:34; Phil 4:19)**

Result if biblical truth is applied (how do I change?): **I trust the Lord with my future knowing that he is working for my good and that he is with me; I act out of confidence and trust rather than fear and despair**

These heart and mind restructuring activities, paired with basic counseling skills like motivational interviewing, active listening, and empathy go a long way to help a woman struggling with depression, but it is not the only course of action. Paired with regulating her body and spiritual life, the counselor should also consider what support system she has in place. God created us to live relationally from the very beginning (see chapter 1) and designed the church to serve as a family, bearing one another's burdens and meeting each other's needs. Is this counselee connected to a church family who can support her, who can proclaim the truth of the Scriptures to her in both word and action, and who can encourage her regularly? Is there also an area in which she can serve, to focus on others rather than her own struggles? If not, these must be priorities for the counselor.

Additionally, it may be worth considering whether physiological factors could be at play and if/how medication might be useful. It is my opinion that medication is not a first resort unless physiological factors are overtly evident (such as with postpartum depression, or cyclical hormonal issues around her monthly period); instead, it might be considered if and when other interventions fall short.[7] When we work with a counselee for a significant amount of time and see that, while progress is being made, she is still struggling despite her best efforts, or she is struggling to even function or focus on the tasks laid out for her, the counselor might recommend an evaluation for medication by her general practitioner or psychiatrist.[8]

Because of the nature of depression, it is essential that the counselor be aware of and screen often for suicidality. Suicidal thoughts and intentions can change in an instant, and while the counselor cannot be there for every change in thought throughout the week, she can open lines of communication with the counselee about suicidal thoughts. For more information about this topic, see chapter 12.

Possible Homework Assignments

Here are some homework assignments a counselor might introduce to help between sessions:

- Journal problematic thoughts and appropriate responses (as demonstrated above).
- Set a weekly schedule for physical and spiritual care and stick to it.
- Find two or three people who can act as a support system for day-to-day struggles or needs.
- Engage in service in a ministry of choice.
- Read through the Psalms noted in this chapter (13, 22, 34, 69, 102, and 143); meditate on each one and write a personal psalm that is reflective of her struggle.
- Make a list of things she is thankful for, concrete examples of God's goodness to her and provision for her.
- Particularly when feelings of hopelessness or despair arise, practice the thankfulness list but specifically pair with a grounding exercise, such as "I'm thankful for the ability to see God's creation," or "I'm grateful for the way it feels to hold my child."

Conclusion

Depression is difficult for any woman to walk through; recovery is often long and takes much patience on the part of the counselee and counselor. Sometimes depression is long-lasting. In these situations especially, the ultimate aim is to help the counselee know God and glorify him, not a (possibly) unrealistic expectation of their depression ending. We can have fullness of life and flourish in spite of suffering, but this requires that we trust God in the midst of it. Thankfully, the Lord has given us adequate tools for ministering and caring for women who are struggling with depression. He demonstrates in his Word that hope is found in him, peace is available through him, and deliverance will be given to his children, though ultimately each of those is satisfied in eternity. As we counsel, let us point our sisters to these truths and pray the Spirit would allow them to take root in the hearts of our counselees.

Recommended Resources

Berger, Daniel, *Rethinking Depression: Not a Sickness Not a Sin* (Taylors, SC: Alethia International, 2019).

Bridge, William, *A Lifting Up for the Downcast* (Louisville: GLH, 2014).

Eswine, Zack, *Spurgeon's Sorrows: Realistic Hope for Those Who Suffer from Depression* (Fearn, UK: Christian Focus, 2015).

Greene-McCreight, Kathryn, *Darkness Is My Only Companion: A Christian Response to Mental Illness* (Ada, MI: Brazos Press, 2015).

Hodges, Charles, *Good Mood, Bad Mood: Help and Hope for Depression and Bipolar Disorder* (Wapwallopen, PA: Shepherd Press, 2012).

Lloyd-Jones, D. Martyn, *Spiritual Depression: Its Cause and Its Cure* (London: HarperCollins, 1998).

Piper, John, *When the Darkness Will Not Lift: Doing What We Can While We Wait for God and Joy* (Wheaton, IL: Crossway, 2006).

Welch, Ed, *Depression: Looking Up from the Stubborn Darkness* (Greensboro, NC: New Growth Press, 2011).

8

Fear and Anxiety

Lydia comes to see you for counseling and is visibly tense. You can tell she has had a lot on her mind lately. She shares with you that recently she has felt more anxious than usual with "all that's going on in the world." Though much of what she seems worried about is what she sees on the news, it all feels very personal to Lydia. She cannot seem to shake the sense that she is in constant danger and lives in a world where people are "out to get me for no good reason." She struggles even to put her finger on what exactly she is anxious about, but she shares that she is having trouble sleeping despite feeling exhausted, she feels tense all the time, and her mind is always racing. She wants help to "just calm down" and "stop feeling so afraid all the time."

Fear and anxiety are common experiences for us. We live in a world filled with sin and threats of danger; one need only turn on the news for a few minutes to see this is an ever-present reality. And yet, sometimes fears transition into unhealthy worry and anxiety. They extend beyond an immediate threat of harm. And for some, the anxiety becomes consuming, debilitating the person and leading to struggles with functioning or relating to others. When faced with this as counselors, how can we best help the women we seek to serve? What answers does the Bible give for these struggles? This chapter addresses what fear, worry, and anxiety look like, what the Bible has to say, and how we might counsel women struggling in this area.

What Do Fear, Worry, and Anxiety Look Like?

Most of us have a sense of what fear and anxiety are, but the experience of each is often varied and complex. Let's start with some definitions to frame our discussion.

Fear

Fear is a normal response to real or perceived threats. A sense of fear is inborn in us; it is natural. And fear was designed in us to serve a purpose: to keep us safe. Fear produces both physical and nonphysical responses. Upon encountering a significant threat, physically we experience the fight-or-flight sensation: a flood of hormones preparing the body to either flee or fight, accompanied by a rapid heart rate or breathing, muscles tensing, and a focus on the threat. In extreme cases, instead of a fight-or-flight response, the person may experience a "freeze" response, in which the body and mind shut down out of self-protection. Often the person becomes narrowly focused on the threat, blocking out everything else, like a sense of panic or being overwhelmed. A flood of emotions may accompany the threat. Once safe, the person is often tired physically, mentally, and emotionally.

Fear contributes to both concern (or awareness) and worry/anxiety, but one is an appropriate response while the other is not. Think of it this way:

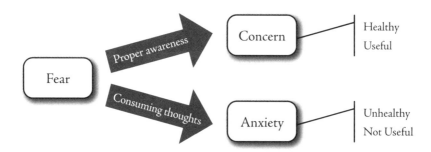

In one direction is what we call concern or awareness. This is not quite worry or anxiety; rather, it is an acknowledgment of potential dangers or real threats, but it is not consuming and typically does not produce the effects noted above. At times, it can be quite wise. Understanding the risks of engaging in certain dangerous behaviors would be considered pertinent. Concern is acknowledging actions and their consequences.

Worry or anxiety, on the other hand, is a lingering sense of fear or concern over a potential future event. At times, worry or anxiety might become consuming or debilitating, impacting a woman's functioning or ability to carry out normal tasks. Anxiety and worry are the continual manifestation of fear, focused on an unknown future threat. Consider the difference, for instance, between not being able to drive out of the potential threat of being in a car accident versus the immediate fear experienced as an accident is beginning. The latter is a natural, expected response to a real and present threat; the former is consuming and debilitating, yet focuses on a *potential* threat that has not come to pass.

These manifestations are both physical and nonphysical. It might be helpful to briefly review the *DSM-5*'s criteria for Generalized Anxiety Disorder,[1] as generally observed commonalities for anxiety:

a. excessive anxiety and worry for at least six months (i.e., the anxiety is long-lasting)
b. individual finds it difficult to control the worry
c. anxiety and worry are associated with three (or more) of the following six symptoms:

      i.   restlessness, feeling keyed up or on edge

     ii.   being easily fatigued

    iii.   difficulty concentrating or mind going blank

    iv.   irritability

     v.   muscle tension

    vi.   sleep disturbance (difficulty falling or staying asleep, or restless, unsatisfying sleep)

   d.   anxiety, worry, or physical symptoms cause significant distress or impaired functioning

   e.   anxiety is not better explained by another disorder or condition

Though anxiety primarily takes place in the nonphysical realm (thoughts, beliefs, desires, behaviors), it produces and may be then furthered by physical manifestations as well. It is a whole-person experience.

For the purposes of this chapter, we will focus on the unhealthy (sinful) responses to fear—worry and anxiety—but include how those responses differ from an appropriate (nonsinful) level of concern.

What the Bible Has to Say about Fear and Anxiety

Given the reality that we live in a sin-filled world full of danger and potential threats, it is no surprise that fear and anxiety plague us. There are over 300 references to fear and worry/anxiety in the Scriptures, perhaps because the Lord knows our tendency toward it in the middle of danger and uncertainty. Scripture's teachings about fear tend to circle around three key themes.

First, God's Word demonstrates to us properly placed fear: the fear of the Lord. Ecclesiastes 12:13 (ESV) says, "The end of the matter; all has been heard. Fear God and keep his commandments, for this is the whole duty of man." In wrapping up his teachings, the author summarizes everything he has written with this one statement: our sole purpose is to fear God and obey him. The obedience, it seems, flows out of our fear of God. Not an unhealthy, running-away-afraid sort of fear, but a reverent awareness of who God is. To this point, the psalmist says in Ps 33:8, "Let the whole earth fear the LORD;

let all the inhabitants of the world stand in awe of him." Rightly placed fear
is fear of God.

Second, we are commanded not to fear/worry/be anxious; in almost every
case, the verb given is an imperative, something we are to *do*. For example,
Isa 41:10 says, "Do not fear, for I am with you; do not be afraid, for I am your
God. I will strengthen you; I will help you; I will hold on to you with my righteous right hand." Twice in this verse we are commanded not to be afraid. And
the reason is clear: God is present and will help us. In the New Testament,
perhaps the most commonly used passage on anxiety is Phil 4:5–9. Paul
writes in verse 6, "Don't worry about anything, but in everything, through
prayer and petition with thanksgiving, present your requests to God." Again,
the command is clear not to be anxious and the proper response is provided:
present the needs to God through prayer. In verse 7, he promises peace that
surpasses understanding.

Last, the Scriptures speak at length to the proper response to threats
or uncertainty: trust in the Lord. In Prov 29:25, we read, "The fear of mankind is a snare, but the one who trusts in the Lord is protected." The writer
of Proverbs is telling us that fear is a trap that can easily entangle us; help
and protection are found in the Lord. David gives us clear teaching as well in
Ps 56:3–4, where he writes, "When I am afraid, I will trust in you. In God,
whose word I praise, in God I trust; I will not be afraid. What can mere
mortals do to me?" David recognized that man ultimately held little power
over him. His God, our God, is trustworthy and therefore we have no reason
to fear. David reminds us that fear is not primarily an emotion, but a belief
system that presents itself as a feeling or behavior. For David, his belief in the
protection of the Lord combated feelings of fear or anxiety.

Several truths are apparent from Scripture as we fight fear, worry, and
anxiety:

Fear in and of itself is not sinful; improperly placed fear is. Fear must be
held in proper perspective. We are to fear the Lord, but this fear is more an
awe and awareness of his might. He is not a threat to us, his children, but
a compassionate Father. Conversely, we can confront fears of earthly threats,

even legitimate ones, with truths about God's sovereignty and power. He is present with his people and will not forsake them. This means even the greatest of threats can be met with certainty that the Lord is present and in control.[2]

The Bible gives clear commands not to be anxious; anxiety reveals a lack of trust in God. Remember Jesus's teaching in Matt 6:25–34 about the lilies of the field and the birds of the air. He teaches that God provides for their needs and he will for ours; worry over needs (even legitimate ones) reveals a lack of trust in our loving Father. This passage is bookended by explicit commands not to worry. Instead, we are to seek his kingdom and he will provide what we need.

The answer to our worries and anxieties is ultimately to trust our Provider. Remember the example above of David from the Bible. He often had cause for fear and worry: he faced a giant who could easily end his life, he led armies into battle, Saul chased him to kill him, and he had a host of family problems to deal with. And yet, over and over in the Psalms David writes that he will trust in God. He held real concerns over his and his family's well-being, but they did not consume him. Instead, they drove him to the feet of his Savior and forced him to act on his belief that God would help him in his moment of need. David understood that he was powerless to remove these threats or meet his own needs, so he must trust the Lord to do it for him. This went beyond simply a cognitive affirmation of who God is; instead, it was a deep, heart-held belief that God was on his side. God is sovereign (1 Chron 29:11–12), he is trustworthy (Ps 9:10), and he provides (Matt 6:31–33), so we can always count on him.

God will meet our needs in his time, not ours. Recall the time that the Israelites spent in the desert waiting for the Promised Land. How did God provide for them? He sent manna and quail *daily* to meet *that day's* needs. One day a week, he sent a double portion so they could rest on the seventh day. God knew what they needed and he provided it; they did not have to worry about the food coming the next day because they knew he was faithful to provide it. But the food would spoil if they tried to store it up; God was teaching them to trust him to meet their needs in his time rather than theirs.

Care for the Anxious Woman

So, what do we make of all of this? How do we fight worry and anxiety when legitimate needs or threats exist? The following responses may prove useful for counselors:

Acknowledge that legitimate needs, threats, and concerns are present. In each of the above examples from Scripture, a real need existed, like food or safety. All women have needs, and as women living in a sin-filled world, there are real threats against us. We must recognize this reality, not dismiss the woman's concerns as if they do not matter.

Acknowledge that our responses might be appropriate, but they might also be sinful. As we explored above, we can appropriately respond to a present threat with fear or hold an awareness of dangers that exist. These are not sinful responses; they keep us safe and serve a purpose. But we might also respond to fears/needs with anxiety or worry, essentially a lack of trust in our Provider. This goes against God's commands for us in his Word, so it is a sinful response.

Address the whole person. Anxiety is multifaceted and complex; we cannot simply stop *feeling* anxious or force our heart rates to slow. As counselors, we must seek to address worry and anxiety, driven by underlying fear, as holistically as possible, treating both the inner and outer person. This means, perhaps, that we deal with underlying beliefs or a lack of trust *while* seeking to lessen panic attacks or regulate sleep (see more below). One is not done at the expense of the other.

Explore the underlying fears that contribute to the counselee's anxiety. Anxiety always has a message. Those messages might be:

- I need _____ and do not have it.
- I may lose _____ that is valuable to me.
- I am or will be in danger if _____ happens.

As counselors, we should seek to evaluate these underlying fears. What is driving this counselee's anxiety? What specifically is she afraid of? Only after we discover her fears can we seek to address her worries.

Seek to revise any improper beliefs. As Luke 6:45 reminds us that it is out of the abundance of the heart that one's mouth speaks. In other words, we say and do (and think) as a direct reflection of what is in our hearts (beliefs, desires, and motivations). The same is true of anxiety. As counselors, and as it relates to these underlying matters, we can evaluate the following in our counselee:

- Does she believe that God is not capable?
- Does she believe that it is completely up to her?
- Does she see herself wrongly (as inadequate or weak) despite the promises in God's Word?
- Does she believe that circumstances are beyond God's control?
- Is her view of herself completely wrapped up in another's approval?

When these or other falsehoods are present, we can seek to correct the underlying beliefs.

Teach her about biblical truths related to her fears. We explored several key ways the Bible speaks to our fears, worries, and anxieties. These realities can and should be communicated clearly to our counselees. She can be reminded that God is present with believers continually and is trustworthy. He will meet her needs in his time. Jesus knows our struggles intimately and is there to provide grace and mercy in time of need (Heb 4:14–16). These truths can bring comfort in the midst of anxiety.

Help her repent of false beliefs or a failure to trust the Lord. The diagram above demonstrated that while concern is healthy and proper (nonsinful), worry and anxiety are not. They directly go against the Lord's commands and, most often, demonstrate a lack of trust in the Lord and his provision. Because of that, we must take sin seriously. As counselors, we can help our counselees walk through repentance, turning and trusting that the Lord is gracious and kind, granting forgiveness and help with her anxiety. This does not mean that she will no longer struggle; we all deal with ongoing sins that we must fight daily. But it does mean that she is acknowledging her wrong and she desires, with the Lord's help, to turn from that wrong.

Slowly walk her through dealing with her anxiety while teaching her how to respond well. Help her practice! Talk through situations or fears that lead to her anxiety and teach her how to respond rightly to that particular struggle. For instance, if her fear is driving, talk through the various aspects of driving and address bit by bit what leads to anxiety and why. In each, discuss the truths shared above and help her think and behave appropriately with each piece. This gives her the tools to do the same when faced with that stressor on her own.

Consider the inclusion of physical interventions. While these should not be done at the exclusion of the interventions above, as counselors we may consider treatment specifically for her body. We might teach muscle relaxation exercises to help calm the physiological responses that accompany her anxiety. We might teach her how to handle an impending panic attack[3] as she feels it coming on. Or we might connect her with a physician to discuss the possible place of antianxiety medication[4] to help stabilize her emotions or intrusive thoughts.[5] We must recognize that habituated fear or anxiety that took a long time to develop, might take a long time to treat as we, in part, must retrain our habituated brain with a new habit.[6]

Helpful Homework Exercises

The following exercises are useful both in session and as between-session homework assignments:

Memorize passages related to anxiety and work toward actively connecting them to everyday anxiety. As with many life struggles, reminding ourselves often of the truths of Scripture can actively combat problematic thoughts, feelings, behaviors, and desires. The anxious woman can memorize and meditate on any of the passages listed above (specifically Isa 41:10, Phil 4:5–9, and Ps 56:3–4), but also passages like Matt 6:34, Ps 34:4, John 14:27, and Ps 23. We can encourage the counselee to pray in line with the truths contained in these verses, journal her personal thoughts, or even write her own personal reminder cards to carry with her for when she is fearful or anxious.

Journal about anxious thoughts and feelings. The counselee can be encouraged to journal when anxious feelings arise. It is helpful for the counselor to first demonstrate this approach, but then the counselee can begin doing her own exercises as anxious thoughts or feelings come up through the week. Her journal may look something like this:

Thoughts and emotions journal entry:

Situation in which I was anxious: _____

Problematic thought/behavior: _____

Potential underlying motivation, desire, or trigger: _____

Biblical truth related to motivation/thought/behavior/emotion: _____

Result if biblical truth is applied (how do I change?): _____

Example:

Situation in which I was anxious: **Driving to the store**

Potential underlying motivation or trigger: **I think that I am in danger; I will get in an accident and die**

Biblical truth related to motivation/thought/behavior/emotion: **God is trustworthy, sovereign, and is for my good; even if the worst happens (I get in an accident and die), God is still good**

Result if biblical truth is applied (how do I change?): **I trust the Lord as I drive; I act out of confidence and trust rather than fear and worry**

Practice thinking about things that lead to anxiety and rehearse responding rightly. Taking meditating on Scripture and journaling a bit further into action, counselors can encourage women to practice doing the last aspect of the journal entry: the practical change when biblical truth is applied. Using the example given in the journal entry above, the counselee can walk through a series of practice exercises, such as playing out in her mind how she might drive somewhere, drive a short distance (such as through her neighborhood), then drive farther and farther. In each situation, she can consistently remind herself of what she has been taught from the Scriptures and rehearse how she can respond rightly to her fears. This might include leveraging a support person to reflect what she has learned in counseling and help her respond appropriately.

Regulate physical contributors such as sleeping, eating, and exercising. Because of the role of the body in anxiety, it might be helpful to regulate her body as much as possible, reducing physical stress and strain. All of us understand, for instance, that a lack of sleep increases stress and inability to focus. By helping her set a schedule for sleeping, eating, and exercising consistently, we are caring for her body and establishing norms that reduce unnecessary physical stress.

Practice relaxation and calming exercises. We discussed the role of the fight-or-flight mechanism in the body that flows out of fear and contributes to anxiety. One way to combat the fight-or-flight response is to consciously relax and create a sense of physical calm and safety—fighting fear with calm. After being instructed and modeled in session, a counselor can instruct the counselee to do grounding or relaxation exercises on her own when her anxiety arises. While these should not be done at the exclusion of dealing with underlying fears, when used along with the techniques above, grounding/relaxation exercises can make those interventions more effective. When the body is calm, the mind can think more clearly and evaluate emotions more easily. She can therefore more easily discern her emotions and thoughts, then determine how to align them with God's desires for her life.

Conclusion

While fear and anxiety are common, they are experiences that are addressed clearly in God's Word. He has much to say about where our fear should and should not be placed and how to rightly combat our worry. The counseling points and exercises in this chapter can significantly aid a woman struggling with worry or anxiety. With the Lord's help, using this approach, anxiety can be overcome.

Recommended Resources

Fitzpatrick, Elyse, *Overcoming Fear, Worry, and Anxiety: Becoming a Woman of Faith and Confidence* (Irvine, CA: Harvest House, 2001).

Jones, Robert, *Why Worry?: Getting to the Heart of Your Anxiety*, Resources for Changing Lives (Phillipsburg, NJ: P&R, 2018).

Lane, Tim, *Living without Worry: How to Replace Anxiety with Peace* (Epsom, UK: Good Book, 2015).

Powlison, David, *Overcoming Anxiety: Relief for Worried People* (Greensboro, NC: New Growth Press, 2012).

Thompson, Jessica, *How to Help Your Anxious Teen: Discovering the Surprising Sources of Their Worries and Fears* (Irvine, CA: Harvest House, 2019).

Wallace, Jocelyn, *Anxiety and Panic Attacks: Trusting God When You're Afraid* (Greensboro, NC: New Growth Press, 2013).

Welch, Ed, *Running Scared: Fear, Worry, and the God of Rest* (Greensboro, NC: New Growth Press, 2007).

———, *When I Am Afraid: A Step-by-Step Guide Away from Fear and Anxiety* (Greensboro, NC: New Growth Press, 2008).

9

Grief

Karen is a sixty-two-year-old woman who has been married for thirty-four years to her husband, Bill. They have three grown children, all married with kids of their own. About two weeks ago, Karen woke up one morning to find that Bill had passed away unexpectedly during the night. She tried to wake him, but when the medics arrived they said he had likely suffered a heart attack in his sleep. The doctors confirmed the heart attack shortly after his death. Bill was generally in good health; there were no indications he was having heart problems.

For the past two weeks, Karen has felt like she is in a daze. She barely eats, finds it hard to get out of bed, and struggles to even put her thoughts together. Her children and her church family have been supportive, stepping in to help her with funeral arrangements and daily tasks such as meals and laundry. Everyone is trying to encourage her and remind her that Bill is with the Lord, but Karen often finds herself angry at God and at Bill's doctors for missing the impending heart attack. Once or twice, she has lashed out at those around her,

*only to quickly realize what she has done and apologize. She feels like she will
never get out of this fog; she doesn't know who she is without Bill. Even looking
at pictures of him feels like a reminder that he is never coming back.*

Grief is a normal part of life. At some point in our lives, we will experience grief as a response to some sort of loss. While grief is typical, it is still an
experience that often leaves us in a state of confusion or emotional upheaval.
Time heals many wounds, but it doesn't make the present grief-filled reality
any more bearable.

This chapter walks through several topics, including a description of
grief, how it presents itself in counseling, a biblical/theological perspective
of grief, some points of counsel as the counselor seeks to come alongside the
grieving counselee, some practical exercises, and some practical resources for
further study.

Keep in mind that it is not the experience of grief that is our primary
focus, though that is certainly important; rather, it is our response to the trig-
gering event. How might we, counselor and counselee, respond in faith despite
immense pain? Will we grieve loss in a way that acknowledges pain yet honors
the Lord? In the face of losing a loved one, will we grieve like those who have
no hope (1 Thess 4:13)? Our understanding of grief, whether it aligns with
a biblical understanding of grief or not, will drive our response and counsel.

The Connection of Grief and Loss

There are a multitude of definitions of grief available.[1] For our purposes here,
grief is defined as a whole-person response to a real or perceived loss, including emotions/affect, thoughts/cognition, and physical/bodily responses.
Grief encompasses the entire person, physical and nonphysical, yet is clearly
related to some sort of event. That event, the loss, may be either real or perceived, tangible or intangible.

Some categories of loss that may lead to grief include the following:

Material or physical loss: the loss of material possessions or a person

Abstract loss: the loss of love, the loss of hope, the loss of ambition; the loss of a dream or perceived future

Relational loss: loss of a relationship, such as a marriage, due to an event such as death or divorce

Role loss: life changes that result in loss of a social/relational role, such as becoming a widow after being a wife or becoming an empty nester

Functional loss: the loss of functional capabilities, such as with a physical or mental impairment

Ambiguous loss: a loss that brings uncertainty or confusion, such as one's experience upon an Alzheimer's diagnosis

Each of these is indeed a loss. We often tend to focus on the more tangible losses; however, the loss of a perceived future and memories with the recent passing of a loved one may bring more grief than the loss of the actual person. The counselor, then, must aim to understand not only the various types of losses, but the respective impact that each of those losses has on our counselee.

Grief is typically proportionate to the loss; the perception of the loss matters greatly. Two people may experience the same event, the same loss, and yet perceive its impact in completely different ways. There are many factors that contribute to one's perception, and therefore experience, of loss (such as personal resiliency, impact on everyday life, whether the loss was expected or unexpected), which directly translates into their experience of grief. The wise counselor, then, should be aware of these factors when working with a grieving counselee.

What Does Grief Look Like?

It may be tempting to believe it is obvious when a person is grieving, because most often what is associated with grieving is outward expressions of sadness, such as weeping or what the Scriptures describe as a soul dejected and in turmoil (Ps 42:5). Even the psalmist in the same passage talks about mourning, that his "tears have been [his] food day and night" (v. 3). This is what we typically expect when someone is grieving.

There are various positions on the stages of grief and whether one should be expected to walk through the stages methodically.[2] However, grief is both complex and, in many ways, unpredictable. One woman may walk methodically through clear stages of grief, while another may vacillate between various emotional responses. Still another may accept and adjust to a loss quickly. The counselor's concern therefore is not so much with the progression itself, but with abnormal presentations of the expression of grief.[3] For instance, it would be cause for concern if the counselee continually denies the traumatic event or the loss, in an attempt to put off dealing with her grief. Or a counselee for whom the grief is intensified or prolonged beyond what is deemed appropriate for the loss may not be dealing with her grief in a way that is healthy or helpful. This understandably brings a level of subjectivity to the counselor's evaluation.

There are other presentations of grief that are normal, yet often unexpected. For instance, along with sadness, a woman may feel despair, hopelessness, numbness, or emptiness. Sometimes a grieving woman may find it hard to focus on mundane, everyday tasks; what used to be automatic is no longer. She might have lapses in memory, particularly short-term memory. In addition, the grieving woman might experience nightmares or flashbacks centered on the loss. Since humans are both body and soul, our bodies are not exempt from the effects of grief. A woman may experience changes in sleeping or eating patterns, even changes in how much she wants to talk to or interact with others. The physical stress that comes with grief may cause exhaustion, headaches, even illnesses in a weakened body. Grief is a whole-person experience, not just an outwardly expressed behavior. This is especially true for children, who may experience more physical symptoms, like stomachaches or developmental regressions, than emotional or mental struggles.

In the spiritual realm, grief can cause us to wrestle with our theology, bringing with it a host of questions, particularly if the loss was intensely personal and unexpected. A counselee is likely to ask questions such as, Is God really good? Is he truly sovereign? Is he worth my trust? These questions are normal and not to be feared. They are not indicative of a lack of faith; rather, they are evidence of wrestling with one's faith and wanting to hold on to it.

Remember that the emotions of a grieving woman may come and go and, at times, may even seem contradictory. We must be able to hold all of these in tandem. An adult caregiver may feel sadness over the loss of a parent, and at the same time she might feel relief that her parent is no longer in pain. The caregiver might also feel relief that the burden of caring for this parent no longer falls on her. It is not uncommon for this second form of relief to usher in feelings of guilt, as if the relief from a personal burden being lifted indicates something negative about her feelings toward her parent. Thus, in this one example, the counselee may be presenting with emotions of sadness, relief, and guilt all at the same time over the loss of her parent.

Grief typically does not happen in ways that are expected. One way this presents is in recurring emotions and responses; we do not simply grieve once over a loss and never grieve again. Triggers and reminders will lead to reexperiencing grief over time. As counselors, we should expect responses to grief to return time after time and communicate that expectation to our counselees.

Biblical and Theological Perspectives

In considering how to care for grieving women, we first look to Scripture's descriptions and prescriptions for how we are to grieve. Women are not alone in our experience of grief; God experiences it as well. But like other emotions, for instance, anger, it is important to note *under what circumstances* God grieves and *how he responds* to that emotion. Both are pertinent to counselors and counselees.

God's Expressions of Grief

In Scripture, we primarily see God's grief over sin or the impact of sin on his creation. In Gen 6:5–6, God is grieving over the wickedness of man and the evil in his heart. God grieved that sinfulness; the passage says he regretted making man. Jesus demonstrates grief over the death of Lazarus—the effects of sin on someone he cared about deeply—in John 11:32–36. And in Eph 4:30, Paul tells us that we grieve the Holy Spirit when we sin. In each of these examples, the resounding theme is that the triune God grieves over sin itself and the impact of sin on his creation, especially on his image bearers. Sin results in death: not only our physical death, but also the need for Christ to die on our behalf. God grieves these things just like we do.

Scripture also speaks at length about God's responses to our grief. Isaiah 53:3–5, a passage prophesying the Messiah, connects God's experiences of grief with our own. Not only was Christ "a man of sorrows and acquainted with grief," he "has borne our griefs and carried our sorrows" (ESV). He carried our grief alongside his own; he both experiences and responds to sorrow. Hebrews 4:15–16 indicates that we can be comforted knowing that he has experienced temptations, even in grief, just as we have.

The Scriptures are clear that grief is not an eternal reality. Isaiah talks of the new heaven and the new earth in Isaiah 65. Revelation 21:4 gives us a picture of eternity, saying "He will wipe away every tear from their eyes. Death will be no more; grief, crying, and pain will be no more, because the previous things have passed away." Grief, one day, will be gone forever because sin will no longer be a reality in God's kingdom.

What does this mean for us, both as counselors and counselees? First, it should bring comfort that God grieves over sin, and we may as well. We can weep over our own sin and the sin of others. Just as God grieves over the impact of sin, we can too. We may grieve when a loved one dies, when injustice is committed, or we are sinned against. We may also grieve when something good is lost or taken from us. We can take comfort in knowing God sees our sorrow; he has experienced it and cares deeply when we experience it as well.

Important Distinctions for Our Own Grief

There are some differences between godly grief and sinful grief. Although God does not sin, we do; this means our experience or expression of grief may be tainted by sin also. A few comparisons, then, are in order.

First, God grieves knowing the rest of the story. He knows the outcome. Paul wrote of losing loved ones that we should not grieve as those who have no hope (1 Thess 4:13). We can grieve knowing our God is in control. Second, God is wise and we are not. In God's expressions of grief, he rested in his own wisdom, sovereignty, and plans for the future. He knew he had control of the outcome. As believers, we must rest knowing that these truths do not depend on our losses or our experience of grief. God remains good, sovereign, and wise. Third, God's responses to grief are always good and appropriate. While he grieves, he does not sin; he is not anxious, fearful, or hopeless. And yet, many times our grief is accompanied by these emotions, and sinfully so. Therefore, we must be aware that we might sin in our grief and repent of that sin, aligning ourselves more closely to God's examples of grief experiences in Scripture.

Scripture's Direct Teachings on Grief

We also have examples in the Scriptures of how the people of God grieved. One example is in the book of Job. Job had experienced tremendous loss, more than many of us can fathom. We see the proper and improper responses of those around him to Job's experiences. On the positive side, when his friends learned of his loss, they came and sat in silence with him for seven days, openly weeping with him. And yet, those same friends, along with Job's wife, gave him very poor counsel soon afterward. At the end of the book, we see God's response. In the last several chapters, God provides the answer to Job's grief: remembering God's sovereignty, wisdom, and provision.

Another helpful example is David's grief over his sin before God. After he was confronted about his sin with Bathsheba, taking her as his own and having her husband killed, he was overcome with grief about his sin. Psalm 51, in which David repents at length before the Lord, is the outpouring of that grief. Similarly, in 2 Samuel 12, after the death of his son, we see David's outward expressions of grief: refusing to eat, lying on the ground, unwilling to take part in his kingly duties. Such responses are typical of grief, even today.

Along with these examples, of which many more could be shared, Scripture speaks clear encouragement to those who are grieving. Psalm 34:18 says, "The Lord is near the brokenhearted; he saves those crushed in spirit." Those who are grieving can be assured the Lord is near to them. Psalm 23, familiar to many of us, is a reminder that even through the "valley of the shadow of death," there is no fear because the Lord is with us. Many who are grieving feel as if they are walking through a valley of death, but they can rest knowing that God is ever present with them. Additionally, Isaiah 40 speaks about suffering and comfort. Those who are grieving need strength because they are faint and weary, and they can find comfort in our God.

Finally, passages like 2 Cor 4:17 and Rom 8:18 remind the New Testament believers that future glory will far outweigh current suffering. The believer is encouraged to have a godly, eternal perspective rather than a temporal one. Essentially, we are to remember the future outcome that we are told about, the reality that God will establish his kingdom, free of grief and sorrow.

Counseling Steps

While grief and the process of working through grief is highly individualized, there are some commonalities that counselors must keep in mind as they seek to minister to women who find themselves dealing with loss. Many of the following reminders are simply good practices for any counseling situation; however, in the midst of a loss, the impact of counseling well or not counseling well is in some ways magnified. It is imperative, then, that counselors seek to do the following as they minister to the grieving woman.

Be patient. Grief is complex and often comes upon us unexpectedly. Reminders of the loss, and therefore a revisiting of the grief, often come unexpectedly as well. There is no set timeline for when grief should be complete. For counseling, this means counselors may be in it for the long haul.

Weep with those who weep. Empathy is an essential skill for counseling, and even more so for walking with another woman through grief and loss. Counselors must intentionally enter the world of the counselee, understand the loss from their perspective, and feel that loss with them. Only then can the counselor truly weep with them and weep with understanding.

Affirm the reality of their loss and grief. While there is certainly the capacity to sin while grieving, one thing that counselors can consistently affirm is the reality of the loss and the reality of their resulting emotions. A distinction can be made with regard to the *appropriateness* of the response, but the real, felt experience of the counselee should be acknowledged and affirmed. This includes changes to their identity. Profound losses (like the death of a spouse or child) almost always impact the identity of the woman. We must acknowledge this reality and give the woman the space she needs to reflect on the change to her identity.

Be quick to listen, slow to speak, and slow to respond. Scripture is full of reminders that we are to listen and listen well before we respond. For instance, Prov 18:13 says, "The one who gives an answer before he listens—this is foolishness and disgrace for him." Also, James 1:19 reminds all believers that we are to be "quick to listen, slow to speak, and slow to anger." In each case, the authors are reminding us of the wisdom of listening well and carefully thinking through our response. The same is true for counseling grief: counselors should listen and listen well, speak but speak with wisdom, and be careful of their own responses to the counselee's grief.

Get practical. Get the church involved in practically loving a grieving sister or brother. Set up meals, have someone run errands, ask several people to visit regularly. In all of these, the counselee receives the message that she is cared for and her pain is not forgotten. These practical acts of love and service can speak volumes to someone who feels alone in her grief.

As a side note, it is also helpful for the church to care for a woman on the anniversaries of her loss, particularly profound losses, such as the death of a spouse or child. Such "anniversary care" demonstrates ongoing awareness of and love for her.

Encourage grieving rituals if they are helpful. Often, it is hard to think about practical ways to bring closure to a loss. Events like a funeral help in the case of losing a loved one, but what about intangible losses? The counselor can help the counselee think through ways to memorialize a particular loss, like a memory book or remembering anniversaries. This communicates that the memory is still there, despite the sense of loss.

When wise, gently challenge false beliefs. We have the capacity to sin in the midst of expressing grief. One of those ways may be a false understanding of where God was in their loss. Or the counselee may be placing an undue responsibility on themselves for the loss. When those things happen, the counselor can gently but clearly seek to correct false beliefs, intentionally encouraging the counselee as that confrontation happens.

Encourage the counselee to look outward. Paul tells us in 2 Cor 1:3–4, "Blessed be the God and Father of our Lord Jesus Christ, the Father of mercies and the God of all comfort. He comforts us in all our affliction, so that we may be able to comfort those who are in any kind of affliction, through the comfort we ourselves receive from God." In these verses, Paul is reminding his readers their suffering is not about them; they are expected to minister to others in similar circumstances. The counselor can encourage the counselee to be an example of Christ to another person, since we all experience grief and suffering.

For the counselor: be mindful of your own internal responses or triggers. While this reminder is pertinent for many of the topics covered in this text (particularly trauma or abuse), the reality is that many of us have experienced grief in our own lives. Sometimes it might be that our experience of grief is very similar to that of a counselee. In that case, as counselors we must be aware of how we have dealt with our own grief and sorrow, so that it will not negatively impact our care for our sister. We can grieve alongside another woman in her grief, but it is not appropriate to shift the focus to our own loss when we are serving as the caregiver.

Suggested Growth Assignments

The following may be helpful as growth assignments for the counselee:

a. **Grief emotion scales.** While not necessarily an assignment, it may be useful for counselors to employ formal or informal grief scales to help the counselee more easily understand the impact or expression of their grief. These can explore levels of grief (such as on a scale of 1 to 10). Journaling when and how feelings of grief arise throughout the week may also give perspective.

b. **Writing a letter to a loved one she has lost.** The counselee may benefit from practical exercises like writing a letter to the loved one or creating a memory book. Such exercises may bring closure and help the counselee accept the permanence of the loss.

c. **Writing a psalm, focusing on both lament and worship.** In writing her own psalm, primarily following the examples in Psalms 42, 43, or 88, the counselee is not only expressing how she feels and her views about God or others, she is also encouraging herself to remember God in the midst of her struggle.

d. **Sharing the loss with someone, transparently and openly.** The counselee is doing this with the counselor, but sharing losses within the body of Christ allows us to both weep and rejoice with one another. It minimizes the sense of isolation.

e. **Connecting them with ongoing, corporate care.** Continual community care also helps the counselee not feel isolated in their grief, and it also serves as encouragement to remember biblical truths about grief and loss. This care can be accomplished through small groups, support groups, church-based ministry/care, or reading the testimonies of others who have walked through similar experiences.

Conclusion

We have only scratched the surface on ministering to a grieving counselee. Grief is complex and oftentimes messy; it is also something no one can escape. We will all, at some time, experience the loss of something precious. Most of the time, that loss is unexpected. Therefore, counselors must always be ready to speak biblical truth to a counselee, with sensitivity and wisdom.

Recommended Resources

Eareckson Tada, Joni, *A Place of Healing: Wrestling with the Mysteries of Suffering, Pain, and God's Sovereignty* (Colorado Springs: David C. Cook, 2010).

———, *When God Weeps: Why Our Sufferings Matter to the Almighty* (Grand Rapids: Zondervan, 2010).

Hodges, Samuel J., IV, and Kathy Leonard, *Grieving with Hope: Finding Comfort as You Journey through Loss* (Ada, MI: Baker Books, 2011).

Kellemen, Bob, *Grief: Walking with Jesus*, 31-Day Devotionals for Life (Phillipsburg, NJ: P&R, 2018).

Piper, John, *When the Darkness Will Not Lift: Doing What We Can While We Wait for God—and Joy* (Wheaton, IL: Crossway, 2006).

Randolph, Paul, "Grief: It's Not about a Process; It's about *the* Person," *Journal of Biblical Counseling* 23, no.1 (Winter 2005): 14–20.

Tripp, Paul David, *Grief: Finding Hope Again* (Greensboro, NC: New Growth Press, 2020).

Tautges, Paul, *Comfort the Grieving: Ministering God's Grace in Times of Loss* (Grand Rapids: Zondervan, 2015).

Tautges, Paul, *A Small Book for the Hurting Heart: Meditations on Loss, Grief, and Healing* (Greensboro, NC: New Growth Press, 2020).

Wright, H. Norman, *Experiencing Grief* (Nashville: B&H, 2004).

10

Disordered Eating

Tabitha is already an accomplished ballet dancer at fifteen. She is also a perfectionist. Every movement she makes draws attention to her body, and she wants to look flawless. To maintain what she believed to be perfect, she began skipping meals. After a few months, she could not remember what it was like to eat a full meal three times a day, and her body became ill any time she ate "too much."

Derrick is a wrestler, and a good one. But to maintain his weight class, he has to be conscious about what he eats. As Derrick gets better and better, more pressure comes to stay in his weight class to compete. He finds himself fasting before matches, then throwing up after the meals he does eat. He notices that he has less energy, but that seems a fair price to pay to win.

Brittany is seventeen years old, and has been on her own since she was a young child. Her father left when she was an infant, and her mother had a string of live-in boyfriends while Brittany was growing up. Most of the time, she was neglected, but several of her mother's boyfriends molested her. She felt out of control and alone. As she grew, she realized that one thing she could control was how she looked, which she controlled through her eating habits. At seventeen, Brittany weighs just ninety-five pounds.

What Does Disordered Eating Look Like?

In each of the scenarios above, we see an example of disordered eating. Though the "causes" are varied, each one stems from an improper belief about food. In all three cases, food is used as a tool to achieve something the person desires, whether it be perfection, success, or control.

And yet, as we consider those cases, each of them is complex. There are physical, emotional, mental, and spiritual issues at play. In the physical realm, there are consequences for a lack of eating: low energy, likely chronic fatigue, and a weight that cannot be safely maintained. In the mental realm, specific thoughts contribute to the disordered eating. Though the case studies are not lengthy enough to draw them out, there are likely emotional and spiritual components present as well.

Disordered eating, very simply, is the misuse of food. Food is most generally misused to accomplish some sort of goal: a certain body type or weight, control, coping with difficult emotions, a response to trauma, or something else entirely. Recent studies by the NIMH put current prevalence rates of diagnosable eating disorders in adults between 1 and 2 percent, depending on gender and age group.[1] The NIMH also reports that the lifetime prevalence in adolescents is close to 3 percent, with rates twice as high in females than males.

Eating disorders have a high rate of comorbidity with other mental health struggles. More than half (56.2 percent) of respondents with anorexia nervosa, 94.5 percent with bulimia nervosa, and 78.9 percent with binge eating disorder met criteria for at least one of the core *DSM-5* disorders, the most common being some type of anxiety disorder.[2] Another recent study showed that over a third of studied adolescents with an eating disorder (ages twelve to twenty-two, 92 percent female) had experienced some sort of traumatic event that was related to the disordered eating.[3] What does this mean for counselors? Eating disorders are complex and are often accompanied by some other significant life struggle, such as anxiety, depression, or a traumatic experience. The approach to treatment, therefore, would also need to be complex and comprehensive.

Symptoms, Manifestations, and Diagnosis

There are three commonly known eating disorders, though disordered eating as a whole goes beyond the three main diagnoses. The first, anorexia nervosa (AN) is the practice of restricting food intake, characterized by extreme thinness, a pursuit of increased thinness, a distorted self-image, and self-esteem that is highly influenced by perception of body weight or shape. Along with the comorbid conditions noted above, there is also a significantly higher rate of suicide that accompanies anorexia, more than any other mental illness. The *DSM-5* criteria for AN follows:

1. Restriction of energy intake relative to requirements leading to a significantly low body weight in the context of age, sex, developmental trajectory, and physical health. Significantly low weight is defined as a weight that is less than minimally normal or, for children and adolescents, less than that minimally expected.

2. Intense fear of gaining weight or becoming fat, or persistent behavior that interferes with weight gain, even at a significantly low weight.

3. Disturbance in the way in which one's body weight or shape is experienced, undue influence of body weight or shape on self-evaluation, or persistent lack of recognition of the seriousness of the current low body weight.

The effects of AN range from health issues like thinning bones, anemia, muscle weakness, and low blood pressure to heart problems, organ failure, fatigue, and infertility.

Similarly, bulimia nervosa (BN) is a lack of control over eating large amounts, followed by behavior that compensates for the eating (vomiting, taking laxatives, fasting, exercising, etc.), with the counselee generally maintaining a relatively healthy body weight. Per the *DSM-5*, BN is characterized by:

1. Recurrent episodes of binge eating. An episode of binge eating is characterized by both of the following:
    a. Eating in a discrete amount of time (e.g., within a two-hour period) an amount of food that is definitely larger than most individuals would eat in a similar period of time under similar circumstances.
    b. Sense of being unable to control overeating (i.e., stopping; what or how much is eaten) during an episode.
2. Recurrent inappropriate compensatory behavior to prevent weight gain, such as self-induced vomiting; misuse of laxatives, diuretics, or other medications; fasting; or excessive exercise.
3. The binge eating and inappropriate compensatory behaviors both occur, on average, at least once a week for three months.
4. Self-evaluation is unduly influenced by body shape and weight.
5. The disturbance does not occur exclusively during episodes of anorexia nervosa.

The effects of BN are similar to AN, but also include throat and teeth issues, acid reflux, GI problems, dehydration, and an electrolyte imbalance.

Last, binge-eating disorder (BED) is a lack of control over eating large amounts, but there is no purging that follows like there is with BN. Most counselees in this category are overweight, given the lack of purging. Following are the *DSM-5* criteria:

1. Recurrent episodes of binge eating. An episode of binge eating is characterized by both of the following:
    a. Eating, in a discrete period of time (e.g., within any two–hour period), an amount of food that is definitely larger than most people would eat in a similar period of time under similar circumstances.

     b. A sense of lack of control over eating during the episode (e.g., a feeling that one cannot stop eating or control what or how much one is eating).

  2. The binge-eating episodes are associated with three (or more) of the following:

     a. Eating much more rapidly than normal

     b. Eating until feeling uncomfortably full

     c. Eating large amounts of food when not feeling physically hungry

     d. Eating alone because of feeling embarrassed by how much one is eating

     e. Feeling disgusted with oneself, depressed, or very guilty afterward

  3. Marked distress regarding binge eating is present.

  4. The binge eating occurs, on average, at least once a week for three months.

  5. The binge eating is not associated with the recurrent use of inappropriate compensatory behavior as in bulimia nervosa and does not occur exclusively during the course of bulimia nervosa or anorexia nervosa.

Like AN and BN, BED has some significant side effects, though less severe than in other forms of eating disorders. They include eating even when full to the point of discomfort, eating alone, and frequent dieting to compensate for weight gain. In all three forms of disordered eating, quite often the counselee will also present with struggles like distress, shame, guilt, embarrassment, withdrawal, and isolation.

Biblical and Theological Perspectives

The Scriptures are full of references to food, from the provision of food to eat in the garden of Eden to the feast in Revelation, and there are a few key ideas the Bible draws out as it relates to food. Most clearly, the Bible indicates that food is given as physical sustenance from the Lord, and it is good. This idea is evident in passages like Gen 9:3 (paralleled in Gen 1:29), in which God tells Noah, "Every creature that lives and moves will be food for you; as I gave the green plants, I have given you everything." Every animal and plant are good for food and useful to mankind for physical sustenance. This theme is later echoed by Mark 7:18–19 in which Jesus declares all foods clean, amending the dietary restrictions given to Israel, returning to this proclamation given to Noah.

Further, the Bible indicates that food is not to be a source of anxiety for us. In Matt 6:25, Jesus teaches, "Therefore I tell you: Don't worry about your life, what you will eat or what you will drink; or about your body, what you will wear. Isn't life more than food and the body more than clothing?" He goes on in verse 31, "So don't worry, saying, 'What will we eat?' or 'What will we drink?' or 'What will we wear?'" because "all these things will be provided for you" (v. 33). The Lord is faithful to provide for our basic needs. Food does not need to be hoarded or binged; God will meet our needs.

Finally, the eating of food is an active part of honoring God. This is most clearly seen in 1 Cor 10:31, where Paul wrote, "So, whether you eat or drink, or whatever you do, do everything for the glory of God." Bringing glory to God is an integral part of the life of a believer, and Paul's mention of it in this verse should not be overlooked. For the counselee struggling with disordered eating, the Bible's teaching should be a significant part of counseling.

Not only does the Bible speak directly to the place of food, several key themes relate to disordered eating. While space does not allow for an extensive discussion about each of these, the following is a list of potential emotional/mental/spiritual aspects of disordered eating that the Bible addresses:

A distorted sense of self. Often, counselees struggling with an eating disorder do not view themselves properly. This may be a distortion of how they view themselves physically in a mirror, or it may be pushing themselves to be thinner and thinner, placing their value in their weight.

Misplaced identity. Many women who struggle with disordered eating place their identity in their physical bodies, rather than in both body and soul, their inner and outer person. They wrongly believe they have less worth if they do not conform to a particular ideal, or they might even place part of their identity in the diagnosis itself.

Self-idolatry. Ultimately, all sin comes down to idolatry, typically of self. Eating disorders are no exception. Often, the counselee is elevating an ideal self above a healthy and God-honoring self. This ideal self may stem from the counselee's own view of how she should be or may be influenced by the thoughts of others, such as a family member or peer.

Fear of man. Matthew 10:28 is a firm reminder that we are to fear God rather than man, and yet many counselees who struggle with disordered eating find themselves driven primarily by what they believe others think of them.

Distorted sense of value for the body. Though the body is a key aspect of who we are as physical persons, for the woman struggling with disordered eating, the body is something to be controlled or used to accomplish some end. Those ends may be immensely varied, much like our vignettes above, but the body is a tool in each of these cases.

Addiction. Over time, disordered eating becomes habitual, and may become addictive. But the Scriptures speak at length about being sober-minded (1 Pet 5:8) and self-controlled (Titus 2:12 ESV; 2 Tim 1:7 ESV), and reminds us that we are free from enslavement to sin (John 8:36; 1 Cor 6:12).

Lack of control, but a sense of being overpowered. Many with an eating disorder report feeling that they are unable to control their urges, particularly overeating or purging. While we understand that the sinful nature remains, and therefore the struggle with sin is ongoing, the Bible teaches that believers have been set free from that bondage (Gal 5:1). Therefore, the woman struggling with disordered eating in any form can be affirmed that she has a choice in her desires, thoughts, and behaviors as they relate to eating, just as she does in any other area of life.

Improper response to stress or anxiety. While stress is a normal part of life, disordered eating may arise in response to what seems to be overwhelming stress or anxiety. This is tied closely, at times, to feeling a lack of control over one's circumstances; in response, the struggling young woman begins to habitually use food as her refuge or to cope with these difficult emotions.

Misplaced contentment. Like many sinful habits, disordered eating might stem from a lack of contentment. It might also be general discontent with life's circumstances. A woman struggling with disordered eating may seek contentment in a particular appearance or weight, or in the ability to control her environment.

Improper response to trauma or crisis. A 2018 article in *Appetite* reported that over a third of adolescents with an eating disorder had experienced a traumatic event.[4] For the counselee struggling with an eating disorder, it may be that it arose in direct response to a crisis situation; rather than running to the Father, the counselee sought to cope with the situation through her eating habits. While we affirm the direct correlation between trauma and disordered eating, we must also uphold the woman's choice in how she responds to traumatic event(s). We must also recognize that if trauma is an underlying cause, it will need to be addressed and resolved first, before she can make significant strides toward resolving the disordered eating. We cannot just deal with the symptom (disordered eating) without addressing the underlying wound (trauma).

While the heart (specifically sinful thoughts and desires) is certainly at play with disordered eating, eating disorders may also have some sort of biological underpinning. Suzanne Mazzeo and Cynthia Bulik reported on research into how environmental and genetic risk factors influence eating disorders.[5] The body may be a contributing factor. Consider another example: a woman with severe food allergies physically feels better if she does not eat, but she goes to the extreme of not eating much at all to avoid pain. The inability of her body to accept certain foods, causing pain when she eats them, is directly correlated to her disordered eating. And yet, she is responsible for her choices of what and when to eat. The impact of sin on the human body is real and at times significant. The Scriptures affirm the brokenness of the body; therefore, consider that the broken body might be at play in an eating disorder.

A related concept with special importance for the discussion on eating disorders is the idea from 1 Cor 6:19–20 that our body is a temple for the Holy Spirit. Paul writes, "Don't you know that your body is a temple of the Holy Spirit who is in you, whom you have from God? You are not your own, for you were bought at a price. So glorify God with your body." Paul referred to the literal dwelling place of God in the Old Testament, relocating that dwelling place in the individual believer. Our bodies matter significantly. Further, Paul noted in this passage that the struggling believer was "bought at a price," a theme he echoed in Rom 14:7–8. The believer "is not [their] own"; rather, she is accountable and subject to her Master.

The believer has been set free from the bondage of sin. The effects of sin remain, and the struggle with sin is ongoing, but the Christian is no longer enslaved (Gal 5:1; 1 Cor 6:12). The counselee struggling with disordered eating need not be controlled by it; there is hope found in the freeing power of the Spirit dwelling within her.

Counseling Steps and Practical Procedures

First and foremost, the counselor must recognize that an eating disorder affects all parts of the struggling counselee: physical, spiritual, mental, emotional, and relational. It is important to pursue holistic care, including those specifically trained in treating disordered eating. Many times, cases of eating disorders (particularly AN and BN) are treated in a medical facility where there is consistent oversight, regulation of intake/output, and ongoing counseling. These facilities include all aspects of the counselee in their treatment plan.

For counselors seeking to treat a counselee with an eating disorder as an outpatient, it is wise to involve a medical professional in the treatment, and to include a nutritionist. As a part of the additional medical care, the counselor might opt to use an eating plan created in conjunction with the nutritional care team and that the counselee agrees to. When the counselee fails to comply, an agreed-upon higher level of care is pursued. This ensures the counselee's buy-in and communicates the severity of the struggle. It is also a way to honor the counselee and recognize the importance of her physical health.

Given that the biblical counselor will be most equipped to speak to the spiritual/emotional/mental realms of disordered eating, the counselor should spend the most time focused on a few key areas. First, the counselor can lovingly challenge the misplaced counselee's desires and identity, drawing from the discussion above. Counseling may focus on aligning her beliefs with Scripture's teachings about food; checking any sinful desires surrounding food; and affirming and defining who she is in Christ, the role of the Spirit in her battle, a proper, biblical perception of self, and sanctification. There is much to explore in these areas.

Further, given that much of disordered eating centers around one's thoughts, the counselor can encourage the counselee to think truthful thoughts. In Phil 4:8, Paul urges the believer, "Whatever is true, whatever is honorable, whatever is just, whatever is pure, whatever is lovely, whatever is commendable—if there is any moral excellence and if there is anything praiseworthy—dwell on these things." The counselee's true, honorable, just, pure, lovely, and commendable thoughts should be particularly related to herself and her view of food, seeking to align those thoughts with biblical teachings.

Similarly, the counselor can help the counselee seek to make God-honoring choices one at a time, day by day. Disordered eating impacts every area of life, not just mealtime, but schedule planning, social interactions (avoiding eating around others), and conversations. The counselor and counselee can celebrate each victory, no matter how small, rejoicing in God's work in even the minute details. Accountability comes into play here as well, when appropriate for the counseling relationship.

When a woman is struggling with disordered eating, her focus is inward. She is consumed by thoughts of herself, when and what to eat, what others think of her, how she can exercise control over her circumstances. A helpful exercise, then, is to help her focus outward on others. Identify areas where she can meet the needs of other women in service to them, shifting the focus from herself to someone else.

Working with a medical professional, the biblical counselor can also seek to *wisely* and *appropriately* regulate intake and output. This includes assistance from parents when caring for a teenage woman. Some examples of this might include encouraging the counselee to eat in the presence of others or be accompanied to the grocery store or a restaurant. Eventually, this may also include diet regulation or changes in tracking intake and output. An important note here: it will not suffice to simply tell the counselee to "eat more" or "stop purging." This approach is largely ineffective. It is wise to exercise great patience in this area, focusing first on thought patterns and beliefs before seeking to radically change behaviors. The help of a physician or a nutritionist might also be helpful here.

Last, the counselor should keep in mind the higher risk for comorbid conditions and treat as appropriate. In particular, be aware of the potential for emotional struggles like anxiety or depression. The counselor should also regularly screen for suicidal thoughts or self-harm behaviors, again due to the high rates of comorbidity. Rarely will a counselee present with just disordered eating; most often, there will be other life struggles as well. Treating the disordered eating, then, becomes only a part of counseling rather than the sole issue or focus.

Suggested Growth Assignments

Among the growth assignments that might be useful for the counselee struggling with disordered eating, the counselor might first focus on the passages noted above, particularly exercises centered on Phil 4:8. One exercise is asking the counselee to list problematic thought patterns and replacement thoughts that are in line with biblical teaching, then work through what it looks like to choose to live in line with biblical teaching. Or the counselee might memorize and meditate on passages like 1 Cor 6:19–20 or Matt 6:25–33, specifically to combat underlying desires or thought patterns contributing to her disordered eating. Third, the counselor may also opt to have the counselee keep a journal or food diary to track both behaviors and thoughts, with any noticeable triggers (e.g., stress, upcoming weigh-in, a feeling of not being in control, etc.). Then the counselor and counselee can work through areas of struggle on multiple levels: heart (desires/motivations), thoughts/emotions, and behaviors. Last, the counselor can ask the counselee to include others in her walk, providing accountability and encouragement as they move toward healing and right living.

Conclusion

Disordered eating is complex and most often multifaceted. It is rarely as simple as a young woman saying she wants to look like the women she sees on television or social media. We as counselors must take the time and care needed to consider the *individual* woman we're treating, her *specific situation*, and how to help *her*, rather than making any blanket assumptions simply because she might have an eating disorder diagnosis. And while we acknowledge her context, such as a history of trauma or potential physiological factors, we must uphold her power to choose how and what she eats. This is a delicate balance, one that must be filled with compassion, patience, and grace.

Recommended Resources

Alexander, June, and Janet Treasure, *A Collaborative Approach to Eating Disorders* (New York: Routledge, 2012).

Arterburn, Stephen, and David Stoop, *The Life Recovery Workbook for Eating Disorders: A Bible-Centered Approach for Taking Your Life Back* (Carol Stream, IL: Tyndale House, 2020).

Emlet, Michael, *Overeating: When Enough Isn't Enough* (Greensboro, NC: New Growth Press, 2020).

Grilo, Carlos M., and James E. Mitchell, *The Treatment of Eating Disorders: A Clinical Handbook* (New York City: Guilford Press, 2011).

Street, John D., and Janie Street, "Eating Disorder: Anorexia," in *The Biblical Counseling Guide for Women* (Eugene, OR: Harvest House, 2016), 135–51.

Welch, Ed, *Eating Disorders: The Quest for Thinness* (Greensboro, NC: New Growth Press, 2020).

———, *Just One More: When Desires Don't Take No for an Answer* (Phillipsburg, NJ: P&R, 2002).

11

Same-Sex Attraction and Gender Dysphoria

Ann comes to counseling to reconcile an internal struggle: she is attracted to women, but faces significant backlash from her family if she were to share that struggle with them. They speak openly about "the gays" and the LGBT movement, often following comments or conversations at church about homosexuality. They are not exactly understanding. Though Ann is only sixteen, she has wrestled with these feelings for some time now, and the few friends she has told have been accepting and affirming of her. As a Christian, Ann firmly believes that it goes against God's design, and yet she continues to struggle with whether or not she can act on her feelings. She is beginning to recognize what it might mean for her to continue in life attracted to women but not acting on it: not getting married or having children, potentially living as a single woman for the rest of her life. She is seeking help to work through what she should do and how to share her struggle with others.

The current American culture, like most of the West, celebrates individuality and personal happiness. It should come as no surprise that these celebrations also occur in the area of human sexuality. Unlike a century ago, or even fifty years ago, our culture now affirms (and at time encourages) things like homosexuality and a fluid gender identity.

The church has remained fairly outspoken about these issues, affirming that God has created gender and sexuality as good things within proper bounds, but sin has distorted it immensely. Where does this leave the Christian struggling with homosexual attraction or gender dysphoria? How might we counsel in a way that is both faithful to Scripture and compassionate toward the counselee?

This chapter covers same-sex attraction (SSA) and gender dysphoria (GD), including a definition/description of what each looks like, some diagnostic history, what Scripture has to say about each, and some counseling approaches. The goal is to help the reader become better prepared to speak clearly and yet graciously to those struggling with either situation.

Definitions, Descriptions, and Diagnostic History

Before defining and describing SSA and GD, it is important to note that clear definitions are essential to this discussion. We must distinguish between *attraction* or *feeling* and one's *lifestyle* or *identity*. A distinction must be made between an internal state versus outward behavior and lifestyle. While this may seem like splitting hairs, it is tremendously important. We might draw the parallel between someone who *desires* to harm another person versus one who *actually hurts* someone else versus someone who *identifies* as a murderer. While all three are impacted and ultimately driven by a sinful human heart (a distortion of what God created as good), the behavior and claim of identity matter tremendously.

Within this discussion, when the term "same-sex attraction" is used, it indicates someone who is attracted to a member of the same sex, whether that attraction is acted upon or not. When one claims to be homosexual/

gay/lesbian/bisexual, that person is acknowledging the same-sex attraction, but that identity also generally includes acting upon the attraction or identifying with those behaviors. Similarly, someone who struggles with gender dysphoria acknowledges the feelings of disconnect between their given biological sex and the gender they feel they are; a transgender designation, on the other hand, identifies a person who is choosing to live as their felt gender rather than their biological sex. These differences matter significantly: feelings/attractions come from within us,[1] whereas identities are constructed (volitionally) by us.

Same-sex attraction is essentially what it sounds like: sexual interest and attraction to those of the same gender, with or without attraction to the opposite gender as well. SSA for a male involves attraction to other males and SSA for a female involves attraction to other females. Numerous struggles come along with SSA, some paralleling the struggles of those without SSA. For instance, dealing with impure thoughts, feeling different, feeling ashamed, grief over the inability to be "normal," setting appropriate physical boundaries, and perhaps internal conflict from feeling accepted by some and rejected by others. Those with SSA may wrestle with spiritual realities like whether the attraction itself is sinful, why God would allow their SSA, the surety of their salvation, and perhaps even how to respond when the church responds poorly. We saw many of these struggles above with Ann.

In many ways, gender dysphoria is distinct in its presentation and yet quite similar to SSA with regard to struggles. GD, by definition, is a felt incongruence between one's biological sex and one's felt gender; for example, being born as a biological female but with an internal sense of being male. It includes things like disgust for their body (beyond genitalia), emotional disturbances, feelings of isolation or "feeling different," confusion, and anxiety. Like those with SSA, those with GD may struggle with internal conflict and suffering (looking one way on the outside but feeling like that appearance is wrong, with little she can do to change it), uncomfortable boundaries for behavior and dress, feeling different and/or ashamed, grief over those differences and the inability to be "normal," and the spiritual questions already mentioned. Each counselee is an individual, but generally speaking, these feelings of incongruence begin fairly early in life, usually between eight and fourteen years of age.

It is difficult to find true prevalence rates of those struggling with SSA and GD within the church, in part because one's sexual attraction or felt gender is deeply personal. Pair this with the church's outspokenness on these issues and many do not feel they can share these struggles with others. The struggles may be unrecognized, but they are still present and often the individual receives no support.

With regard to a formal diagnosis, SSA/homosexuality is no longer included in the *DSM* manuals, though it was present in some respect through the *DSM-III-R* (1994). However, gender dysphoria is in the current version of the manual, the *DSM-5*; in the last revision, the condition shifted from gender identity disorder to gender dysphoria, to soften the language away from a formalized disorder and focus on the emotional distress (dysphoria). At least two of the following criteria for gender dysphoria must be experienced for at least six months' duration in adolescents or adults for diagnosis:

1. A strong desire to be of a gender other than one's assigned gender
2. A strong desire to be treated as a gender other than one's assigned gender
3. A significant incongruence between one's experienced or expressed gender and one's sexual characteristics
4. A strong desire for the sexual characteristics of a gender other than one's assigned gender
5. A strong desire to be rid of one's sexual characteristics due to incongruence with one's experienced or expressed gender
6. A strong conviction that one has the typical reactions and feelings of a gender other than one's assigned gender

In addition, the condition must be associated with clinically significant distress or impairment. One note of importance is the higher rates of comorbidity with other struggles, primarily suicidal thoughts, anxiety, depression, and eating disorders.

Biblical and Theological Perspectives

The Bible is clear on both homosexuality and gender. Passages such as the following are commonly cited with regard to both SSA and GD:

- The creation of Adam and Eve in Genesis 1: Many point to the creation of man and woman as indicative of both God's design for marriage (between one man and one woman) and for gender (Adam created as "male/husband" and Eve as "female/wife").
- Leviticus 18:22, "You are not to sleep with a man as with a woman; it is detestable." This passage speaks particularly to God's design for sexual relations between people, and what is out of bounds with regard to sexual behavior.
- Deuteronomy 22:5, "A woman is not to wear male clothing, and a man is not to put on a woman's garment, for everyone who does these things is detestable to the LORD your God." God is stating in this passage that there is a clear male-female binary, not to be confused with one another.
- Romans 1:26–28, "For this reason God delivered them over to disgraceful passions. Their women exchanged natural sexual relations for unnatural ones. The men in the same way also left natural relations with women and were inflamed in their lust for one another. Men committed shameless acts with men and received in their own persons the appropriate penalty of their error. And because they did not think it worthwhile to acknowledge God, God delivered them over to a corrupt mind so that they do what is not right." Phrases such as "dishonorable," "contrary to nature," and "shameless acts" are seen as indicative of God's position on sexual behavior that is outside God's established norms and bounds.

༄ 1 Corinthians 6:9–10, "Don't you know that the unrighteous will not
inherit God's kingdom? Do not be deceived: No sexually immoral people, idolaters, adulterers, or males who have sex with males, no thieves,
greedy people, drunkards, verbally abusive people, or swindlers will
inherit God's kingdom." Several of the sins noted in this list involve
sexual behavior, but the end result for all is separation from God.

Homosexuality and atypical gender identity are products of the fall. Every
person has passions that do not align with God's desires, and for many, these
passions are sexual. But we *choose* whether to act on those passions. In the
texts above, particularly those from Leviticus, Romans, and 1 Corinthians,
the focus is on the *behavior* and the *identity* that flow from the passions. This
is not to say the internal passions do not matter—quite the contrary—but
the focus tends to be on the response as a reflection of what is in the heart.

The Scriptures speak directly and firmly against sexual immorality,
which includes homosexuality and cross-gender self-expressions. It cannot
be missed. To say these passages do not apply to us today or that God is
accepting of these things rejects the notion of a holy and just God. We cannot
explain away sin. But the message of the gospel remains: Jesus came to die for
our sin, to pay the price for our redemption. Acknowledgment of our sin leads
us to acknowledgment of grace.

What does this mean for the counseling conversation with regard to SSA
and GD? We, by his Spirit, have the power to obey God's directives, despite
our passions; the disordered desires may remain and need to be fought day
in and day out, but our behavior and identity matter immensely. God has the
power to change these passions, though he may not; this is true of all forms
of desire. Identity, though, is found in Christ and who he determines we are,
rather than our feelings or struggles.

Counseling Steps and Practical Procedures

SSA and GD should not be confused. SSA and GD are distinct struggles,
and the counselor should not assume, for example, that one who struggles

with GD also struggles with SSA. For the one struggling with GD, given that they see themselves as the opposite gender, their attraction to someone of their gender "feels" appropriate, though it is technically same-sex attraction. While this does not negate the need to address it *at some point* in counseling, the SSA in these circumstances is secondary to the GD.

Counseling Same-Sex Attraction

First and foremost, the counselor must seek to understand the counselee and her unique struggles as fully as possible. Attraction to those of the same sex is often something counselors have little or no personal experience with, so it might take extra effort to understand her perspective and her struggles. Throughout the process of listening and learning, the counselor should affirm Scripture's teachings with grace and compassion. We should acknowledge the brokenness of humanity as well as the weight of sin (both inherent and volitional), but also affirm personal choice with personal responsibility. A counselor cannot force a counselee to live rightly. The counselee is personally responsible before a holy God. The woman is both sinner and sufferer. These truths can and should be communicated with compassion and humility.

Next, the counselor can seek to walk with the counselee to determine how she chooses to live in regard to her struggle, focusing primarily on the response rather than the struggle, though not neglecting things like underlying desires. We are all responsible to obey the Lord's directives, despite feeling otherwise, and to daily fight desires that do not align with God's. But our obedience is made possible by the Spirit of God living within us, not by any power we have on our own.

Third, the counselor should be mindful not to give any false promises. God may choose to relieve them of their desires, aligning them with his desires, but he may not this side of eternity. It might be that this woman struggles with SSA for the rest of her life. The counselor should be cautious about promising relief from this struggle; rather, the focus should be on trusting God's power to help her live rightly in a fallen world.

This may mean a period of grief as the counselee processes feelings of loss. Recall Ann in the opening vignette; she was coming to the realization that to live in obedience to the Lord might mean never marrying or having children. Lament with her over unmet dreams, feelings of being "different," and the realization that she might struggle with these feelings for the rest of her life. Counselors should openly acknowledge these feelings of loss and grieve with the counselee.

For parents of children identifying as homosexual, the counselor's role might be to help them think through a proper response to their child: How can the parent love their child yet not affirm their choices? What might this look like for a teenager versus a young adult? These conversations may involve thinking through family functions or other practical considerations.

Finally, and permeating all the above, the counselor must proclaim the good news of the gospel, as it is especially pertinent here. The gospel impacts life every day; we have suffered and died with Christ, we are to mortify the desires of the flesh, and we are to seek to honor the Lord, but there is eternal victory over sin. These daily struggles are temporary, and the Lord Jesus already paid the price for our sin on the cross. And after his death, he sent his Spirit to dwell within us, empowering us to become more like him. Keeping an eternal, spiritual perspective is key.[2]

Counseling Gender Dysphoria

Though there may be some overlap as it relates to counseling, our approach to GD is different from SSA. Mark Yarhouse outlines four typical approaches in *Understanding Gender Dysphoria*,[3] the first two of which are commonly used in Christian/biblical-counseling circles. The first approach is direct intervention to decrease cross-gender behavior and feelings; the counselor and counselee aim to decrease cross-gender behaviors and identification through intentional speech or counsel. The second approach is known as watchful waiting, taking a somewhat neutral approach that allows for some behaviors while not reinforcing them. A third option is psychosocial facilitation, which is facilitating expression of the gender that aligns with a child or teenager's feelings. Finally, puberty suppression involves the use of hormones to put off puberty until an adolescent can decide more fully. Within each category there is some variation in how the approach is carried out.

The most common approach in broader Christian circles is the watchful waiting, though the approach in part depends on the age of the counselee. The choice is made to not affirm the behaviors, like using a different name or allowing cross-gender dress, as well as generally avoiding intentional conversation. Within this category is also some degree of not directly speaking against it, flowing out of the idea that a child may "grow out of it." The commonality of this approach seems to be in part because we aren't familiar with these issues, so watching and waiting avoids conflict while not affirming.

For the biblical counselor, a wise combination of the first two approaches is recommended. It is clear that Scripture speaks to issues of gender, which cannot be circumvented. And yet, the reality of a woman struggling with GD is a reality of suffering. This struggle consumes her day in and day out, so it is essential that the counselor be full of grace and compassion. The decision lies with the counselor as to what this looks like in practice; perhaps it is that the counselor is wise in both the timing and content of conversations, but also mindful of using the counselee's name or gender identifier ("he" or "she") in their conversations. Such awareness is not condoning the struggle, but it is being intentional not to cause more pain.

For those struggling with GD, much of the counseling advice echoes in the advice for counseling SSA, but nuanced for gender struggles. The counselor must be quick to listen and slow to speak (Prov 18:13; Jas 1:19), taking time to understand the counselee and their struggle. GD is another area where few counselors have struggled themselves. We must understand our counselees well, including where they are in the struggle (i.e., have the feelings developed recently or have they been ongoing; or has the counselee thought extensively about gender-reassignment surgery?) and what they want out of counseling.

Counselors should clearly affirm Scripture's reality of distorted desires because of the fall, with discernment, but also with grace and compassion.

This would look different for a believer versus an unbeliever. An unbeliever will likely not see Scripture as an authority on the topic of gender identity; therefore, counseling would look dramatically different. Take care to understand the weight the counselee places on God's Word. For the believing counselee, appeal to biblical truth is a priority; for unbelievers, the approach may be working through their struggle while pointing them toward a value system that aligns with the Word of God, with the aim of sharing the gospel.

The counselor should decide where she falls on the spectrum of approaches to the issue. The counselor should make this clear in her own mind, according to her conscience before the Lord, before the issue arises in counseling. As with any struggle, it is not loving or kind to the counselee to be unprepared to discuss struggles appropriately, especially such weighty matters as these.

Finally, if it is appropriate, the counselor should grieve this struggle with her. No woman going through this struggle, or any struggle, delights in her suffering. The Lord does not delight in her suffering. He is gracious and kind in our struggles, and uses them to accomplish his purposes; but struggles with gender identity are a product of the fall, and that is to be grieved. The counselee may come to the realization that she might deal with these feelings for the rest of her life and, consequently, might never marry or have children. The counselor can and should grieve these realities with her.

In counseling parents of children struggling with GD, the counselor can educate them on the struggles of those with gender dysphoria. It is about more than just the behaviors or the feelings; there are practical implications and emotional struggles that come along with it. The counselor should acknowledge the struggle of the parents as well. GD is usually expressed outwardly, which may lead to embarrassment or questions from others within the church. Counselors can help parents think through how to love their children well while not affirming their behaviors, seeking to balance grace and firmness that does not stem from their own frustrations, embarrassment, or legalism.

The counselor can and should affirm the gospel. In counseling struggles over gender identity, we must remember that hope and identity are found in Christ; we will have eternal victory over sin, and God's saving power is mighty. While these struggles might last for a lifetime, they are not eternal.

Remember that both SSA and GD (especially GD) have high comorbidity rates with other mental health struggles, particularly suicidal ideation. We must address these, and often it is wise to address the other struggles first as the relationship is built. Once relational credibility is established, and the woman knows firsthand the genuine care and concern of the counselor, we can speak into the tougher, more deeply held struggles of SSA and GD.

Suggested Growth Assignments

There are several growth assignments that may be useful for counseling both SSA and GD. First, the counselor can walk with the counselee through a study or exploration of identity. The counselee can be instructed to look through Scripture and write out who she is based on Christ and his work rather than her perception of herself. Then, she can think through and write out the practical implications for each aspect of her identity. If she is a believer, she can identify that she is a beloved daughter of God, and what that means in practice is she can rest secure (i.e., not in fear) knowing that he cares for her and desires her good.

Second, the counselee can be instructed to keep a thoughts journal, making a list of thoughts arising throughout the week that relate to her sexuality. She can then notice trends and discuss them with the counselor. The counselee can do a Scripture study on what God's Word has to say about sexuality and sexual expression (starting with passages like Genesis 1, Romans 1, or 1 Corinthians 6), or on how we should put off sin and put on righteousness (Colossians 3).

Finally, the counselee might consider reading the testimony of others, like the texts below written by Rosaria Butterfield. This can help the counselee feel not quite so alone in her struggle. Similarly, she might identify a few "safe" church members for support, those she can feel comfortable talking to when her struggle becomes especially difficult.

Recommended Conceptual and Practical Resources for Counselors and Counselees

Same-Sex Attraction

Allberry, Sam, *Is God Anti-Gay? And Other Questions about Homosexuality, the Bible, and Same-Sex Attraction*, rev. ed. (Epsom, UK: Good Book, 2013).

Black, R. Nicholas, *Homosexuality and the Bible: Outdated Advice or Words of Life?* (Greensboro, NC: New Growth Press, 2014).

Burk, Denny, and Heath Lambert, *Transforming Homosexuality: What the Bible Says about Sexual Orientation* (Phillipsburg, NJ: P&R, 2015).

Butterfield, Rosaria, *Openness Unhindered: Further Thoughts of an Unlikely Convert on Sexual Identity and Union with Christ* (Pittsburgh: Crown & Covenant, 2015).

Butterfield, Rosaria, *The Secret Thoughts of an Unlikely Convert: An English Professor's Journey into Christian Faith* (Pittsburgh: Crown & Covenant, 2012).

DeYoung, Kevin, *What Does the Bible Really Teach about Homosexuality?* (Wheaton, IL: Crossway, 2015).

Hill, Wesley, *Washed and Waiting: Reflections on Christian Faithfulness and Homosexuality* (Grand Rapids: Zondervan, 2016).

Longacre, David, ed., *First Steps of Compassion: Helping Someone Who Struggles with Same-Sex Attraction* (Boone, NC: L'Edge Press, 2009).

Welch, Edward T., *Homosexuality: Speaking the Truth in Love* (Phillipsburg, NJ: P&R, 2000).

White, David, *Can You Change If You're Gay?* (Greensboro, NC: New Growth Press, 2013).

Gender Dysphoria

Yarhouse, Mark, *Understanding Gender Dysphoria: Navigating Transgender Issues in a Changing Culture* (Downers Grove, IL: InterVarsity Press, 2015).

Yarhouse, Mark, and Julia Sadusky, *Emerging Gender Identities: Understanding the Diverse Experiences of Today's Youth* (Ada, MI: Brazos Press, 2020).

Walker, Andrew T., *God and the Transgender Debate: What Does the Bible Actually Say about Gender Identity?* (Epsom, UK: Good Book, 2017).

12

Suicide and Self-Harm

Elise sits in your office in tears. She says, "I just don't know what to do anymore. Things are never going to change, I'm never going to feel better, and there just isn't any use going on anymore. I've lost everything that has ever mattered to me, and I'll never matter to anyone else. I'm just ready to be in heaven where I'll be happy." While she has not shared any plan to take her life, her words and countenance tell you she is close. She has battled with depression for years, but now is hopeless and in great emotional pain. She doesn't know what else to do.

Suicidal thoughts and attempts are far more common than we would like to admit; it is a struggle both within and outside the church. Self-harm, or the purposeful injury to oneself, is increasing in prevalence as well, particularly among young women. As counselors, we must be prepared to counsel through these difficult thoughts. This chapter addresses both suicide and self-harm, including some background information and description, theological foundations, and practical counseling strategies. The struggles with suicidal thoughts and self-harm may overlap, but they are by no means the same thing; one does not necessitate or exclude the other. Therefore, while both topics are included in this chapter because of some areas of overlap, they should be understood separately and not assumed to be indicative of the other.

Suicide

Definition/Description of the Problem and Prevalence within Counseling

Suicide is the taking of one's own life. Suicidal ideation, in comparison, is the thought patterns that surround that event, and a suicidal attempt is the effort to carry it out, whether successful or not. Some typical means of following through with these ideations include the use of a firearm (most prevalent among males), poisoning (most prevalent among females), suffocation/hanging, or other less common approaches such as jumping, cutting, or drowning. According to the CDC, suicide was the tenth leading cause of death in the United States in 2020 and is on the rise in most states.[1] More than half of those who have attempted suicide did not have any sort of mental health diagnosis at the time, and most often, the attempt was related to situational stressors, such as a relationship, finances, job, or physical health. The highest demographic for completed suicide attempts is middle-aged white males, and while four times as many men die by suicide as women, women attempt suicide more often.[2]

Risk Factors

While there is no clear set of criteria to determine if a counselee will or will not have suicidal ideations or attempts, the following are common risk factors the counselor should be aware of, several of which we see in Elise above:

- Prior suicidal attempts or self-harm behaviors
- Expressed feelings of hopelessness or helplessness

- Comorbid mental health issues (such as depression, substance abuse, ADHD, etc.)
- Significant life stressors
- A history of abuse
- Family history of suicide
- Lack of consistent mental health treatment

Although none of these are fully indicative of someone who *will* attempt suicide, the presence of any of these risk factors should increase the counselor's awareness and precipitate an intentional conversation around suicidal thoughts or ideations.

Common "Reasons" for Suicide Attempts

A counselee may express many reasons for her desire to end her life. The most commonly shared reason is some sort of internal emotional pain, including feelings of despair, hopelessness, deep sadness, or unrelenting suffering with no prognosis for change. She may also express feelings of guilt or shame over a particular event or a personal failure in her life. Some cultures view suicide as honorable and preferable to bringing shame to one's family, or the counselee may feel that way herself; the counselor must understand this reality properly to counsel well.

The counselee may feel there is an unmet need in her life; this is typically an intangible need such as love or acceptance, but it may also be a physical need like income or protection. Particularly with the elderly, a woman might have suicidal thoughts after the loss of a loved one, like a spouse; in these cases, the suicidal thoughts often come in response to a feeling of emptiness or despair of having to live life without that loved one. Some may express that their suicidal thoughts come out of anger or bitterness; the attempt to take their life is actually an attempt to hurt another person or for revenge.

It is important for the counselor to discover the underlying motivation for the suicidal thoughts, as treating someone with deep emotional pain will look vastly different than treating someone who feels lost without their spouse of fifty years. The wise counselor spends a significant amount of time seeking to understand the counselee's reasoning for wanting to take her life and responds accordingly. Counselors must remember that a woman's desire to take her own life is always logical to her; we must seek to understand that logic.

Symptoms and Manifestation of Suicidal Ideations

Often, it is difficult to determine clear "symptoms" of someone's suicidal thoughts unless told outright; counselees are good at hiding their distress. However, we may see indicators of that distress in several ways. First, the woman may talk about her intentions directly or indirectly, perhaps by making statements about not being around, that she is a burden to others, she feels trapped, or she has no reason to live. She may also get her affairs in order, giving things away or writing a will. We might see indicators like withdrawing from others or significant mood changes; this would include things like sleeping changes, acting anxious or depressed, or being aggressive or reckless. Sometimes substance use is indicative of their attempts to deal with problematic and overwhelming emotions.

Biblical and Theological Perspectives

While suicide is listed several times in the Bible (Samson, Saul, Saul's armorbearer, Judas, and others), in no case do we see direct teachings about it within those accounts. Despite the lack of prescriptive teaching about the issue, the commonality is these were people who were not walking with the Lord, who faced imminent death from mortal injury, and who evidenced great fear. These situations do not typically align with what we see in counseling, so there is little that we can glean *directly* from Scripture related to suicidal thoughts or intentions.

However, there are several key theological teachings that speak to the issue of suicide and suicidal ideation. First and foremost, Scripture is clear about the value of human life; we are image bearers, precious and valuable to God, and our value is not based on capacity or ability. Therefore, human life should be upheld as tremendously valuable. Second, Scripture is clear that God alone is Creator, Sustainer, and Author of life; he gives and sustains life, so he and he alone is the authority over when life begins and ends.

Next, the Bible includes several commands against murder; self-murder is included under that umbrella and is sinful and disobedient to these commands. Therefore, suicide carries with it a clear moral component: it is not about honor versus dishonor, rather it is clearly a sinful act. As counselors, we can talk about morality of suicide. It is disobedient to commands, it is an act of unbelief (desiring to do things one's own way), and it is self-centered.

We must be clear that suicide does not make someone lose their salvation, though it is a serious sin. One act of rebellion, by God's grace, does not forfeit a person's eternal security. And yet, we would not want to take suicidal thoughts or attempts lightly, because they are sinful, as noted above. Therefore, the wise counselor is careful to assert all truths of Scripture, holding both the seriousness of this sin and the grace of God in tandem.

Counseling Steps and Practical Procedures

First, the counselor should not be afraid to speak openly about suicidal thoughts/ideations (SI). Talking about suicide isn't going to lead a woman to take her life; but avoiding that discussion may mean missing clear indicators and be a danger to the counselee. Therefore, the topic of suicide and suicidal thoughts should be discussed *at the very least* in the beginning session(s), but if there is any indication of ongoing struggles in this area, conversations should happen frequently.

Second, as soon as a counselee shares suicidal thoughts or intentions, a suicidal ideation action plan should be put in place. This contract should contain a clause wherein the counselee agrees to be honest and forthright in each session and to bring any and all relevant events or thoughts to the attention of the counselor, specifying whether the event or thought best falls into the category of feelings of hopelessness, SI with no intent to act, or specific plans of suicide. Additionally, the counselee must agree to inform the counselor when she feels as if she may not be safe. The contract should also include plans (developed together) of what the counselee must do if SI arises while she is in counseling, including who to call in case of an emergency.

In addition to the contract and the contact list, it is advisable to send the counselee home with a list (created with the help of counselor) of self-soothing resources to use well before reaching the stage of SI with intent to act. These can include any calming and/or relationally engaging activity: walking, calling a friend (listing names is helpful), using relaxation techniques, writing or journaling, heading to a familiar place that the counselee enjoys, reading specific Scripture passages, listening to worship music, or something else the counselee enjoys.

In counseling the suicidal counselee, above all, the counselor must be compassionate. We must not talk down to or assume the woman has not already wrestled with the morality of her decision. We must speak with grace and kindness, yet firmly. We should remind her often of the gospel; we are to love her well, but expose lies and wrong thinking. The following list of passages may aid the counselor with this situation:

- 1 Corinthians 10:13–14: We are never tempted beyond what we can bear. Even thoughts of suicide, or strong temptations toward it, are not beyond temptations we can bear with the help of the Lord.
- 2 Corinthians 4:7–18: We are to keep an eternal focus in our suffering. While suffering is real and pressing, it is still temporal. It will pass away.
- Hebrews 4:12–16: Jesus sympathizes in our weakness. Jesus faced immense hardship and he knows intimately the suffering our counselees bear.
- Lamentations 3:18–26: His mercies are new every morning. Each day, the counselee can receive those mercies to face the day ahead, including the struggles it brings.

- Psalm 46:1–11: "God is our refuge and strength" (v. 1). Because our strength comes from the Lord of hosts, "we will not fear though the earth gives way" (v. 2 ESV).
- Psalm 73:1–28: "God is the strength of my heart and my portion forever" (v. 26 ESV). This psalm reminds us that he guides us with his counsel, and afterward will take us up in glory. He receives us despite our weaknesses.
- John 10:1–18: Jesus is our good Shepherd. It is he who leads us to safety, rest, and provision (see Psalm 23). He protects and cares for his own.

Throughout these passages and in counseling, the counselor should lean on three key themes. First, we can have hope because God is ever-present, compassionate, merciful, and forgiving. He will never leave us and he is always working for our good, even when we do not see or understand. Second, God retains sovereign control despite our chaos. Elise's statements that things will never get better miss this reality. Finally, we continually provide genuine care and concern, taking her thoughts and feelings seriously, but specifically combating feelings of worthlessness and hopelessness. God sees her as a being of infinite worth and he is the God of all hope who fills us with joy and peace as we trust in him (Rom 15:13); as her counselor, I should assign her great worth and hold out great hope.

Remember that for the suicidal counselee, taking her life has an internal logic. As an outsider, it might not make sense to us, but be assured that it makes sense to her. Recall the example of Elise; her logic led her to the belief that heaven is much better than this hopeless, pain-filled world she lives in. As the counselor, we must seek to understand this logic rather than immediately dismissing it.

The counselor should listen, and listen well, assessing as she goes. The counselor can ask questions like:

- What is her pain?
- What circumstances are contributing to her thoughts?

     Why does she believe she would be better off not living?

     Does she have a plan and means?

     Has she made a recent attempt?

     What emotions is she experiencing?

     Where does she see God in her situation?

These questions in particular aim to get at the internal logic as they seek to understand the individual and her motivations.

The Role of Risk Assessments

The questions above help the counselor evaluate for suicide risk. There are tools available to help assess suicide risk; the counselor may choose one of her liking, but should use an assessment that incorporates intent, plan, and means; contributing risk factors such as their history of suicidal thoughts/attempts, problematic emotions or relationships, and life stressors; and any emotional, behavioral, or thought patterns that are indicative of their intent. Tools such as the Columbia Suicide Severity Rating Scale (C-SSRS), Suicide Behaviors Questionnaire (SBQ-R), Suicide Assessment Five-Step Evaluation and Triage (SAF-T), and the Kessler Psychological Distress Scale (K10), among others, may be useful to assess for suicide risk.

    While it is helpful to have categories, the counselor should be aware that a counselee can transition from low risk to medium or high risk rather quickly, so it is best to hold these categories somewhat loosely. For conceptualization though, a low-risk counselee would be one who perhaps deals well with stress, and has a passive intent with no real plan, no previous attempts, a strong support system, and clear thoughts about the impact of her own moral stance on suicide. The medium-risk counselee, like Elise above, likely has a more active intent, a greater sense of hopelessness, has communicated one or more times her intent to others, has a general plan or means, and chronic stressors that are not easily managed. Finally, the high-risk counselee has clear intent, plan, and means, sometimes with an indicated time or date. She may have previous suicide attempts, lack of support from others, little if any awareness of the implications of her death, and a low stress tolerance or high stressors that aren't managed. Again, while these categories may be helpful, it is important to remember these are momentary and temporary categories; one cannot assume because a counselee leaves an appointment lower in risk that she may not transition quickly at some point into being high risk.

In many ways, the response to a suicidal counselee is contingent upon the risk. For (consistently) lower-risk counselees, the intervention may simply be continued monitoring or securing a verbal no-harm agreement (i.e., an agreement not to take her life, documented in the counselor's case notes), along with continued counseling, and a SI plan as outlined above. In this case, counseling may be short term, focused on removing methods of harm, assessing and establishing support, meeting immediate needs, and so forth. Medium-risk counselees require more intentional and frequent conversations, and perhaps a written no-harm agreement. Counseling for this category is likely a bit longer term. Higher-risk counselees might require interventions such as hospitalization and involuntary intervention to ensure their safety, and dealing with deep-seated hopelessness or sinful thoughts, and perhaps a lack of support in various areas of life. Particularly for medium- to high-risk women, it is important to involve a full care team, typically including those trained in crisis/trauma and suicide intervention. The counselor should create, alongside the counselee, a comprehensive plan of care (SI plan explained previously), including ways to reduce stressors, the key persons within a support team, and a plan in place in case the counselee does attempt to take her life. This is best done in writing and given to the counselee, with a copy kept for the counselor.

The counselor should take counseling day by day, week by week, while immediately addressing practical needs. This would include helping her remove any means of harm (like pills and weapons), establishing a suicide watch if necessary, and establishing a regular counseling schedule to continually assess and respond to the counselee's risk level and stressors. If possible and when appropriate, the counselor can and should also involve family members (or those she lives with) and the church in the support of the counselee.

Suggested Growth Assignments

There are growth assignments suitable to each counselee. A theme noted above was hopelessness; in response, the counselor can lead the counselee to read passages from the Psalms that deal with hopelessness and God's response to it (e.g., Ps 34:17–20; 94:1–16; 13:1–6). The counselee might also find it helpful to write her own psalm, expressing her emotions and concerns clearly and frankly to the Lord, or meditate and journal on the eternal kingdom that is to come (Revelation 21 and 22). The counselor might also have the counselee memorize and meditate on passages that relate directly to her underlying fears, worries, or grief.

The counselee will generally benefit from having a care plan in place, including who she might reach out to or where she might find support in the difficult moments. Another practical assignment is for the counselee to find opportunities to serve others. This intentionally shifts her focus from self to other people. Last, it can be tremendously helpful for the counselee to journal her thoughts as they arise, then either with or without the counselor, look for patterns of unbelief or wrong thinking, underlying longings/desires, toppled idols, failed dreams, or losses (tangible or intangible).

This section closes with a final reminder: ultimately, the counselee is responsible for any decision that she makes to take her own life. She has autonomy. You can plead with her not to take her life, you can provide counsel, wisdom, prayer, and care, and you can help her get committed to a hospital for care and supervision, but you cannot own her choice. It is her own.

Recommended Resources

Black, Jeffrey S., *Suicide: Understanding and Intervening* (Phillipsburg, NJ: P&R, 2003).

Powlison, David, *I Just Want to Die: Replacing Suicidal Thoughts with Hope* (Greensboro, NC: New Growth Press, 2010).

Self-Harm

Definition/Description of the Problem and Prevalence within Counseling

Self-harm, by definition, is intentional physical harm caused to a woman's own body, and may include things like cutting her arms, legs, or stomach, carving words into her body, hitting herself with her fist or a hammer, burning herself, or other means of inflicting harm or pain. Self-harm may or may not be related to suicidal ideation; the counselor should not assume, but should assess for risk of suicide in cases of self-harm.

Statistically, self-injury is on the rise and is most common in adolescent and young adult females. Overwhelmingly, most people who self-harm begin during their teen or preteen years, and nearly half have been abused in some way. Many who self-injure report learning how to do it from friends or pro-self-injury websites. The reality is that the current teen subculture in many ways affirms and propagates self-harm as an acceptable method of dealing with problematic emotions or situations. Notice the correlation of age (teen/preteen) and developmental realities such as the influx of emotions without fully developed emotional regulation. This does not alleviate personal responsibility, but does provide insight for the counselor working with a young woman struggling in this way.

Symptoms and Manifestation

Quite often, but not always, self-harm wounds are hidden, since there is sometimes a level of shame associated with this behavior. More important are the reasons behind the behaviors, which are pivotal to treatment. The most common reasons include:

- An attempt to stop or cover negative emotional feelings; self-harm may give a sense of control over one's feelings
- If experiencing emotional numbness, a desire to at least feel something
- To punish oneself
- To relieve feelings of emptiness
- A way to relax
- Something to do when alone

Another reason is the need for attention, but this almost always comes in tandem with one or more of the reasons listed above. The current youth culture has an increased awareness of these behaviors, and some teens desire to stand out or be viewed a particular way. Or the teen might feel like her parents will only take her emotional struggles seriously if she is self-harming. In either case, it is behaviorally reinforcing to have attention focused on her despite any negative connotations associated with the behavior.

Common risk factors for self-harm may include an inability to cope with negative emotions (i.e., difficulty with emotional expression), prior exposure to self-harming behaviors, simply being an adolescent, lack of a strong support network, and having a comorbid mental health struggle, such as depression. Self-injury is also strongly linked to other mental health diagnoses like borderline personality disorder.

Biblical-Theological Perspectives

Many of the same biblical and theological foundations regarding suicide apply to self-harm. Specifically, we are to view the individual as valuable and see God as the authority over all things, including our bodies. Further, believers understand that the body is the literal temple for the Holy Spirit; it is not our own (1 Cor 6:19–20). God has the authority over our bodies, because he made us and we were bought with a price. The blood of Christ was shed on our behalf to pay our debt of sin.

Regarding the struggle with problematic emotions, we must remember that God's Word is the truth (John 17:17), and therefore, it is the ultimate authority over our emotions. Furthermore, the Lord himself is our rest and peace (Matt 11:28–30). Both of these truths can lead the counselee to combat many of the common struggles related to self-harm. These teachings can and should be applied individually to her individual struggle and internal logic/feelings.

The Bible speaks at length about the struggles between flesh and spirit. Paul writes in Rom 8:6, "Now the mindset of the flesh is death, but the mindset of the Spirit is life and peace." When we follow the (sinful) desires of our heart, it only leads to destruction and death. We are harmed. But when our mind is set on the things of God, led by his Spirit, we find life and peace. For the self-harming counselee, life and peace are often missing, but God provides the solution in his Word: setting our hearts on him rather than ourselves.

Finally, in 1 Pet 2:24, we are reminded that he bore our sins on the cross so that we might live and live righteously. He did the work, and it is finished. The Bible reassures the counselee engaging in self-harm that living rightly is possible because of what Christ already accomplished on the cross and by the power of the Spirit living within them.

Counseling Steps and Practical Procedures

Assessment is an important aspect of counseling those engaging in self-harm behaviors, including an assessment for suicide.[3] The counselor should assess the counselee's history of injury, the means, frequency, reasons, openness, any triggers or stressors, and any other struggles like depression, anxiety, OCD, and so forth. In particular, the counselor should seek to understand the reasons or motivation behind the behaviors, because only when we understand the motivation can we get at the heart of the problem. As counselors, we do not want to just stop the behavior, but to deal with the underlying issue(s). Typically, these conversations will focus on motivations and desires, emotional recognition and regulation, recurring thought patterns, teaching other means of dealing with stress or emotions, and if possible, removing or minimizing stressors. When faced with comorbid conditions, dealing with those struggles tends to further reduce the self-harm behaviors.

In the short-term, the counselor should seek to help her (or her parents) to remove any methods of self-harm, such as knives, razors, pencils, and the like, while still acknowledging that this is limited (e.g., the counselee may use her fingernails to inflict harm). The counselor can encourage supervision, if and when possible, and should involve parents with any underage counselee. This can be done while still maintaining the trust of the counselee, particularly by encouraging the counselee to disclose to her parents directly. The counselor should also be quick to document disclosures of self-harm and any suicidal thoughts that may accompany her actions.

For ongoing counseling, the counselor must be patient; the behaviors will not stop overnight. Self-harm is almost like an addiction in that the use of self-harm becomes an "effective" way of coping with emotions that the counselee cannot handle. In some sense, the counselee must relearn coping mechanisms that are more appropriate and honoring to the Lord as she shifts her understanding of the Lord and herself in light of the truths of God's Word. In parallel, the counselor should talk openly and frequently about submission to the Lord. It is sinful to harm oneself and the counselee must work toward both thinking and acting in a way that is honoring to God. The counselor can also continually share theological truths pertinent to this struggle: God is near to the brokenhearted; he gives comfort, hope, and peace; and by his power these sinful patterns can be changed. There is hope.

Suggested Growth Assignments

There is a variety of growth assignments that may be helpful. First and foremost, it is helpful for the counselee to keep a log of self-harm incidents between sessions, including the setting, triggers, any feelings before and after (if completed), coping mechanisms in place, and thought patterns. This will allow better assessment and discussion in the counseling session as well as treatment planning moving forward.

Second, the counselee can meditate on passages such as 1 Cor 6:20—we were bought with a price and should use our bodies to glorify God—as well as Isa 53:5—that by his wounds (not our own) we are healed. In light of Phil 4:8, the counselee may benefit from listing biblical truths related to her triggers; for example: "I am his, not my own" (1 Cor 6:20) and "Because the Son has set me free, I am free indeed!" (John 8:36). Similarly, she can journal and meditate on remaining steadfast through trials (Jas 1:12, 5:11; Rom 5:3–5; Gal 6:9). Along these same lines, the counselee can practice other methods of coping with stressors, such as reading a psalm or thinking on truthful thoughts as explored above.

Finally, the counselee may be encouraged to journal through questions that reveal heart motives, such as:

- What am I getting from this? (Sometimes this question is easy to answer partially but difficult to answer with complete honesty. I have often had counselees who immediately give the usual suspects—control, relief, and so on [all true of them individually]—but later they let me know that they purposefully concealed that they are also getting love, care, and attention from their struggles.)
- What am I afraid I might lose if I were to give up self-harm?
- What could replace this practice in a moment of difficulty?
- What lie am I believing that allows me to continue this practice, and what truth do I need to act on by faith?
- What might life be like without this practice? What might I be missing by holding on to this?

The answers to these questions can then be discussed in the next counseling session.

Conclusion

This chapter has sought to provide a high-level understanding of both suicide and self-harm, including how each is manifested, addressed in Scripture, and treated in counseling. However, the seriousness of each of these struggles cannot be overstated. The beginning counselor in particular is encouraged to engage with others who have more training in this area when the struggle arises in counseling, to be better equipped to walk with those who are struggling in these ways.

Recommended Resources

Baker, Amy, *Relief without Cutting: Taking Your Negative Feelings to God* (Greensboro, NC: New Growth Press, 2011).

Ganschow, Julie, *Toward a Biblical Understanding of Self-Injury*, 2nd ed. (n.p.: Pure Water Press, 2013).

Lelek, Jeremy, *Cutting: A Healing Response*, Gospel for Real Life Series (Phillipsburg, NJ: P&R, 2012).

Welch, Edward T., *Self-Injury: When Pain Feels Good* (Phillipsburg, NJ: P&R, 2004).

13

Addiction and Pornography

Bridgette, a single woman in her thirties, comes to counseling stating that her main problem is guilt over her "occasional use" of pornography. Upon further conversation, she shares that her use of porn is quite frequent, several times a week in fact. Bridgette says it relieves stress (she has a highly stressful job) and helps minimize feelings of loneliness and isolation. She started out watching movies with scenes that were inappropriate, but quickly escalated to seeking out videos and masturbating as she watched. She feels guilty, but also wrestles with feelings that it is "normal" and "not hurting anyone" because no one else really knows about it.

Isabelle has been married to Mark for about two years, but she recently discovered that his pornography use has resurfaced. She knew he struggled before they were married, but he assured her it was over and was not a temptation anymore. Turns out, he has been looking at pornography consistently over the last four months. She feels betrayed and angry, not sure where to go from here.

> *She wants to trust him again, but constantly fights thoughts wondering what*
> *he is doing if he's alone or if she can believe him when she brings it up. Mark*
> *has confessed his sin to their pastor and several men are helping to hold him*
> *accountable, but she feels left out and in need of care and support.*

Addiction is rampant in American society, including addiction to pornography. Studies estimate that over half of men regularly watch pornography,[1] and while numbers seem to vary on the percentage of women, that number has been steadily rising in recent years. Even within the church, the pervasiveness of substance use and abuse, including pornography, is close to that of the broader culture.

This chapter addresses both addiction and pornography, seeing addiction as the umbrella concept and pornography use as one type of addiction. Admittedly, we cannot cover everything, but will discuss some general principles. We will also primarily focus on pornography addiction, like the vignettes above, since this is the most common form of addiction and one rarely discussed openly. Counselors may be called on to care for either the addict herself or the family member of the addict. Both are significant struggles, so this chapter aims to give direction for counseling in either category.

Description/Presentation of the Problem

The Bible does not use the term "addiction" formally; it has no concept of the secular approach to the disease model of addiction. However, it does speak at length about enslaving sins, a much more appropriate category for understanding addiction and pornography use. Building on Ed Welch's writings, *The Gospel for Disordered Lives* provides a helpful working definition: "Arising out of our alienation from the Living God, addiction is bondage to the rule of a substance, activity, or state of mind, which then becomes the center of life, defending itself from the truth so that even bad consequences don't bring repentance, and leading to further estrangement from God."[2] This definition goes beyond the *DSM-5*'s use of "substance use disorder" instead of "addiction" and deviates from the APA's assertion that it is a complex "brain disorder" that leads to compulsive behavior. Importantly, this definition recognizes the separation from God that addiction brings.

Another important dynamic with addiction is that the counselee has become both a rebel and a slave. There is a choice to be disobedient (rebel), but eventually as use moves to addiction, the counselee also feels out of control and enslaved by the compulsion toward the substance or activity.[3] We typically think of addiction to a substance within this dynamic, but pornography use is no different. What begins innocently (like with Bridgette above) quickly becomes compulsory, almost as if it is necessary to life.

An addiction, to pornography or something else, is not simply behavioral. It is not just something we *do*, but something we *crave*. It is a matter of the heart. Desires (for satisfaction or control), beliefs ("I won't get caught" or "It isn't that bad"), and attitudes (justification for sin and pride) directly fuel one's use of a substance or pornography. The physiological response affirms the use, but it begins much deeper than that.

Further, deception is almost always present. As the saying goes, "If you've met an addict, you've met a liar." With pornography, one deceives oneself by minimizing porn's sinfulness and feeling a false sense of control, and deceives others by covering up or hiding his sin. It is not uncommon for addicts to deny their addiction or even their use to those around them (including counselors), and while guilt may rightly accompany these lies, they continue to lie.

For the wife of an addict, particularly the pornography user, the impact is tremendous. Remember Isabelle above; she felt betrayal, rejection, anger, hurt, confusion, and a lack of control over her situation. In short, she feels like she has been dropped into chaos. She is trying to figure out how to respond appropriately, fighting extremes of overregulation versus ignoring the issue or jumping to quick forgiveness to avoid more pain. But quite often, the secrecy of the porn use trickles into her life as well and leads to a lack of receiving care for her struggle. She feels alone, possibly embarrassed by her husband's actions, and unable to reach out to others for help.

What the Bible Has to Say

The Bible speaks at length about the condition of the human heart and our sinful tendencies. Apart from Christ, we are enslaved to our sin (Rom 6:6), and even though believers are set free from that enslavement through Christ (John 8:36), we still fight a pull toward sin. Addiction is part of that pull. Jesus taught that we act out of our heart's desires (Luke 6:45). He said, "A good person produces good out of the good stored up in his heart. An evil person produces evil out of the evil stored up in his heart, for his mouth speaks from the overflow of the heart." In other words, our external behaviors are direct reflections of our hearts. Want to know the state of someone's heart? Look at what they say and do. Addictive behavior reveals a desire to meet a need that cannot be met outside of God, and a (false) belief that the addicting substance or activity can meet that need.

The Bible also teaches that we are to love God first and others as ourselves (Matt 22:37–40). Addictive behavior, in contrast, puts oneself on the throne rather than God or others; it is self-serving rather than God-serving or others-serving. Addiction and pornography use are attempts to meet a personal desire despite the negative impact on others. Specifically with pornography use, it violates another person at their expense for one's own personal pleasure.

We are also to be self-controlled (Eph 5:15–18), which is not a characteristic of addiction. Recall the discussion above about the counselee as both rebel and slave. A slave is not able to exercise self-determination or control over her choices; she is controlled by whatever has enslaved her. Addiction is not about the use of the substance or engagement in the activity; it is ultimately about self-control to choose to honor the Lord and others over oneself. It is about practicing those characteristics Paul, in Col 3:12–16, tells us to put on (e.g., compassion, kindness, humility, love) rather than those he tells us to put off in Col 3:5, 8 (sexual immorality, lust, greed, etc.).

Specific to pornography, we must also remember Scripture's teachings about proper sexual expression. The Lord's design is that sexual activity happens only within the bounds of biblical marriage (Heb 13:4; 1 Cor 6:18). The use of pornography directly violates these directives. Sex is something to be enjoyed between a husband and wife, not between a husband, wife, and others. Marriage, including sexuality within marriage, mirrors the unique, intimate relationship between Christ and his bride, the church. Anything outside God's design, then, goes against his intentions.

The use of pornography also views people wrongly. In Gen 1:27, we read that God created man and woman in his own image, which means they have value. People are not objects to be used but are image bearers of the Almighty God. Pornography, though, sees people as tools to bring personal satisfaction rather than fellow image bearers worthy of dignity, honor, and respect.

Finally, the Bible is clear that we are to repent of our sin and turn from it (Acts 17:30–31; Rom 2:4). This certainly includes any addictive behavior or pornography use. Addiction and pornography use are wrong; they violate God's commands and are sinful against him and others. Those caught in these sins must repent and turn from them. The good news of the gospel is that when we repent of sin, God is faithful and just to forgive us through Christ (1 John 1:9), and he helps us move toward change.

How Should Counselors Respond to Addiction and Pornography Use?

After reading the above, someone struggling might feel hopeless, thinking, "I know, but how do I change? I feel so helpless." Or the tendency of a counselor might be to think that it's *simply* a sin issue in need of repentance. While that is true—we should repent and turn from our sin—we must acknowledge that addiction is more complex than that, evidenced by high relapse rates even in Christian circles. People are both body and soul and realistically, when someone becomes a slave to their addiction, both body and soul are at war. An appropriate response considers this reality.

For the Addict/Porn User

Several measures can be put into place to counsel the addict or pornography user:

Foster a greater love than that of the substance/activity. Our hearts were made to worship: it is how we were created and how we continually live. Because of sin, we tend to worship things other than God, most often worshipping ourselves or things we desire. Addiction disorders, then, are worship disorders: the addict worships something over God and ultimately worships herself over God. The best way to combat this is to foster a love for something greater (God). The treatment for addiction (a worship disorder) is worship realignment. The counselor must explore this dynamic with the counselee and help her properly align her worshipping heart.

Acknowledge the seriousness of her sin. The user must realize (1) that her actions are continually sinful against both God and others, and (2) that she needs help overcoming it. She also must be committed to turning from her sin with the help of God and others. While minimizing or deception continues (to herself or others), there is little hope of change. Alternatively, when a counselee realizes the weight of her sin against God and others and is committed to change, she has a much greater likelihood of overcoming her addiction.

Repent specifically of sin to those offended. Part of acknowledging the weight of sin is a willingness to repent of it. The counselor should help the addict/ pornography user work through the list of those she has offended (God and others) and determine how she might specifically repent of her sins against them. This is not an easy process; it pushes up against pride and requires an acknowledgment of wrongdoing. But the balance of sin is grace; through Christ, when we repent, we are forgiven of our sins immediately and fully.

Recognize potential triggers or times of temptation. The counselor should help the counselee explore any triggers or common times of temptation for her to fall back into her addiction or pornography use. These might be times of higher stress, times when she is alone, or circumstances where other emotions seem overwhelming to her. In tracking these situations (see homework exercises below), the counselor and counselee can discuss a proper response or practical barriers to the substance/activity.

Put practical measures in place to minimize access. For any sort of addiction, including pornography, access to the substance or material can be alleviated. For instance, if the counselee is addicted to alcohol, the counselor and counselee might consider removing any access to alcohol and possibly initiating oversight of her finances (accountability). With pornography, placing restrictions on electronic devices to block certain websites and send alerts to accountability partners is a practical measure that can be taken. Further, the counselor and counselee might consider consequences of evading these precautions, such as disclosure to others (like a spouse or pastoral team) or more stringent oversight. The role of the counselor may vary significantly depending on context (i.e., licensed therapist vs. church-based ministry), but counsel can and should be given related to setting up practical barriers to access.

Get support from others. The fight against addiction and pornography is strengthened tremendously when others come alongside the counselee to help her fight the battle. Ideally, her church has a pastoral care team or an accountability group in place to help her, but if not, several groups exist for support (Celebrate Recovery, Alcoholics Anonymous, etc.).[4] The counselor is only one member of the care team.

Be patient, understanding that lapses happen. The road out of addiction and pornography use is a hard one, a battle that is often long fought, with several lapses or relapses. But this is not a failure. Most addicts will relapse several times before overcoming their addiction; the counselor should not be surprised when a lapse or relapse happens. Instead, the counselor should address it clearly and directly, acknowledging the sin but extending grace as the counselee recommits to change.

For the Wife of a Pornography User

Slow down and help her grieve the betrayal. The tendency may be for an offended wife to jump toward forgiveness and "forgetting" that it ever happened. In some ways, this feels easier than dealing with rejection and betrayal. However, the offense was real and significant, one that brings with it grief and a need for healing. This healing takes time and, given the nature of lapses that often happen with addicts, may have to be revisited several times.

Acknowledge the seriousness of the sin and place responsibility on the offender. Sometimes wives want to blame themselves for their husband's pornography use, which ultimately comes from a desire to control the outcome or future hurt. The reality is that the *offender* chose to use pornography, she didn't. She is not responsible for his choices. The counselor should rightly place blame on the offender and actively combat inappropriate assumption of personal responsibility by the wife.[5]

Discuss biblical forgiveness and reconciliation, including consequences for sin.[6] Forgiveness is the one-directional pardoning of an offender, while reconciliation is the two-directional acknowledgment of sin, forgiveness for that sin, and restitution of the relationship. We are required to forgive (Matt 18:21–22; Matt 6:14–15), but we are only required to move toward reconciliation as far as possible (Rom 12:18). Despite these requirements, there are still consequences for our sin. In the case of pornography use, consequences for the relationship between a husband and wife. This might be the rebuilding of trust, more constraints or oversight after disclosure, or even church discipline. The counselor should help the offended wife work through each of these concepts and evaluate her role in them.

Determine her responsibilities and role moving forward. Most often, it is not wise for the wife to be the accountability partner for her husband; this is better left to men who have walked with others, perhaps even themselves, through this struggle before. Sometimes wives must fight the urge to police their husbands, looking over his shoulder constantly or not letting him be alone. While these feelings and tendencies are understandable, they are generally not helpful. The counselor should help the offended wife work through what is appropriate for her in his struggle with pornography, given their unique situation and her own temptations.

Work through her response and help her respond in a way that honors the Lord. While an offended wife might not have much control over her husband's sin, nor is she responsible for it, she is responsible for her own response. She can control her reaction in both thoughts and actions. Her aim, with the help of the counselor, should be to respond in a way that is loving to the Lord and loving toward her husband (Matt 22:37) and is a response that she would desire if she were in his place (Matt 7:12). This means kind and gracious words despite her anger, acting justly, and trusting the Lord to do his work in her husband's heart.

Homework Exercises

For the Addict/Pornography User

The following exercises may be helpful for the addict or pornography user:

1. Keep track throughout the week of times or situations when the temptation arises to use the substance or engage in pornography. Make note of whether it was a temptation only or temptation and use, as well as any situational stressors or triggers. The counselee may choose to use an hourly calendar or simply daily notations in a journal, but the journal/tracking sheet should be brought to the next counseling session for discussion.

2. With guidance from the counselor, develop an appropriate response plan for times of both temptation and use. This includes accountability partners[7] or potential consequences for engaging in the addictive behavior. While much of this can be discussed in session with the counselor, the counselee can spend some time on her own thinking through who might be best to come alongside her and the potential impact of her choices. This gives her ownership over her care and reinforces the significance of her actions.

3. Reading, meditating, praying through, and journaling about fruits of the Spirit from Gal 5:22–23 can help her contrast right action

and characteristics with sinful choices that come with addiction or pornography use. In particular, she should draw out characteristics of each fruit and how those can and should manifest in her own life, specifically as it relates to her addiction. For instance, one fruit of the spirit is peace: addiction promises peace (or relief from pain) but always falls short. In contrast, the Lord brings true peace that cannot be taken away. Meditating on these realities directly confronts underlying desires and counters them with biblical truth.

4.   Make a list of positive outlets to pursue. Most often, the use of pornography is in response to something, for instance, stress or temptations toward inappropriate sexual behavior outside of marriage. In either case, the counselee can think through positive ways to manage her stress or temptations that do not include the use of pornography. Giving her options outside those moments of temptation helps her prepare for when the moments of struggle come.

For the Wife of a Pornography User

These activities may be helpful for an offended wife:

1.   Ask the counselee to write down any ways she blames herself or takes responsibility for his actions. This might be withholding sexual intimacy, failing to be around when he is alone, having priorities higher than him, or others. The counselee can bring this list to her counseling session and discuss proper responsibility with the counselor as well as ways that she can appropriately help with his struggle.

2.   She can also note throughout the week the times that she feels the tendency to police her husband or check in on him. She can discuss those occasions and how to properly combat them with the counselor. The two can also discuss ways to rebuild trust or appropriate ways to guard herself against these tendencies.

Conclusion

Addiction and pornography use are tough situations to work through, but by God's grace and through his Spirit, they can be overcome. As counselors, we must be sensitive to the dynamics of addiction and pornography, confronting them directly and firmly, while still showing grace and patience as the addict pushes forward in the struggle. For the offended wife, counselors can show great compassion, grieving with her and supporting her as she walks alongside her husband. In either situation, the aim should be to honor the Lord and live rightly before him.

Recommended Resources

Lambert, Heath, *Finally Free: Fighting for Purity with the Power of Grace* (Grand Rapids: Zondervan, 2013).

Lasser, Deborah, *Shattered Vows: Hope and Healing for Women Who Have Been Sexually Betrayed* (Grand Rapids: Zondervan, 2008).

Reju, Deepak, *Pornography: Fighting for Purity* (Phillipsburg, NJ: P&R, 2018).

Shaw, Mark E., *The Heart of Addiction* (Bemidji, MN: Focus, 2008).

Tiede, Vicky, *Your Husband Is Addicted to Porn: Healing after Betrayal* (Greensboro, NC: New Growth Press, 2012).

Welch, Edward T., *Addictions: A Banquet in the Grave: Finding Hope in the Power of the Gospel* (Phillipsburg, NJ: P&R, 2001).

Welch, Edward T., *Crossroads: A Step-By-Step Guide Away from Addiction, Study Guide* (Greensboro, NC: New Growth Press, 2008).

14

Singleness

Mary has come to counseling for several sessions now, but today she shares that much of her feelings of sadness and discontentment seem to be stemming from the reality that she is still unmarried at thirty-two years old. Her friends are all married and have young children, and she often feels left out or a third wheel. Friends and family ask often if there are any new guys in her life or if she has met anyone, which reminds her again that she hasn't found "the one." She is starting to believe that she never will, that she's destined for a life of singleness and will never be a mother. When she expresses her discontentment to others, she always receives a pat answer: "It'll happen one day," "Just be patient," or her favorite, "Well, are you being too picky?" This just is not where she saw herself in life at this point.

In 2016, 45.2 percent of the US adult population was unmarried; 63.5 percent of those had never been married.[1] This number has risen over the last several decades and is expected to continue increasing. Many who are single are perfectly content to be so, either desiring to never marry or because it is simply something they don't think about often. But many others within this population desire marriage and have not yet gotten married, much like Mary above. Singleness, particularly for women, becomes a struggle that often grows as the woman ages. As counselors, we must be prepared to counsel this issue, especially as more and more women find themselves single and getting older.

What Is Singleness Like?

Singleness may seem to be an odd chapter in a text where the other topics more clearly align with problems in living. And yet, the longer I counsel, the more I speak with young women who are still single and do not wish to be. These desires grow and the struggle intensifies when she sees her friends, roommates, and perhaps sisters getting married, and she is not. She develops a sense of loneliness and hopelessness that feels like it cannot be satisfied by anything other than marriage. Sometimes this struggle is also amplified by her desire to have children and a ticking biological clock, so much so that her singleness feels like an impairment or a hindrance to moving forward in life. Despite how common it is, singleness can cause great distress, hence its inclusion in our text.

Before exploring what the Bible has to say about these struggles, and how we as counselors might respond to them, it is helpful to make a few distinctions. The impact of a woman's singleness may depend, in large part, on her desire to marry. Some have little desire to marry, so the struggle is not significant. For others, it is a main priority in life: marrying and having children has been their plan since childhood. The level of desire matters immensely.

There is a significant difference in being single at various ages. For those in their twenties, singleness is the norm. Many of these young ladies have not settled down yet and are busy getting their life in order. Singleness in this stage may be on their radar, but likely is not a pressing issue just yet. Conversely, women in their thirties are often starting to feel the pressure of not being married and likely are starting to lose hope of ever marrying, particularly as they move into their forties. Friends are getting married and having children, moving on to another stage of life the single woman has not entered. By the time a woman gets to her fifties, most single people in her age group are divorcees who have been married and are no longer. The struggles for women who are single now after being married are different than for those who have never married. And finally, a single woman in her seventies may very well be a widow, which again brings with it different struggles than a never-married single woman in her twenties or thirties experiences.

In counseling, we will typically see someone who either deeply desires to be married and has not yet, or who has walked through a divorce or death of a spouse and now finds herself single again. Those who have not yet married often struggle with hopelessness or frustration. She likely finds herself discontent and longing for marriage. Those who have divorced or lost a spouse may find themselves feeling like wanderers, grieving the loss and struggling to get their bearings after years of companionship.

We may also see the young woman who struggles with same-sex attraction and recognizes the limitations on biblical marriage that this struggle carries with it, though this is a minority of the single women seeking counseling. The woman in this category is likely struggling with her singleness as it relates to her SSA, which can bring grief and wrestling with questions about why she has to struggle in these ways.

What the Bible Has to Say about Singleness

It is not hard to find examples of single people in the Bible; Jesus and Paul are perhaps the most common examples, but it can be safely presumed that several other biblical authors and prophets were likely single as well. A multitude of teachings in Scripture are directly applicable to the struggle with singleness.

First, for some, singleness is a gift (1 Cor 7:7, 17; Matt 19:11) to be used to further God's kingdom, just as marriage is a gift to be used to further the kingdom. Paul spoke to this explicitly in 1 Cor 7:7–8, "I wish that all people were as I am. But each has his own gift from God, one person has this gift, another has that. I say to the unmarried and to widows: It is good for them if they remain as I am." The gift of singleness, as Paul noted here, is given to some and not to others, just as the gift of marriage is given to some and not to others. Paul even went so far as to say it is good to remain single, as he was, because he was able to do the Lord's work more freely.[2]

Because it is a gift from God, singleness is also God's plan for some, like Paul. This means that singleness is not inferior to marriage or that a single person is somehow incomplete or less than her married friends. Every man and woman, in marriage or not, is a full image bearer of God and reflects him, with or without a spouse.

Third, Paul noted in the same 1 Corinthians 7 passage that single people have advantages married couples do not (1 Cor 7:32–35). Singles have time that can be devoted to ministry that married couples do not have, because they have more responsibilities. Paul wrote, "I want you to be without concerns. The unmarried man is concerned about the things of the Lord—how he may please the Lord. But the married man is concerned about the things of the world—how he may please his wife—and his interests are divided. The unmarried woman or virgin is concerned about the things of the Lord, so that she may be holy both in body and in spirit. But the married woman is concerned about the things of the world—how she may please her husband" (1 Cor 7:32–34). A single person simply has fewer people to worry about, so more focus can be placed on kingdom work.

Fourth, singleness is also not easy and for many, not preferred. God declared in Gen 2:18 that it was not good for man to be alone; we were made for companionship and intimacy with one another. Marriage can satisfy this need for companionship. Also, sexual attraction and temptations exist and for a single person, the outlet of sex in marriage is not present. This was part of Paul's argument toward marriage in 1 Corinthians 7: a lack of self-control leads a person toward marriage as the proper expression of sexuality.

Next, the Bible indicates that the church is to be the place of relationships that are eternal. As brothers and sisters through Christ, our family in the

Lord is permanent and should hold a primary place in our lives. The church cannot replace marriage, but it is a setting where singles can develop deep and meaningful relationships with other believers until eternity, when marriage is no longer a reality (Matt 22:30).

God's Word reminds us our identity lies in Christ as his daughters. As believers, we are first and foremost image bearers of God (Gen 1:26–27), saved by the grace of Jesus (Eph 2:8), and sent out to fulfill his mission (Matt 28:19). Marital status is a secondary characteristic, not a primary one. It does not define who we are. The single woman is not a "single Christian," but a "Christian." We must not allow marital status to become a primary identifier of who we are when the Bible says otherwise.

Our first priority is meant to be how to honor God, not how we can find a husband. God knows well our desires and delights in meeting them, but he is not a vending machine; he does not simply dispense what we want if we obey him. Rather, our desires begin to align with his when we aim to honor and please him rather than to satisfy our own wants (Ps 37:4). This is especially true with singleness and potential temptations to honor God *for the purpose of* finding a husband.

Counseling Singleness

Several key principles are appropriate as we seek to minister to the struggling single counselee:

Recognize the struggle that is present in your counselee. Especially if a woman has sought out a counselor to help with her singleness, she is wrestling with this reality in her life. She probably is not happy about being single and desires marriage. For counselors who are married and do not struggle with singleness, it is often easy to forget just how pressing this struggle is. When her car breaks down, she wonders who to call; after church, she likely goes home to eat alone. Singleness impacts a woman's life day in and day out. We can recognize and affirm the reality of that struggle.

Acknowledge that the desire for marriage or companionship is a good, God-honoring desire, but it cannot become a demand. In the early chapters of Genesis, we learn that God recognized Adam's need for someone like him (Gen 2:18) and God created marriage to satisfy that need. The desire for marriage or a life companion is an innate, good, and proper desire. But when it becomes a demand or leads to sinful responses, such as bitterness, jealousy, or anger, it has moved beyond a good and proper desire. As counselors, we can help our counselee think through whether her desire for a husband has moved to a demand or an expectation, and if so, how to hold it properly.

For those who are single because of divorce or losing a spouse, grieve those losses. Sometimes singleness comes after a marriage ends through divorce or death. In these cases, a counselor can help the counselee grieve that loss. The divorced or widowed woman is likely struggling with feeling like herself again, figuring out who she is now that her husband is no longer part of her everyday life. This means things she used to rely on him for are no longer possible, from fixing things around the house to listening to how her day went. Singleness was likely not part of her plan. The counselor can help identify those needs and help connect her with others who can help fill that gap, but she can also simply weep with her over her newfound reality.

Provide gospel hope in the middle of these struggles. In particular, the counselor can and should affirm God's goodness, presence, and sovereignty. Whatever the way this woman became single, the counselor can affirm that God is still good. He is still for her. He is still present with her and sovereign over her life, though she may feel otherwise. It is also helpful to encourage the counselee that this is not God's plan B for her; he is not responding to something that caught him off guard and he has not forgotten about her. He knows the plans he has for his people, including her (Jer 29:11), and they are good (Rom 8:28). These gospel truths must remain at the forefront of her mind as she fights untrue thoughts or beliefs.

Explore ways to combat feelings of loneliness and isolation, particularly within the church. Encourage the counselee to be a part of a community where she invests in others and others invest in her. This might be a small group or Sunday school class, or it may be a particular ministry that she is interested in. The counselor should encourage her to engage with other singles and married people, not only those in her stage of life. Women who are married and/ or have children can speak wisdom into her life that she just doesn't have yet. And she can do the same for them. In most cases, the counselee should avoid singles ministries that are specifically designed to arrange marriages. If she participates in a singles ministry that happens to foster relationships as they study God's Word and serve others, that is appropriate, but a singles ministry should not serve as a dating site.

Help the counselee align herself with biblical teaching on singleness and marriage. We want to help our counselees see marriage and singleness correctly, as God sees them. We can help her view others first as brothers and sisters instead of married or single, seeing their value not in their marital status but in how they work together to further God's kingdom. We can also help her think through how singleness is a gift in this season of her life, rather than seeing it as a punishment or something she has to walk through to learn something from. Help her embrace and use her singleness for God's glory.

Work through any sinful responses such as jealousy or bitterness. Singleness has the potential to bring negative emotions toward those who are married, like anger, jealousy, or bitterness. However, these are not pleasing to the Lord (Eph 4:31) and are sinful. As counselors, despite being compassionate toward the counselee who deeply desires marriage, we should help counselees put away any of these sinful responses. This includes repentance and actively fighting this sin. Paired with the recommendations above, we can guide the counselee toward active engagement with others without any expectations (especially with single men) and help her fight any sinful emotions when she sees others entering relationships while she is not. This is particularly pertinent when, for instance, she is asked to be in or attend a wedding or hears of a new relation-ship that has formed. Such events are common triggers for sinful responses.

Help the counselee separate her identity from her marital status. The sec-tion above discussed the reality that a person's identity is not primarily tied to her marital status, but quite often our tendency is to see marital status before unique individuals. Many activities and ministries in the church are centered around marriage and families (children's ministry, small groups, marriage retreats or workshops, etc.). And we tend to identify with and be around peo-ple who are in a stage of life similar to ours. But this does not mean it is who we are entirely. The single woman may struggle to separate who she is as a child of God from her marital status; linking the two exacerbates her struggle. As counselors, we can talk through identity and how to view ourselves prop-erly in accordance with God's teachings.

If needed, put accountability in place to combat sexual temptation. Men and women were created, in part, as sexual beings. Sexual desires, like the desire for marriage and companionship, are not inherently sinful, but they were created to be expressed only in marriage. For the single woman, sex-ual temptation exists[3] and our culture encourages sexual expression outside marriage, making that temptation even greater. However, the counselor and counselee must acknowledge God's bounds for sexual expression and set boundaries in place to keep those desires in check. We need not ignore them; rather, we must help our counselees understand their proper place and how to fight temptations to express them in ways that are sinful.

Possible Homework or Growth Exercises

Much growth in this area happens from intentional conversations about a woman's singleness and her struggles related to it. However, a few assign-ments outside of counseling sessions can be helpful:

   ❧ The counselee can journal about why singleness is a struggle for her. In particular, she should write about the relational and emotional impact singleness has had on her life. Then in the counseling session, the counselor and counselee can walk through the specific struggles that she encounters regularly and how/why they are significant. When appropriate, the counselor can correct any faulty thoughts or behaviors that come in response to her struggles.

- ❧ Ask the counselee to make a list of areas that bring her discontentment, including singleness if that is the case. Have her pray specifically for the Lord to bring contentment in these areas. She can also read through texts like 1 Tim 6:6–8, Phil 4:11, and 2 Cor 9:8, meditating on what these verses have to say about contentment in the Lord's provisions.

- ❧ The counselee can be instructed to be intentional about being part of a church community and developing purposeful, deep relationships with people of all marital statuses. This specifically combats feelings of isolation and loneliness and better aligns with God's design for relationships (i.e., we should not only be in a relationship with our spouse).

Conclusion

Singleness is a common struggle among women in the church; the desire for marriage can be great. The Bible has much to say on the matter, encouraging women to see themselves and their marital situation correctly. As counselors, we can minister to single women regardless of how they arrived at their singleness, speaking wisdom and truth to bring comfort and a God-honoring response.

Recommended Resources

Allberry, Sam, *Seven Myths about Singleness* (Wheaton, IL: Crossway, 2019).
Danylak, Barry, *Redeeming Singleness: How the Storyline of Scripture Affirms the Single Life* (Wheaton, IL: Crossway, 2010).

Dykas, Ellen, *Sex and the Single Girl: Smart Ways to Care for Your Heart* (Greensboro, NC: New Growth Press, 2012).

McCulley, Carolyn, *Did I Kiss Marriage Goodbye?: Trusting God with a Hope Deferred* (Wheaton, IL: Crossway, 2004).

Segal, Marshall, *Not Yet Married: The Pursuit of Joy in Singleness and Dating* (Wheaton, IL: Crossway, 2017).

15

Trauma and Abuse

As you read through Tamara's forms, you notice a recurring theme: since she was a young child, she has been physically and sexually abused by those close to her. In fact, you are amazed at how much detail she includes on such a short intake form. From her stepfather to her uncle, boyfriends, and acquaintances, it seems she has been taken advantage of throughout her life. She has come to counseling asking for help, but she says it is because she can't seem to focus and she has trouble keeping friends, which is beginning to cause her a lot of distress. Tamara also is not sleeping well. She connects these struggles with her trauma, but isn't quite ready to "dive that deep" just yet.

In recent years, the topics of trauma and abuse have come into the spotlight in the evangelical world. While this is a tragic phenomenon, which we will discuss momentarily, these conversations have brought to light a topic that believers must be prepared to deal with. Trauma and abuse are pervasive, but quite often the events themselves and their effects are hidden. The Bible is not silent on these topics. Not only are there many examples of traumatic events in the Scriptures (the rape of Tamar, the murder of Abel, the killing of baby boys), but the Bible speaks at length about the effects of sin, suffering in a fallen world, and the future redemption that awaits us.

This chapter will focus on the larger concept of trauma and hone in on traumatic abuse.[1] We cannot address every type of trauma and abuse; but most forms of trauma, including abuse, follow a typical pattern that can be applied in many different scenarios. This chapter gives an overview of trauma and abuse, along with some biblical teaching and counseling helps on the topic.

I intentionally draw from secular resources on trauma. The field of trauma recovery has had particular focus in the secular arena in recent years and great strides have been made that may be beneficial for Christian counselors. As one example, the ACE (Adverse Childhood Experiences) study, with resulting research, has demonstrated significant findings that are pertinent for our field. Specifically, the study has shown the high correlation between experiences of trauma in childhood and increases in mental illness, rates of suicide and self-harm, drug and alcohol use, and various physical health conditions. Given that childhood abuse and neglect are in most cases preventable, it naturally follows that the increased risk does not have to be a reality. In other words, if we prevent the potentially traumatic event and reduce its effects (i.e., becoming *traumatized*), we directly lower the risks of depression, anxiety, suicidal thoughts, drug and alcohol use, heart disease, and a shorter life expectancy.

What Are Trauma and Abuse?

"Trauma" as a larger concept may be defined as "a normal reaction to abnormal events that overwhelm a person's ability to adapt to life."[2] There are three components worth noting here. First, there is a precipitating event that is abnormal, what we would call the "traumatic event" or "potentially traumatic event." Trauma does not flow out of normal, everyday life experiences; something out of the ordinary happens. Second, trauma involves a response that is typical, understandable, or justified. In other words, the average person may react in this way, because it is the event that is abnormal, not the response. The response to the event is in many ways subjective, since it is perceived and processed through a person's individual lens. Finally, the event and response combined are overwhelming, impacting the whole person (emotions, functionality, thought processes, relationships, etc.). Trauma, by its very nature, overwhelms one's ability to cope. However, just because someone experiences a potentially traumatic event, that does not mean the person will be *traumatized*. A potentially traumatic event and being traumatized, though similar, are different things (the experience versus the response or result).

To narrow our focus, "abuse" means mistreatment or misuse of something. When applied to a person, it is the dynamic of an unhealthy relationship that is marked by mistreatment, power, or control rather than mutual honor and value. Abuse can be categorized in various ways; for instance, age (child abuse versus abuse of an adult) and type (e.g., physical versus verbal). Child abuse is the mistreatment of someone under eighteen, including neglect or abandonment. Child abuse falls under mandatory reporting laws in all fifty states.[3] In contrast, domestic violence is violence or abuse within the home, typically between adult spouses or partners.

The following list, though not exhaustive, is a starting place for understanding some types of abuse:

- Physical: physical harm to another person, such as hitting, pinching, punching, or throwing
- Verbal/Mental/Emotional: injury to the psychological capacity or emotional stability of a person, including put-downs, criticisms, and other harsh words meant to diminish the person's self-worth
- Spiritual: distortion of biblical teaching to elevate self and degrade another, or for the purposes of forced submission/obedience
- Sexual: engaging in inappropriate or unwanted sexual behavior, including both touching and nontouching (verbal; forced observation) offenses

In all these situations, there are two parties involved (the abuser and the victim) and there is an injustice or a violation taking place. Psalm 58:2 may be a helpful descriptor: "All your dealings are crooked; you hand out violence instead of justice" (NLT). In the Old Testament, the term "justice" means to make something right or as it should be. The abuser, instead of living correctly with God and others, violates fellow image bearers. He is crooked, turning away from God, in all his ways.[4] Contrary to Isa 1:17, the abuser does not do good, he does not pursue justice, and he does not defend those who cannot defend themselves. He is the oppressor against whom we are to guard.

As noted previously, though, the experience of abuse or a traumatic event does not necessitate that a woman be *traumatized*. By God's grace, for many women, the experience of abuse or a potentially traumatic event is dealt with in a healthy way and has little long-term impact. There are many factors at play when it comes to the outcome of being traumatized, including the event itself, a history of trauma or abuse, the severity of the offense, and the woman's ability to respond in a way that she chooses. This chapter speaks primarily to cases where a woman is traumatized, the full understanding of the word "trauma," though that necessitates the inclusion of the actual event.

Impact of Trauma or Abuse on a Person

Trauma can have a tremendous, sometimes lifelong, impact on a victim, and on that person as a whole. For instance, a person may learn distorted thought patterns or hold wrong beliefs because of repeated abuse (Stockholm syndrome; misunderstandings about proper relationships) or live perpetually in a state of fear, worry, and anxiety. Relationally, the traumatized or abused person may withdraw or isolate, or fail to understand how to live in right relationship with another person. Spiritual questions about the sovereignty of God or his goodness may also arise.

Much of the secular research on trauma in recent years has focused on its physical and neurophysiological implications. Given that we are persons made up of body and soul, both of which are impacted by sin, this research is important for us. On a basic level, trauma and abuse may leave physical wounds, but on a more complex level, evidence demonstrates that it impacts the very structure of our brains. The brain is physically changed by trauma, in ways that affect functioning, behavior, and thought patterns.[5] For example, with repeated trauma, fight-or-flight pathways within the brain begin to activate sooner; this means that physiological responses to events or triggers happen faster, often before we can think clearly. So, although our bodies were meant to deal with sporadic, limited fight-or-flight situations, and God designed those functions within us even before they became necessary (after the fall), our bodies were not meant to live in a perpetual state of fear or danger. When we do, our sympathetic nervous systems go on overdrive and stay there, or they are activated more quickly; adrenaline continues to be released, our hearts continue to race, and the thought centers of our brains (the prefrontal cortex) struggle to function.

Judith Herman, a pioneer in trauma research, described the effects of childhood trauma in *Trauma and Recovery*:

> Repeated trauma in childhood forms and deforms the personality. The child trapped in an abusive environment is faced with formidable tasks of adaptation. She must find a way to preserve a sense of trust in people who are untrustworthy, safety in a situation that is unsafe, control in a situation that is terrifyingly unpredictable, power in a situation of helplessness. Unable to care for or protect herself, she must compensate for the failures of adult care and protection with the only means at her disposal, an immature system of psychological defenses.[6]

Here, Herman is addressing the multifaceted, complex nature of trauma. As believers, we would go even further than Herman does and acknowledge the added complexity of sin; abuse happens because one person sins against another, and yet the victim also has the choice to sin in response. Trauma, then, is incredibly complex. Trauma and abuse overwhelm, confuse, and distort what is good and can impact every area of life moving forward.

Symptoms, Manifestations, and Diagnosis

So how do we recognize cases of trauma and abuse? First, there is an abnormal, precipitating event that takes place; it may be an occasion of abuse, witnessing violence, a significant physical injury, or something similar. The event evokes a normal, fight-or-flight response. With more severe events, it might activate a freeze response, in which the woman is so overwhelmed that her body shuts down. In any of these responses (fight, flight, or freeze) the person responds to the abnormal event in a normal way: a physical stress response, cognitive dissonance, or relational conflict. Finally, these events and responses become maladaptive, or they create problems in living. There may be constant feelings of danger or problematic patterns, including thoughts, beliefs, or behaviors, that form in response to the events.

Bessel A. van der Kolk, in his book *The Body Keeps the Score*, provides some helpful understanding in this arena:

> We have learned that trauma is not just an event that took place sometime in the past; it is also the imprint left by that experience on mind, brain, and body. This imprint has ongoing consequences for how the human organism manages to survive in the present. Trauma results in a fundamental reorganization of the way mind and brain manage perceptions. It changes not only how we think and what we think about, but also our very capacity to think.[7]

While, as Christians, we would certainly want to uphold personal responsibility and the choice of response, van der Kolk aptly describes the manifestation of trauma: it fundamentally changes a person and those changes are often evident from the outside. It may be as subtle as illogical thinking demonstrated outwardly, or it may be as overt as withdrawal and isolation.

With abuse, there often is also a level of secrecy that hides what is happening. The secrecy is sinfully used by the abuser to continue inflicting trauma on the victim. While secrecy by virtue of what it is may be a hidden manifestation, it is very common. Secrecy might be enforced through manipulation

("If someone finds out, you'll be the one in trouble") or outright lies ("This is your fault"). But the words of Prov 10:11 ring true as it relates to secrecy of abuse: "The mouth of the righteous is a fountain of life, but the mouth of the wicked conceals violence." The abuser's words are not life-giving; they hide violence and are life-taking.

How Does the Bible Describe and Speak to Trauma and Abuse?

Examples in Scripture of both trauma and abuse—murder, rape, war, genocide, slavery, and more—fill many pages of the Bible. This is so because of the depth and pervasiveness of sin: one brother murders another because of jealousy, a man rapes his half-sister out of lust, and three men are thrown into a furnace because of a desire for ultimate power. In each of these accounts, trauma, specifically abuse, happens because one person desires something that they should not desire and mistreats another to fulfill that desire.

At its very core, abuse is about power and control. An abuser assumes improper power and control over another human being at their direct expense. Put another way, the experience of abuse is an experience of the impact of the sin of another person directed toward oneself. It is a failure to treat another image bearer with dignity and honor. And quite often, it involves pain and manipulation.

Looking at trauma as a whole, although Scripture gives many examples, it clearly teaches that those events should not have occurred. Remember our definition of trauma: it is a normal reaction to an *abnormal* event that overwhelms one's ability to cope. It is not the response that is abnormal;[8] the precipitating event is outside common experience. And though we experience the effects of sin every moment of every day, a traumatic event (usually involving the sin of another directed toward us) is uncommon, unexpected, and difficult to cope with.

Another way Scripture speaks to the experiences of trauma and abuse is it acknowledges that our bodies were created in particular ways to do specific things. Remember, for instance, the command to work in Gen 2:15. God created man and woman as capable of working the ground, even down to the physiology of our bodies. Similarly, God created our bodies to respond in particular ways to experiences. Recent research on emotion demonstrates that physiological processes take place when we experience or express certain emotions. One of the features God created in our bodies, even before the entrance of threat, was the ability to respond to it. God created what we know as the "fight-or-flight system" (our sympathetic nervous system). When employed correctly, it leads us to protect ourselves without relying on logical thought to respond. For example, if I come across a lion, I do not have to consciously think, "Run away, I'm in danger!" I simply run.

In the case of trauma, though, especially complex trauma, this system gets overwhelmed. Rather than being a temporary state, the fight-or-flight system remains activated. As Judith Herman notes, "After a traumatic experience, the human system of self-preservation seems to go onto permanent alert, as if the danger might return at any moment."[9] Recent research demonstrates physical changes in the brain in response to trauma, as the body and brain react to experiances of trauma or abuse. In perpetual trauma, these changes become ingrained and more fixed physiologically in the brain. Sin has real impacts on the whole person, including the body and the brain.

The Scriptures also teach us about the only ultimate hope: the gospel. Part of the message of the gospel is that one day all things will be made new. As Rev 21:4 reminds us, "He will wipe away every tear from their eyes. Death will be no more; grief, crying, and pain will be no more, because the previous things have passed away." There will be no more trauma, no more abuse.

How Do We Counsel Trauma and Abuse?

Because of the potential complexity of counseling trauma, particularly repetitive abuse, both wisdom and competency in this area are required. Treating complex trauma or recurrent abuse, and sometimes treating more straightforward cases of trauma or a one-time incident of abuse, is not a basic, entry-level counseling issue. Poorly done counseling has the potential to do great harm. Therefore, it is imperative that a counselor ensure she is properly equipped to treat trauma and abuse cases; this may necessitate more extensive training or consultation with another professional, but it should not be undertaken hastily or unwisely.

Because of the nature of treating trauma and abuse, if the counselor has a history of trauma or abuse as well, she must be aware of potential triggers in treating the traumatized counselee. For instance, if a counselor was subjected to verbal abuse from a parent as a child, and a counselee recounts specific phrases she has heard that very closely mirror the counselor's experience, these phrases may trigger a physiological, fight-or-flight response in the counselor or they may trigger more memories for the counselor in the midst of a session. If the counselor has not sufficiently worked through her own trauma or abuse, it can significantly impact the treatment of the counselee.[10]

In counseling trauma or abuse, there are three primary steps or tiers of treatment. First, and most important before moving forward, is safety and stabilization. Here, the counselee's safety is ensured and her basic needs are met. If the counselee is not safe and is lacking in basic needs, any counseling will be insufficient. (Remember, Jesus often met physical needs of his hearers as he taught about spiritual realities.) The aim here is to get support for daily living, including the involvement of the church or community resources. During case management, the counselor would also evaluate for suicidality or self-harm and respond as appropriate.

In the next step, the counselor would address the trauma/abuse more directly, but in a holistic way. This may include teaching practical skills like relaxation (minimizing the fight-or-flight sensation) and self-control in the midst of strong emotions, basic skills for living and stress management, self-regulation, how to maintain a calm body, problem-solving, and self-care. These lessons can be modeled for the counselee. Building the counseling relationship also happens in this second stage, to develop trust and a sense of safety, before any trauma processing begins.

Addressing the trauma, then, includes, with appropriate training,[11] patiently exploring the traumatic events and their impact on her everyday life. This is done carefully and very patiently, taking great care not to overwhelm the counselee. The counselor should regularly weave in relaxation or grounding exercises, pausing where needed to go at a safe and wise pace. In this exploration, the counselor should speak the truth in love, acknowledging sin and grieving the offenses against the counselee where appropriate. This includes the sin of the abuser but also gently confronting any sinful responses in the counselee. The counselor would also work through any spiritual questions or struggles that may arise, bringing encouragement and biblical truth (e.g., pointing often to Ps 9:9, "The Lord is a stronghold for the oppressed, a stronghold in times of trouble" [ESV]).

Finally, the counselor moves toward helping the counselee with right living and, in some cases, helps the counselee learn how to live with a sense of "normalcy" again (though that might look very different after her trauma). The counselor can patiently teach appropriate responses, if needed, aiming to counter unwarranted feelings of danger or fear. The counselor can work through thinking on truth (Phil 4:8) rather than uncertainties and living correctly in response to those truths, aiming toward a heart aligned with the truth of Scripture. The counselor might also need to help the counselee learn what God-honoring relationships look like, including healthy boundaries, proper communication, and establishing trust/respect/mutual honor, particularly if these have not been modeled in the counselee's life. Drawing on 1 Cor 13:4–7, the counselor can walk through what it means to love one another—what authentic, God-honoring love looks like. In doing all this, the aim is to move toward normalcy, breaking the unhealthy or sinful patterns that have developed in response to the trauma. Last, with great wisdom and patience, the counselor may need to explore forgiveness and reconciliation (though not necessarily forgoing consequences like legal action or a restraining order) between the counselee and her offender, as well as wise boundaries moving forward.

Suggested Growth Assignments

Often, traumatic events become overwhelming to a counselee; by their very nature they lead us to look inward and be self-focused. To combat this, as well as potential feelings of isolation, the counselee should be encouraged to meditate on Jesus, particularly what he went through as he endured the cross on our behalf. He is our perfect example of suffering—with all that suffering entails—while responding rightly. This leads the counselee to two truths: Jesus knows our suffering and we are not alone. Hebrews 4:14–16 becomes much more real when we consider the cross.

Particularly in cases of abuse, the counselee can read and meditate on Ps 10:17–18: "Lord, you have heard the desire of the humble; you will strengthen their hearts. You will listen carefully, doing justice for the fatherless and the oppressed so that mere humans from the earth may terrify them no more." These verses remind us the Lord is just and hears our cries, and he also brings strength and protection.

There are many other psalms that the counselee can incorporate into her healing. Psalms of lament (like 42 and 43), psalms of hope (91 and 121), and psalms of thanksgiving and worship (34 and 118) should regularly be in our hearts and on our tongues. Counselees can read, meditate on, journal, and pray through these and others like them. The aim is for the truths of God's Word to get at our hearts and shape the way we think about even traumatic events like abuse.

Finally, in addressing the traumatic event(s), the counselor leads the counselee through physical relaxation exercises like deep breathing and grounding, including meditation on Scripture when triggers arise. During a session, and paired with these relaxation techniques, the counselee can create a visual timeline of the trauma/abuse with the counselor, which can be a useful technique for organizing thoughts. Further, the counselee can write out a narrative of the event(s) and share it in a counseling session. Over time, the counselee can share the narrative with someone else, like her mentor, inviting her friend to know about her trauma. Then, after writing a narrative, the counselee can go back through and rewrite it, adding ways that the Lord was present or showed grace during the trial(s), even if it was not evident at the time. This helps the counselee organize the event(s), and begin to see God's grace in the midst of her trauma.

As a final note here, I mentioned earlier that counselors should be wise in choosing if and how they walk with a counselee through her trauma. While we did not explore this at great length, much harm can be done through an inexperienced counselor taking on more than she is trained to do. This is especially true in cases of complex trauma/complex PTSD. I strongly recommend that the counselor tread carefully and refer quickly if she recognizes that her counselee's trauma is complex and beyond her skills.

Conclusion

Counseling trauma and abuse is a difficult and often draining process, but it is also an area in which much healing can take place. By God's grace, with the help of his Spirit and the truth of his Word, we can come alongside our sisters who have been mistreated, comforting them in their affliction. In cases of trauma and abuse, we can "bear one another's burdens, and so fulfill the law of Christ" (Gal 6:2 ESV).

Recommended Resources

Gingrich, Heather Davediuk, and Fred C. Gingrich, eds., *Treating Trauma in Christian Counseling* (Downers Grove, IL: InterVarsity Press, 2017).

Herman, Judith, *Trauma and Recovery: The Aftermath of Violence—From Domestic Abuse to Political Terror* (New York: Basic Books, 1997; epilogue, 2015).

Langberg, Diane, *Suffering and the Heart of God: How Trauma Destroys and Christ Restores* (Greensboro, NC: New Growth Press, 2015).

van der Kolk, Bessel A., *The Body Keeps the Score: Brain, Mind, and Body in the Healing of Trauma* (New York: Penguin Books, 2014).

Wright, H. Norman, *The Complete Guide to Crisis and Trauma Counseling* (Minneapolis: Bethany House, 2011).

16

❦

Domestic Violence and Abuse

Sitting in your office in tears, Alice shares that her marriage is not what it seems to everyone on the outside. At home, her husband Jeff is a completely different person: his anger is explosive and unpredictable; at the smallest thing, he will blow up and start throwing things across the room. This week, he broke a vase from Alice's grandmother. Most of the time, he justifies his anger, quite often saying it is her fault because she didn't do something he asked or she didn't anticipate an inconvenience that came along. Sometimes, he will call her names, things she'd rather not repeat. But a day or two after each episode, he apologizes, saying he isn't sure what came over him. He says he wants to change. Up until the vase being broken, Alice kept telling herself that because he has never physically harmed her, it isn't really abuse. That seems like such a heavy word and she doesn't want that label. At the recommendation of her friend, she has come to see you for counsel, though she's not sure it will be of much help.

What Is Domestic Violence and Abuse?

Domestic violence and abuse, also known as intimate partner violence or coercive control, is violent, aggressive, or harmful behavior within the home, most often by one spouse toward the other.[1] It is the cycle of fear, power, and control by one partner over another. In the United States, it is unfortunately quite common; as the NCADV reports, "Nearly 20 people per minute are physically abused by an intimate partner."[2] In one year, this amounts to more than 10 million women and men. Most often, violence is directed at women, with severe results such as physical injuries, depression, suicidal thoughts, and PTSD.

Domestic violence often follows a common pattern: the tension stage, in which the offender becomes more and more agitated and the victim is walking on eggshells, followed by the explosion, when the acts of abuse happen. Then comes the "honeymoon" stage, when the offender apologizes, promises not to do it again, and things seem normal again. For the victim, the pattern progresses from attempts to calm or placate during the tension stage to self-protection, fighting back, or trying to reason with the offender in the explosion stage. During the honeymoon period, the victim is often happy and hopeful, agreeing to stay and trying to get help for the abuser. She wants to believe his apologies and his promises to change. Through each of these stages, the victim operates out of denial or justification; eventually, she may find herself acknowledging the cycle, but hopeless that things will ever change or that she can get out. Sometimes, this, in part, is because of her abuser's threats and manipulation. Domestic abuse erases a woman's personhood, eliminates her preferences, and indoctrinates her into believing she deserves this treatment.

Helpful tools in this discussion are the Power and Control Wheel[3] or a controlling-behavior checklist.[4] While some domestic violence is physical, not all of it is, like with Alice above. The abuser may use threats of harm, threats of taking the children, coercion, emotional or economic abuse, twisting of Scripture to maintain dominance, or minimizing/denying there is a problem. Each of these behaviors falls under the category of domestic abuse and should be acknowledged as such. Many women recognize the abuse for the first time upon seeing the Power and Control Wheel or a behavioral checklist.

Domestic violence carries with it several co-occurring problems, the most common of which is anger. Quite often, the offender will blame his anger for his abusive behavior, attempting to justify it. Other problems include pride or a sense of entitlement, selfishness, an elevated sense of self above others, and a desire for power. These may be explicitly stated or hard to identify, but they are common. Substance use is not uncommon in domestic violence situations.

Domestic violence is tremendously harmful to the victim. Justin and Lindsey Holcomb say it well in their book *Is It My Fault? Hope and Healing for Those Suffering Domestic Violence*: "Abusers often find ways to hurt the whole person. They shred their victim's sense of self-worth, crush their wills, and violate their bodies. The effects are widespread and catastrophic—including physical, social, emotional, psychological, and spiritual damage. If left untended, these effects will be ongoing, no matter how long ago the abuse happened. This is why it is important to deal with them honestly now."[5] Until we recognize the weight of this struggle, and the many ways in which it harms women, we will fall short of helping in a meaningful way.

What the Bible Has to Say About Domestic Violence and Abuse

God in his Word gives us a wealth of information as it relates to marriage and how husbands and wives are to live with one another before God. First and foremost, we know that marriage was established by God at creation; it is an institution lived out before God and designed by him, not mankind. Adam and Eve were declared "very good" at creation because they lived perfectly with one another, without shame (Gen 2:25). There was no conflict, no harm from one toward the other, and they cooperated fully in fulfilling their purposes.

The Bible also teaches us that man and woman became "one flesh" at marriage: "This is why a man leaves his father and mother and bonds with his wife, and they become one flesh" (Gen 2:24). In other words, they are to be so unified that they are one. As it relates to domestic violence and abuse, if we uphold the biblical teaching that husband and wife are "one flesh," that means violence against one's spouse is violence against oneself. A man cannot harm his wife without also hurting himself.

The Scriptures are full of teachings about the purpose of marriage, that a biblical marriage is meant to mirror Christ and his bride, the church. In mirroring Christ, the husband self-sacrifices for his wife, loving her and honoring her (Eph 5:25–33). This text instructs husbands to "love" their wife four separate times, which means it's important. We could connect the use of the word "love" here to John 3:16, where we're told that God so loved the world that he sacrificed his Son to save us. Using this model, love equals sacrifice, the giving up of oneself for another. Further, just as Christ seeks to make his bride holy, so too is the husband responsible for his wife's holiness. Violence and abuse are far from holy and certainly do not work toward the holiness of the wife.

Similarly, the wife is called to submit to her husband, as the church submits to Christ (Eph 5:22–24). In the summary of this section on biblical marriage, Eph 5:33, Paul uses the word "respect" in place of "submit." This gives the picture of the wife following the leadership of her husband out of honor toward him, but as a picture of the church's submission to the perfect leadership of Christ. Unfortunately, these verses are often twisted and presented as an ultimatum, with the negative connotation of submission rather than the positive, willful respect and honor of a wife toward her husband. Christ does not force us to follow him; we are called to follow and responsible to respond. Put another way, it is not the husband's role to force submission; he is not entitled to do so.

The Bible is also clear on how we are to treat our brothers and sisters in Christ:

- Matthew 22:39: Love your neighbor.
- Ephesians 4:29: Speak words that build one another up.
- 1 Thessalonians 5:11: Encourage one another.

- Ephesians 4:32: Be kind and tenderhearted toward one another, forgiving each other (ESV)
- Colossians 3:12–13: Be compassionate, kind, humble, meek, patient, and forgiving
- Luke 6:31: Treat others as we wish to be treated
- Romans 12:10: Outdo one another in showing honor (ESV)
- Romans 15:1–2: Bear with the weak
- Philippians 2:3–4: Consider others more important than ourselves, and look out for the interests of others
- Romans 12:18: Live at peace with everyone

Domestic abuse fails at each one of these things; it is not loving, encouraging, kind, compassionate, or honorable. It is hatred toward the other person, against Christ and the gospel.

We must also remember that God is for us; he is not our enemy. Living in a domestic abuse situation, a woman might come to believe that God has abandoned her. This simply is not so—as Leslie Vernick puts it, "God hates the abuse of power and sin of injustice (Psalm 5, 7, 10, 140; 2 Corinthians 11:20; Acts 14:5–6)."[6] Even when Jesus was betrayed, suffered abuse, and was rejected, he was not abandoned by the Father. Jesus understands what it is like to be treated harshly, and he never leaves or forsakes his daughters, even when they suffer as well.

How Might We Minister to a Woman Living With Domestic Violence and Abuse?

The following steps are helpful as we seek to care for and counsel a woman in a domestic violence situation:

1. **Listen without taking charge.** As counselors, we fight the urge to step in and rescue, and while there is a time and place for rescue, initially we must listen, and listen well. The woman who is a victim of domestic abuse has had her choices taken from her. Even simple

things like choosing to seek help are monumental decisions for her. Her abuser takes charge, removing her choice. From the very beginning of counseling, we must allow her to retain her choices.

2. **Call it what it is**. We should acknowledge the sinfulness of violence and abuse, using words that are appropriate to the weight of what is happening. We should not make excuses for his behavior or add to any justification of his actions. As she is telling her story, we should not question if her behavior prompted it, but simply listen and seek to understand. As we respond, we should call sin what it is: a violation against her and against God. This might include educating her on what abuse is. We also must recognize the power and control that has been exerted over her, calling this out clearly and directly.

3. **Establish safety.** Though we are to listen without taking charge, we should very quickly seek to keep her safe if she is willing and able. This might or might not mean that she does not return home that day; that is her decision and one that she should not make lightly. Establishing safety may take some planning and wise strategy with regard to timing, resources, and where she can go. A team approach is best here. We should help her develop a safety plan even if it is never used, as this communicates the severity of the sin against her. When possible and necessary, engage others to help, including her church, family, or friends. As counselors, we should also help her understand the necessity of safety, assisting her as appropriate as she follows through with any plans. Establishing safety must be done wisely and carefully, since severe consequences can result if it is done hastily. In particular, we must be mindful and prepared when she leaves; a woman is most in danger of harm immediately after she leaves the home. It might take some time and come in slow steps, but we should be moving in this direction from the very first meeting, at least in some way.

4. **Talk through separation options and the purpose of separation.**[7] This includes where she can stay, what happens with her children,

indicators that it is safe to return, a team to care for and counsel her, and a team to observe and confirm change in him. She should understand the goals of separating (to protect herself and her children, to give him a cooling-off period, to communicate the seriousness of his actions, and/or to provide time for him to seek help) and tangibly what that looks like. We should see the marriage as secondary to her individual issue. Domestic violence is not a marriage problem or an anger problem; it stems from the sin in the offender's heart. We are to counsel the individual first, not jump into marriage counseling. Doing marriage counseling in lieu of individual counseling can have drastic consequences for her. At a minimum, she would be hindered in being open and honest; if she is, she risks retribution when she leaves. Our first responsibility is to the woman and how she can move forward.

5. **Acknowledge God's position on domestic abuse and violence.** Many women in abusive marriages find themselves feeling hopeless and wondering where God is in the midst of their struggle. We must remind her of the truths of his Word that are especially pertinent in her suffering: he has not forgotten her, he is near (Ps 34:18); he grieves over sin (Gen 6:5–6); he hates injustice (Prov 6:16–19); he is able to save (Zeph 3:17); he gives strength and power to the powerless (Isa 40:29); he is the God of hope, peace, and comfort (Rom 15:13); and he has overcome death and sin through his Son (Isa 25:8). These truths do not change with her circumstances; instead, they might become more real to her as she walks through these trials.

6. **Explore what biblical love means.** Love is not always accepting and approving, and what is most loving does not always seem the most kind. First Corinthians 13:4–8 gives us a picture of what it means to love: "Love is patient, love is kind. Love does not envy, is not boastful, is not arrogant, is not rude, is not self-seeking, is not irritable, and does not keep a record of wrongs. Love finds no joy in unrighteousness but rejoices in the truth. It bears all things, believes

all things, hopes all things, endures all things. Love never ends." These things should characterize the victim of domestic violence, but nowhere in this passage does it say that love tolerates and does not correct sin. In fact, it "finds no joy in unrighteousness [abuse] but rejoices in truth." In other words, allowing continued violence or abuse is not good for the offender; it is allowing him to continue in his sin, which is unloving. Much like it is unloving for a mother to not correct her wayward child, it is unloving to not hold someone accountable for their sin.

7. **Work through various emotions and responses, including beliefs, thoughts, and behaviors.** A victim of domestic violence and abuse may experience a myriad of emotional responses and thoughts: grief, anger, hopelessness, helplessness, fear, a desire for retribution, and more. As you work through these, acknowledge the strong temptation toward these responses. Domestic violence would test any of us in those ways, but it does not give us permission to sin. We should also explore areas in which the woman is responding wrongly. For instance, anger over sin and grief over suffering is appropriate, but a desire to harm the offender in return or beliefs that God has abandoned her are not. We should help her reject lies and false thinking. Though she is not responsible for the violence directed at her, she is responsible for her response to it, and the Lord will help her overcome the temptations to sin in her response (1 Cor 10:13).

8. **Identify improper shame or guilt.** Despite what the offender tells her, her actions did not deserve violence or abuse. Abuse is never an appropriate response to conflict, including provocation. Therefore, she is not guilty for the actions of the offender and does not need to feel ashamed. However, feelings of guilt and shame are common for victims of domestic violence, perhaps because he blames her or because she is embarrassed that she is "letting this happen." In our counseling, we can work through any feelings of guilt or shame, putting them in their proper place.

9. **Move toward forgiveness and eventual reconciliation.** The Scriptures say clearly that we are to forgive at all times (Matt 18:21–22; Matt 6:14–15), which is unidirectional. Just as God extends forgiveness to us, so we are to forgive others. But also, when possible, we are to pursue reconciliation (Rom 12:18). This reconciliation might take time, since it depends on genuine repentance from the offender, which does not include the typical honeymoon-phase apologies. It is dependent on genuine repentance marked by genuine change. We cannot rush this process. As counselors, we should desire the restitution of a counselee's marriage, a return to biblical marriage as the Lord defines it in his Word, but we can also be very patient for consistent, ongoing demonstrations of repentance before reconciliation takes place.

10. **Help her find ways to draw support from and minister to others.** Many women affected by domestic violence and abuse find significant comfort from support groups and ministry from other women who have been affected by this struggle. They understand the complexity of her situation, including the cycle of abuse, the justification and manipulation that often comes with it, and the weight of the decision to take action. One reason support groups are helpful is that the Lord uses our stories to help and encourage others, and he intended to do so (2 Cor 1:4). Our struggles are not just about us, they are for the building up of God's people. We can help our counselee find specific ways to use her unique story to minister to and encourage other women caught in a similar struggle and also to find support when she needs it.

Walking with another woman through domestic violence and abuse is a complex endeavor, one that is not to be done flippantly or without caution. Unwise decisions (premature departure, lack of a safety system in place, a lack of resources, etc.) can have disastrous consequences for the woman. If possible, it is best to include several others in the care team, ideally at least one person who has been trained and is experienced in dealing with domestic violence situations.

What about Calling the Police?

It has been noted repeatedly that a care team should be put in place to help a woman get out of a domestic violence situation. In many cases, this involves calling the proper legal authorities, such as the police or an attorney, or both. However, typically it is most wise that the woman be the one to make the police report. All counselors should explore the laws in their state, but often, more harm than good can come from a counselor circumventing a counselee and calling the police. The report hinges on the victim's words; if she is not ready to report or to take action, she might suffer significant retribution from the abuser. Therefore, counselors should exercise great wisdom regarding if or when they call the police.

The one exception to this guidance is cases of suspected child abuse. In most states, if there is "reasonable suspicion" of child abuse or neglect, the counselor is mandated by law to report it. Sometimes in domestic violence situations, the children have also been victims of abuse. If the woman discloses during counseling that the child has been harmed or neglected, it must be reported to law enforcement. Again, each counselor should understand the laws of her state, but most often, a report is required.

Growth and Homework Exercises

Because of the nature of domestic abuse, sometimes typical homework exercises are not possible. The offender may not know the woman is in counseling, which is relatively common. The first few exercises below take this into consideration, but the final one may be used when either no secrecy is necessary or as the woman is coming out of an abusive or violent situation and is no longer regularly around the abuser.

The first exercise is to create a safety plan, listing resources and people who can step in when violence happens. The safety plan can be done partly in session and partly out of session, and the counselor can and should keep a copy of this plan. If possible, the safety plan should include hotline numbers, places to go, and a list of people and their roles when something happens. This safety plan serves as a tangible reminder that (1) she is not alone, and (2) she is prepared. In other words, she has some control over her situation, even if she cannot control his actions toward her.

Second, the woman can find others to share her situation with, others who are wise and if possible, have experience ministering in similar situations. In part, she is allowing others to bear her burden with her (Gal 6:2) but it also clues others in for when she does need to remove herself from her home or find a place for her children to go. This is not to say that she should be disparaging her husband; sharing with others should be done in a way that is intended to support her and provide wise counsel and direction.

Third, she can spend some time meditating on 1 Cor 13:4–8, noting ways she is demonstrating love but also specific ways that her spouse is not. She should be encouraged to seek to demonstrate love in all things, but also to be honest about unloving behavior toward her. This is not to build up bitterness, but to instill a true understanding of the unhealthy pattern in her marriage that must be addressed. Often, justification and denial take root in a woman's heart for the sinful behavior toward her; this exercise helps to break those down and face her reality, while at the same time encouraging her to respond in God-honoring ways.

Finally, she can be encouraged to write out her thoughts and feelings about her partner during the week. The counselor and counselee can then together evaluate for any areas of sinful responses. In this event, she should acknowledge the sinfulness of the response and repent, but also acknowledge the hardship leading to that temptation. The counselor can help her take ownership of her part (i.e., her response), but not the hardship itself.

Conclusion

Counseling domestic violence and abuse is often a slow process, and one that is painful and difficult. The counselee is suffering tremendously and is sometimes confused and in denial. But with patience, with the help of God's Word and his Spirit, we can walk with women through this hardship and respond in a way that is honoring to both the Lord and her husband, but in a way that also keeps her safe.

Recommended Resources

Dryburgh, Anne, *Debilitated and Diminished: Help for Christian Women in Emotionally Abusive Marriages* (Phillipsburg, NJ: P&R, 2018).

Forrest, Joy, *Called to Peace: A Survivor's Guide to Finding Peace and Healing after Domestic Abuse* (Raleigh, NC: Blue Ink Press, 2018).

Hambrick, Brad, ed., *Becoming a Church that Cares Well for the Abused* (Nashville: B&H, 2019).

Holcomb, Justin, and Lindsay Holcomb, *Is It My Fault?: Hope and Healing for Those Suffering Domestic Violence* (Chicago: Moody, 2014).

Moles, Chris, *The Heart of Domestic Abuse: Gospel Solutions for Men Who Use Control and Violence in the Home* (Bemidji, MN: Focus, 2015).

Strickland, Darby, *Domestic Abuse: Help for the Sufferer* (Phillipsburg, NJ: P&R, 2018).

Strickland, Darby, *Domestic Abuse: Recognize, Respond, Rescue* (Phillipsburg, NJ: P&R, 2018).

Strickland, Darby, *Is It Abuse?: A Biblical Guide to Identifying Domestic Abuse and Helping Victims* (Phillipsburg, NJ: P&R, 2020).

Welch, Edward T., *Living with an Angry Spouse: Help for Victims of Abuse* (Phillipsburg, NJ: P&R, 2008).

17

Marital Unfaithfulness

Sherri sits in front of you broken, sobbing almost uncontrollably. She explains that this past week, she found text messages on her husband's phone that made her suspect he was having an affair. They were explicit, things he had never said to her. She decided to follow him the next time he went out, and sure enough, instead of going to the gym he ended up in a nearby neighborhood. When she confronted him about the texts, he denied it until she told him she had followed him and knew where he had gone. Eventually, he confirmed that he had been having an affair for the last two months. Sherri shares that she just could not handle it, so she walked out and stayed the night at her sister's house. "My whole world is caving in," she says between tears. She feels rejected and betrayed, like her world is in chaos.

What Is Marital Unfaithfulness?

At first consideration, most of us probably equate adultery with marital unfaithfulness, much like the situation above. But infidelity can be much broader than that; it is an affair of any sort, even those that are not physical or sexual (i.e., adultery). It might be emotional intimacy that goes beyond biblical friendship, or it may be sexual advances or flirtations that have not yet led to intercourse. Some would even include the use of pornography in the category of unfaithfulness, pointing to Jesus's teachings on lust in Matt 5:28. In any case, marital unfaithfulness is the betrayal of a spouse's trust, a violation of the covenant of marriage, and it does great harm, regardless of the type of affair that has happened. Any type of infidelity is a serious problem that cannot be ignored.

Ultimately, marital infidelity is a heart issue, often with attempts made to justify it by the spouse's neglect or their own "needs." It is fueled by pride, selfish desires, and lust. Quite often as well, it is accompanied by self-deception that they won't get caught or justification that it is acceptable because of the state of their marriage. The offending party might blame their spouse to relieve personal guilt or conviction.

As counselors, we might be called on to counsel either the offending party (when the woman had the affair) or the offended party (when the husband had the affair). Both are unfortunately all too common. We might also be called on to counsel during a separation or divorce proceedings, which adds a level of complexity to the struggle.[1] The separation or divorce may or may not be the counselee's desire; it might be that her husband is pursuing separation or divorce, or that she feels she has no other option but to end the marriage.

If possible, it is often wise to include a male and female counselor to co-counsel the couple. When this is done, time can be spent individually as well as together, but focused attention can be given to both the offender and the nonoffender. Each counselor can work through the individual struggles (there are many different struggles depending on the situation) but then come together and both encourage the couple as needed.

What the Bible Has to Say about Marital Unfaithfulness

Before exploring Scripture's teachings on marital unfaithfulness and sexual immorality, we must first establish how marriage was created to be. God's Word is clear that marriage between a man and a woman was intended to be one of unity; the husband and wife are of "one flesh" (Gen 2:24; Matt 19:6). Though they are individual persons, they were created to be so unified that they are considered one.

Further, the marriage unity was not meant to be broken (Matt 19:6). It was established by God, before God, and to serve God and is not a covenant that man should break. More specifically, marriage was intended to mirror Christ and the church (Eph 5:22–33). It is a picture of something much greater than the two individuals.

Regarding intimacy in marriage, the writer of Hebrews says marriage should be held in honor and the marriage bed undefiled (Heb 13:4). Spouses are to be faithful to one another in every way, especially in sexual conduct. Paul echoes this teaching often, particularly in 1 Thess 4:3–5 when he condemns sexual immorality, including sexual relations outside of marriage. He writes as well in Eph 5:3 that sexual immorality, including marital unfaithfulness, is improper among those who call themselves Christ-followers. The name Christian cannot equate to adultery.

The Bible is also clear that sexual immorality is a matter of the heart, it is not just about one's behavior. As Jesus taught in Matt 5:28, "everyone who looks at a woman lustfully has already committed adultery with her in his heart." Marital unfaithfulness, fueled by lust, begins in the heart. It is a work of the flesh, not the Spirit (Gal 5:19) and should be put to death (Col 3:5).

And yet, despite these weighty realities, God is gracious to forgive even when we fall in this way (1 John 1:9). We must not forget the gospel message: God sent his Son to save sinners from themselves, to rescue them from sin and death. The man or woman who is unfaithful in their marriage is no exception. We must uphold the grace of the gospel as we acknowledge its condemnation of sin.

A Lesson from Hosea and Gomer

While the Scriptures give us several examples of marital unfaithfulness,[2] none is perhaps more beautiful and instructive than the instruction God gave to Hosea. Hosea 1:2 tells us, "When the Lord first spoke to Hosea, he said this to him: Go and marry a woman of promiscuity,[3] and have children of promiscuity, for the land is committing blatant acts of promiscuity by abandoning the Lord." Hosea obeyed God, and she bore him several children. For a season, it appeared that she was a faithful wife.

And yet, her faithfulness was short-lived. Hosea 2 is a discourse on Israel's rejection of the Lord, which God compares to infidelity. He rebukes Israel, but then immediately moves into his forgiveness of her unfaithfulness. God is faithful though Israel is not.

In chapter 3 of Hosea, the prophet is instructed, "Go again; show love to a woman who is loved by another man and is an adulteress, just as the Lord loves the Israelites though they turn to other gods" (Hos 3:1). He was told to buy back the woman who rejected him, taking her back as his wife. He did so, as a picture of God's coming restoration of Israel. It is a beautiful picture of obedience and reconciliation, despite Gomer's rejection of Hosea. The rest of the book is an indictment of Israel's sin, several calls to repentance, and yet another reiteration of God's faithfulness to restore his people to himself.

What are we to learn from this prophet's letter, specifically as it relates to marital unfaithfulness but also to our sin in general? First, it is clear Gomer is a picture of Israel, and by extension, us. We are dead in our sin apart from Christ, though he is calling us toward repentance. Through no merit of our own, he sought us out, he purchased us, and he is restoring us to himself.

Second, there are consequences for sin. No doubt Hosea struggled with God's commands to take a wayward wife and then restore her after her unfaithfulness. Her sin impacted him personally and deeply. The same is true with marital unfaithfulness today—the sin of a wayward husband or wife directly impacts his or her spouse in ways that are inescapable.

Next, an important lesson can be drawn from Hosea 6:6: "For I desire faithful love and not sacrifice, the knowledge of God rather than burnt offerings." Here, the Lord is lamenting this relationship with his people, much like our counselee laments over the impact of infidelity. But what does the Lord desire? What should the counselee desire? Relationship. Faithful love and knowledge (intimacy), not particular behaviors "just because." Our aim, as counselors, is to restore that faithful love and intimacy, the same that God desired to restore between him and his people.

Finally, love is a choice and an action, not a feeling. God *chose* to restore his people and Hosea *chose* to restore Gomer at great cost to himself. For the couple walking through infidelity, restoration is a choice; love is a choice. And it is a choice that must be affirmed over and over as they walk the road of restoration.

How Might We Counsel in the Wake of Infidelity?

Counseling conversations about marital unfaithfulness are filled with emotion. These sessions are hard; they require a great deal of patience and perseverance. As counselors seek to minister to a woman after infidelity is discovered, the following steps prove helpful:

First, we should openly acknowledge that the marriage has been changed. Adultery is like dropping a bomb on a couple, and despite existing problems—and usually there already were some—this is a completely different ball game. The one-flesh union between husband and wife has been violated; another person was brought into a union they should never have been part of. Trust has been broken. There probably were lies that accompanied the infidelity, either about where the offender was or a denial of the affair, or both, like in our vignette above. Trust takes time to rebuild. Often, I use the analogy of a brick house when it comes to trust, particularly in the wake of infidelity. While the whole house might be knocked down by the wrecking ball of an affair, the "trust bricks" must be put back one by one. This takes time; it does not happen overnight. And while the marriage will not return to the way it was originally, it can eventually be repaired and restored.

Second, we should grieve over sin alongside the counselee. While it is not necessary to walk through every single indiscretion or have every detail, we should get a picture of what happened and grieve that reality. We should know what led up to the event(s) and how each person responded. Considering those details, we should call sin what it is: sin. We should grieve, like God does, over the unfaithfulness and violation within the marriage, which gravely goes against God's design.

Third, we should gain a commitment that both husband and wife will work to restore the marriage. Restoration after infidelity is a long, hard road, one that is only complicated by one or both having little or no motivation to put in the hard work. Both people must be committed to upholding and fixing the marriage or it will not work. This is especially important to communicate early and often, particularly as time goes on and there are seasons when it feels like there are setbacks. The counselor(s) should remind the couple of their commitment to one another and ask each person, if possible, to affirm their desire to restore their marriage.

Fourth, the counselor should give hope of healing and restoration, through the Lord's power and with his help. However, this should be a realistic hope. It will not happen overnight and may not always be a forward progression; restoration takes time, but we should always be moving in that direction and hopeful that the Lord will work in both of their hearts to bring about healing. We should share the gospel hope that Jesus reconciled us to himself while we were still sinners, so that we can be reconciled to him and to one another. Just as Hosea's restoration to his wayward wife was a picture of God's restoration of Israel to himself, so too can the restoration between spouses bring honor and glory to God.

Fifth, we should spend time working through any ongoing emotions and responses. This will take a lot of time; while some emotions and responses are understandable and not inherently sinful, some might be. In those cases, we should help the counselee repent of her sin, getting rid of any justification she might be holding on to. The following emotions/responses are common:[4]

- Sadness and hurt: She has been violated and is understandably hurt/sad. Sadness and hurt are not inherently sinful, but they can lead to other responses that are.
- Suspicion: She might find herself questioning what he says he is doing or where he says he is going, specifically because trust was broken and lies were told in the past.
- Anger: She might find herself angry over his sin against her or the resulting impact the affair has had on her. Conversely, she might be angry over his lack of forgiveness of her infidelity. While anger over sin, like sadness, is not inherently sinful, we must guard against a self-centered sense of justice.
- Fear: She might also experience fear that the affair is continuing or that it will happen again, leading to distrust. This largely stems from a desire not to experience more hurt, which is understandable, but can also easily shift into a desire to control him or a lack of trust in the Lord.
- Embarrassment or shame: She might feel embarrassed or ashamed that it was *her* husband who had the affair, as if it reflects on her as a wife. Or she might be ashamed that she would commit adultery. In considering who else knows, she might be concerned with how others might view her and want to hide her dirty laundry from others.
- Self-blame: It is not uncommon for a wife to believe the affair was somehow her fault, and sometimes this stems from his justification for the affair. In many ways, self-blame is an attempt to control the situation ("It's my fault, and therefore I should have known and stopped it from happening") when she feels like she has no control.
- Bitterness: She might wonder how he could be unfaithful to her (self-righteousness or entitlement) or become bitter that there are no consequences for his behavior. Bitterness can easily lead to a desire to punish or make him hurt as she has hurt.

❧ Desire to punish: Alongside bitterness, she might desire to make him feel the pain she does, as if that will somehow lessen her own pain. She might desire retribution solely so that she is not the only one hurting. Or she might feel that he deserves to hurt like she does, since he is the one who sinned.

In all these cases, we should evaluate the appropriateness of the response. When they are not honoring to the Lord, the counselor should graciously but firmly hold her accountable. This does not mean that she should be happy about the affair—far from it. Instead, it means that she recognizes her responsibility to respond rightly even during suffering and trial (see chapter 2).

Sixth, we should help the couple deal with any issues that were present before infidelity. Marital unfaithfulness does not happen in a vacuum; it is most often fueled by long-standing issues in the marriage before the actual affair. These might include poor communication, prior conflict, a lack of intimacy (of all forms), isolation, withdrawal, neglect, or a failure to fulfill biblical roles within the marriage. Though usually the affair takes center stage, we must not neglect contributing problems; otherwise, there is a high likelihood the marriage will default back to these "norms" after counseling or that reconciliation will not happen.

Next, we should be intentional to talk through and move toward forgiveness and reconciliation. Though this is not the first conversation that is had in counseling infidelity, it is one we should begin early on, particularly our responsibility of unidirectional forgiveness (Matt 18:21–22). Note that this is not surface-level forgiveness, but genuine forgiveness, not done out of obligation or to escape bad feelings. Neither of those is actual forgiveness, but they are temptations for those who have been sinned against in this way. Beyond forgiveness, we should also encourage bidirectional reconciliation, which requires true repentance on the part of the offender, evidenced by change. This includes, but is not limited to, a willingness to answer reasonable and appropriate questions (as is wise for their situation), transparency, honesty, accountability, patience, and the acceptance of consequences. However, it is not the wife's responsibility to force her husband into these things; they should be done volitionally as he seeks to demonstrate godly sorrow over his offenses. For the offending woman, we as counselors should help her move toward these things.

Finally, good care in counseling involves a care team, including the local church. This is not to punish the offender or make public his or her sin; quite the contrary. It is to support them both and encourage them in their marriage, providing accountability, prayer, and comfort. It is also to connect them with people to give a listening ear on the tougher days, during the day-to-day struggles that infidelity brings. Though many affected by infidelity will want to keep quiet about the indiscretions, involving other wise counsel can support the couple in significant ways.

What about Biblical Grounds for Divorce?

In the wake of infidelity, a counselee might desire to explore her biblical grounds for divorce. Specifically, she might be pointing to Jesus's allowance of divorce for marital infidelity in Matt 19:9. Despite that allowance, it is important to view that verse in context (Matt 19:1–12). In that section, Jesus reiterates God's design of man and woman becoming one flesh, that what God has joined, no one should separate (Matt 19:6). God's design is, and always has been, preservation of the marriage. While divorce is allowable, it is not preferred and should not be encouraged. It seems this allowance is given for those who persist in adulterous relationships, fail to repent of their sin, and are therefore not desiring reconciliation.

We should recognize, however, that another option is available, at least in the United States: separation *for the purpose of reconciliation*. It might be that a time of physical separation is wise to assist with healing, but only with set parameters and common aims. It is not to punish; rather, it may be wise if continued proximity is harmful or a hindrance to restoring the marriage. This is a wisdom issue; it may or may not be a legal separation. When pursued, it should be entered into carefully, again with the expressed purpose of pursuing reconciliation.

Helpful Homework Exercises

The most helpful homework exercises help restore trust and intimacy for the couple, with wise bounds and appropriate to their stage of healing. Early on, one helpful exercise is for the counselee to write a letter to the offending spouse affirming her commitment to work toward reconciliation. This letter can serve as a reminder throughout counseling that she is committed to doing the hard work, and that it is worth it.

Another helpful exercise is for the couple to spend time together in a way that honors each person, like doing something the other likes to do. This rebuilds intimacy and takes the focus off oneself to intentionally foster self-lessness. It also serves as a reminder, if done well, of why they got married in the first place: because they love one another and enjoy being together.

A third helpful exercise is for the counselee to keep a log of emotions and responses throughout the week, such as feelings of anger or desires to punish. She can bring this log to the next counseling session to discuss with the counselor; together, they can evaluate if or when her responses are appropriate and honoring to the Lord, or if she is finding herself being drawn toward those responses that are sinful and self-serving. Over time, she will begin to make these evaluations on her own and can practice responding rightly even during her suffering.

Last, she can seek out others who can provide regular support and encouragement. Again, this is not to air her dirty laundry or disparage her husband, but to find other women who can check on her regularly and hold her heart and mind accountable. This is especially helpful because counseling is not a daily activity, so having others who can fill the gap between sessions will serve her well. For the offending party, involving church leadership for trusted relationships to be built, specifically for accountability, can do much to help the couple move forward.

Conclusion

Counseling in the wake of infidelity is hard work, perhaps one of the toughest counseling issues and certainly one of the lengthier struggles to work through.

But there is great hope: the Lord in his goodness established marriage to be a picture of his relationship with his people, though sometimes that relationship requires great effort. Just as he seeks to restore his people to himself, so should we encourage our counselees to seek reconciliation after an affair.

Recommended Resources

Daughtery, Jonathan, *Secrets: A Story of Addiction, Infidelity, and Second Chances* (Greensboro, NC: New Growth Press, 2017).

Ganschow, Julie, *Living beyond the Heart of Betrayal: Biblically Addressing the Pain of Sexual Sin* (Kansas City, MO: Pure Water Press, 2013).

Jones, Robert, *Restoring Your Broken Marriage: Healing after Adultery* (Greensboro, NC: New Growth Press, 2009).

Smith, Winston, *Help! My Spouse Committed Adultery: First Steps for Dealing with Betrayal* (Greensboro, NC: New Growth Press, 2008).

Summers, Mike, *Help! My Spouse Has Been Unfaithful* (Wapwallopen, PA: Shepherd Press, 2014).

18

Infertility and Pregnancy Loss

Anna and John have been married for about six years; though they married young, they started thinking seriously about having children about four years into marriage. At the time, they decided to stop preventing a pregnancy and allow nature to take its course. After close to a year, however, Anna started noticing disappointment when her cycle would start each month. She wondered why she wasn't getting pregnant like her friends. Wasn't it a natural process? Had she done something wrong? After a little more than a year, Anna and John visited a fertility specialist; a multitude of tests revealed there wasn't an apparent cause for their lack of conception. Now two years after deciding to get pregnant, both Anna and John find themselves disappointed, hopeless, and wondering where they go from here.

Infertility and pregnancy loss are quite common, and yet neither is the topic of regular conversation; often, any discussion around these issues, both in our culture and within the church, is reserved for holidays like Mother's Day or a women's Bible study. For the most part, we have remained silent on this topic, despite its prevalence. Counter this with the elevation of family within the evangelical church, and infertile couples are left with no one to talk to and no clear teaching on how to rightly understand and grieve a lack of children or the loss of their children.

Within the realm of counseling, we must be prepared to counsel infertility for both men and women, but as female counselors, we will primarily be seeing other women walking through this struggle. Around 20–25 percent of pregnancies end in miscarriage and 12 percent of women have some sort of impaired fertility (including recurrent pregnancy loss),[1] which means, of the childbearing women in our churches, one in eight has fertility struggles and the number who have experienced a miscarriage is likely even higher. We must be ready to counsel those who are struggling in this way.

What Do Fertility Struggles Look Like?

There are differences between infertility and pregnancy loss, though both are often considered under the same umbrella. Infertility is the inability to get pregnant within twelve months of unprotected sex (or within six months if the woman is over thirty-five), like Anna in our opening story. There are many possible reasons: the woman is not producing a viable egg, the man is unable to produce viable sperm or high enough sperm count to lead to pregnancy, there is a genetic anomaly in one or both partners, or the woman's body simply will not sustain a fertilized egg. Sometimes, the cause is known, but many times, it is not.

Pregnancy loss, more specifically recurrent miscarriage, is when a couple has experienced three or more miscarriages. While considered under the category of infertility, the reasons for pregnancy loss are generally less clear than with infertility; about half the time, the cause is unknown. When the cause is known, it can typically be attributed to hormonal imbalances in the woman, clotting issues, genetic factors, anatomical anomalies, immune differences between mother and child, poor egg quality, infections, or other reasons.

There is also a distinction between primary and secondary infertility. Primary infertility is the inability to conceive at all, while secondary infertility occurs after the couple has already had a child or children.

Despite these nuances, it is important to note that any type of infertility or pregnancy loss, even one miscarriage, can have tremendous impact on a woman and her husband. While not all couples will seek out medical treatment for their infertility or loss, many find themselves unexpectedly seeking to determine both the causes for their struggles and what their options are moving forward. As counselors, then, we must understand the individual circumstances of each couple walking through this struggle.

Further, while every person will respond differently to infertility or a miscarriage, there are some commonalities. There is likely to be some form of grief present, though grief looks different for each person. For some women, this might look like a search for answers, such as going to a fertility specialist. This includes wrestling with ethical considerations if IVF is being considered. For others, it may be inward or outward mourning, clear expressions of the emotional struggles that come with infertility and pregnancy loss. Still others may experience feelings of failure and disappointment, potentially including a failure to fulfill one's role as a mother. These feelings of grief and disappointment are likely to be felt even more on holidays such as Mother's Day or when invited to a baby shower.

A myriad of other experiences might be present as well. Emotionally, a woman might experience great sadness or disappointment, as noted above. This grief may be over the tangible loss of a child, such as with miscarriage, or with the intangible loss of the idea of children or a perceived future as a mother. It is often quite difficult to imagine life without having children; women and couples then may grieve this change in their view of the future. Along with grief may come hopelessness or a fear that either no answers will be found or that there are no options moving forward, like Anna and John experienced. For recurrent losses, this fear might present itself with each new pregnancy. Last, it is not uncommon for those struggling with infertility and loss to experience anger, either at themselves, their spouse, or others.

With regard to the woman's thoughts, there are some common threads that might be present alongside the emotions listed above. For instance, the woman or couple might find themselves at the extreme conclusion that they are never going to have a baby. They might also feel isolated, like no one understands what they are going through. Or, those thoughts might be directed at God, with questions like how God could let something bad like this happen.

Along those same lines, spiritual struggles are often present in response to infertility or pregnancy loss. For example, the woman or couple might feel like God is distant or does not hear their prayers. Or there might be anger at God for withholding a good gift from his child. The woman or couple might struggle with reconciling God as a good Father with their bad experiences.

While all these struggles will not be present with each counselee, it is essential to understand the responses that may be present and might change from day to day. There might also be triggers that increase these responses, such as seeing a pregnancy announcement on social media, a negative pregnancy test, or even simply a tough day. Counselors must be sensitive to where the counselee is at the moment of counseling and be patient in their approach.

What Does the Bible Say about Fertility?

The Bible has much to say about both infertility and pregnancy loss. First and foremost is the reality of the impact of sin on the person, particularly the physical body. When dealing with infertility and pregnancy loss, some physical aspect(s) is failing to work properly; that might be, as noted above, an anatomical issue, a hormonal or clotting issue, or a structural or genetic issue with the egg or sperm. This might leave the couple physically unable to bear children.

Another important biblical theme is identity. For all people, our identity *in part* is related to who our family is; even our names are directly tied to other people. For many, parenthood is a highly anticipated aspect of their self-identity. Women and men alike simply assume they will be parents one day. Relating this to Scripture, in the Old Testament one's identity was almost inextricably linked to one's family. The Jewish people were descendants of Abraham. With the coming of Christ, a shift happened: one's identity shifted from being based on the earthly (physical, biological) family to being primarily a part of God's (spiritual) family. We become sons and daughters of God (the source of one's identity) through adoption. The biological family becomes secondary to one's spiritual family.[2]

Scripture also describes several incidents of infertility and pregnancy loss, but often, those passages are misunderstood as they relate to those suffering in this way. For instance, Hannah in 1 Samuel 1–2 is pointed to as an example of a barren woman crying out to the Lord for a child. After Hannah promises that any child would be devoted to the Lord's service, her womb is opened and she conceives. In every other case of infertility or barrenness described in Scripture as well, the woman conceives. This might lead readers to the false assumption that one simply must pray or promise enough and she will have a child. However, the purpose in those passages is not to demonstrate a formula for having a healthy child; rather, they describe occasions of the Lord carrying out *his plan* in the life of one of his children. The wise counselor articulates this clearly to her struggling counselee.

Another key passage related to children, specifically God knowing children, is Psalm 139. Most women are familiar with this passage; as it relates to miscarriage and loss, Ps 139:16 provides us a pertinent reminder that is echoed elsewhere in Scripture. Here, David writes, "Your eyes saw me when I was formless; all my days were written in your book and planned before a single one of them began." David was reflecting on God knowing him even when he was in the womb, but he made what may be a jarring statement for a woman who has lost a baby in the womb. And yet the truth remains: God has numbered every day of every person, however long or short they may be. All our days, even when those days are few, are ordained by God well in advance. God remains sovereign over life and death, despite our lack of understanding at times.

Last, and while it is a general biblical truth, it is necessary for counselors to be reminded that we are commanded to rejoice with those who rejoice and weep with those who weep (Rom 12:15). Many women (and men) have deeply desired to have a child; the loss of an unborn child or the inability to have a child can be devastating. To understand this devastation, and therefore to weep with her or them, we must be open and transparent with one another, then lament over the loss (real or potential).

Counseling Infertility

To counsel a woman or couple walking through infertility or pregnancy loss, it is important to set the stage for counseling. Like many life struggles, the counselee is dealing with this struggle on a day-to-day and month-to-month basis, which often includes some level of isolation. She might even be isolated from her husband. But every month, every cycle, proclaims failure; the woman receives regular reminders of her struggle. But it is not common to invite others into the daily, weekly, and monthly struggles. For a woman or couple to share this struggle with a counselor or others is not an easy thing.

Further, infertility or pregnancy loss is often wrongly associated with the idea that something is "wrong" with her. While it should not be so, the assumption is that infertility is something they can control or they could have controlled it in the past. This is particularly true when a woman has chosen to have an abortion in the past. Because of this assumed level of control, it can be (wrongly) embarrassing or hurtful to continually answer questions about when they are having children, or it can be tremendously difficult to attend celebrations like baby showers. In the age of social media, each pregnancy announcement or picture of children is potentially a painful reminder of their struggle.

A final practical reminder is to be sensitive to the uniqueness of the struggle for each woman or couple. If you as a counselor have walked through this struggle in your own marriage, it might be tempting to try to encourage by saying that you understand what she or they are going through or to assume that they will struggle the same way you did. And yet, in any struggle, we recognize the individual nature of the woman; your experience will differ from hers. So too may the husband and wife respond and struggle differently though they are walking through the same thing; sensitivity and flexibility are essential.

As it relates to formal counseling steps, the first thing for the counselor is to grieve openly with her/them. We should acknowledge the pain involved, which may include openly grieving/weeping with them. The counselor should be patient with the counselee's grief and walk at their pace; grief is messy and doesn't always progress the way we expect it to. The counselor can also communicate to both husband and wife that their grief may look different; there is little that is "right" or "wrong" about grieving the loss of a child or the hope of future children.

Second, the counselor should offer encouragement and support for any (biblically) legitimate paths moving forward. For some, this will simply be to grieve the loss; for others it may be the pursuit of medical intervention or the adoption process. This includes, if appropriate given the counselor's context, being willing to attend appointments or follow up afterwards to support and encourage. It is helpful to remember that we must be sure not to step outside our role as counselor. We are not medical doctors or adoption agencies, so we must stay within our ethical bounds as counselors. Context also matters here; a formal, clinical counseling setting would set dual relationship boundaries that a church or ministry-based context might not.

Next is to pray and pray often, particularly around the time of the month that might serve as a reminder of her continued struggle (if applicable). This would include prayer for them physically, but also for their thoughts, desires, hopes, motivations, and potential letdowns. Depending on personal boundaries in counseling, this might include reaching out to the counselee after a doctor's appointment or during key times in her cycle, again remembering the wisdom of appropriate boundaries.

Along with praying often, the counselor should share truths from Scripture that are pertinent to the situation, with grace and compassion. For instance, the following themes especially relate to infertility and pregnancy loss:

- We can grieve the impact of sin. It is appropriate that we grieve the brokenness of our bodies and the reality of being unable to bear children or carry a child to term.

- God's faithfulness despite our circumstances/experiences. Our God remains faithful even in times of hardship. The truth of his Word does not change based on our experiences.

- God's continued nearness despite unanswered prayers. God promises that he is near to the brokenhearted and saves the crushed in Spirit (Ps 34:18).

- Our bodies will one day be restored. The present reality of brokenness is not an eternal reality. We can look forward with hope to the day of restoration.

- Our identity is in Christ, not our family. Despite the desire to be a mother or father, parenthood does not define us. Christ does.

- His plan is good, even in our pain. The book of Job in particular reminds us that even in great pain, the Lord is working all things for our good. He is most wise.

Along with communicating these truths, the counselor should explore any areas of sin in the counselee's heart. For instance, is her hope tied to being a mother? Does she feel she will be incomplete or inadequate if she does not have children? If so, perhaps her grief has shifted into (sinful) hopelessness or even entitlement. Alternatively, if the infertility is primarily "caused" by her husband, is she harboring bitterness or anger? If it is her own body that is not working properly, is she angry at God because she is "broken"? The counselor can compassionately yet directly explore these areas, lovingly correcting any sin in her heart.

Last, the counselor should ensure that the counselee(s) is connected to the support of her church. She/they should be encouraged to invite others into their struggle, so others may support them on a daily basis. This is the responsibility of the church, but the support can only be given when the couple invites them in. The church can pray often for them, weep with them, and potentially rejoice with them in the future. On a practical note, the counselee(s) may be encouraged to take small steps in this direction, perhaps sharing with one or two, or their small group, to start, then opening up gradually as time progresses.

Suggested Growth or Homework Assignments

While the wise counselor will adjust any suggested assignments based on the individual situation of the counselee, there are some overarching areas of focus that may be helpful. One growth assignment focuses on grief. In particular, the counselee can read and meditate on various psalms of lament or struggle, such as Psalms 13, 31, 6, or others, then progress toward reading and meditating on psalms of praise like Psalms 34 and 30. In doing so, the counselee is reminded not only of the necessity of crying out to the Lord in grief, but the importance of ending with hope and praise.

A second growth assignment may be to have the counselee explore her identity as defined in Scripture. As part of this assignment, she can write out biblical truths about who she is as a daughter of God. The counselor, through these assignments, can help her remember that our identity is not in what we do or what kind of family we have; rather, God defines who we are as his children. It will be helpful to a counselee to see this truth rather than focusing primarily on her failure to be a mother.

Next, the counselee should be encouraged to be transparent with others, so another growth assignment may be to help her/them take practical steps in that direction. The counselee can be encouraged to choose one or two people and share her struggle with them, or, if she has shared with a few people, to be more intentionally open with them about day-to-day struggles. This growth assignment may include opportunities to connect with and encourage others who are walking through a similar battle through conversation or reading books about the topic of infertility or miscarriage, drawing from the principle in 2 Cor 1:4. This will also assist the counselee in removing the focus from self to others.

Third, the counselee can read and meditate on passages about spiritual parenthood, like 1 Cor 4:14–15, 1 Tim 1:2, and 3 John 1:4. She can journal about how God views these spiritual family relationships and how she might disciple or teach spiritual children. While this does not replace biological children, it ensures that she is participating properly in God's design for his church.[3]

Last, the counselee can explore what it looks like practically to grieve with hope (1 Thess 4:13). The Scripture reference here is particularly useful when considered for pregnancy loss, but it is certainly applicable to the inability to conceive as well. When we as believers grieve with hope, we are intentionally keeping biblical truth uppermost in our minds, rather than allowing (sinful) hopelessness to creep in. Hope is not found in having children or attaining a particular family structure; instead, it is in the God of all hope (Rom 15:13).

Conclusion

The topic of infertility and pregnancy loss is difficult to walk through and difficult to speak to, in part because of the pain and grief involved. Put quite simply, it should not exist and would not if sin had not entered the world. Paired with the reality that we have little control over this struggle entering our lives, along with family or cultural expectations around having a family, it is understandable that hopelessness may enter the heart of the counselee.

But we are not without hope. The Scriptures are full of teachings about God's faithfulness to his children, his provision in seasons of plenty and of want, and the hope of future restoration because of the gospel. This hope can and should enter our counseling of these struggles.

It is worth reiterating the necessity of sensitivity and compassion on the part of the counselor. The loss of a child or the loss of an anticipated future as a parent is one that is deeply painful. Yet, it is a struggle that we can walk through with hope and certainty.

Recommended Resources

Infertility

Arbo, Matthew, *Walking through Infertility: Biblical, Theological, and Moral Counsel for Those Who Are Struggling* (Wheaton, IL: Crossway, 2018).

Baker, Amy, and Daniel Wickert, *Infertility: Comfort for Your Empty Arms and Heavy Heart* (Greensboro, NC: New Growth Press, 2013).

Glahn, Sandra, and William Cutrer, *When Empty Arms Become a Heavy Burden: Encouragement for Couples Facing Infertility*, rev. ed. (Grand Rapids: Kregel, 2010).

Monroe, Kimberly, and Philip Monroe, "The Bible and the Pain of Infertility," *Journal of Biblical Counseling* 23, no.1 (Winter 2005): 50–58.

Patterson Sobolik, Chelsea, and Russell Moore, *Longing for Motherhood: Holding On to Hope in the Midst of Childlessness* (Chicago: Moody, 2018).

Pregnancy Loss and Early Infant Death

Day, Sandy, *Morning Will Come* (Bemidji, MN: Focus, 2005).

———, "Loss of Baby Bible Study: Learning through Loss," Caleb Ministries, https://www.calebministries.org/loss-baby-bible-study/.

Green, Stephanie, *Miscarriage: You Are Not Alone* (Greensboro, NC: New Growth Press, 2014).

Guthrie, Nancy, *Holding On to Hope: A Pathway through Suffering to the Heart of God* (Carol Stream, IL: Tyndale Momentum, 2015).

Showalter, Ryan, *Grieving the Loss of Your Child: Comfort for Your Broken Heart* (Greensboro, NC: New Growth Press, 2014).

19

❧ ∞ ❧

Parenting Struggles

Isabelle sends you an email about beginning counseling for her and her fourteen-year-old daughter, Ella. Lately, it seems that the two of them are constantly at odds; Ella "has an attitude about everything," but Isabelle can't figure out what has changed and why Ella is suddenly so defiant. Isabelle admits that she has "lost her temper" a few times, speaking harshly to her daughter out of impatience. She is also frustrated because her husband wants to take a harsher approach than she would like. He has already taken Ella's phone and grounded her for the next several weeks. Isabelle knows something needs to change, but she doesn't know what. She's open to counseling for both her and Ella, but she would like to meet with you one-on-one first to get some thoughts about "what's going wrong."

One of the issues that a woman (and perhaps her husband with her) might address in a counseling context is parenting struggles. In such cases, the counselor might be called upon to counsel her as a mother, her husband as the father, and even her children or teenagers, depending on the struggle presented.[1]

In counseling parents and children, it is essential that the counselor understand the context in which they live: the family. For a child, the family is their primary context, and while it is certainly helpful to understand the relationships and dynamics with that family, it is also helpful to keep in mind that the child's context goes beyond simply father, mother, sister, brother. As the child ages, more and more voices enter the conversation: the teenager's friends, social media, and broader culture. Therefore, when considering counseling parents and children/teens, it is helpful for us as counselors to understand the purposes of the family. It is both representative of our spiritual family and is the context for things like learning and disciple making.

We must remember that the family unit ultimately serves as a reflection of God's family. Scripture is full of metaphors; for instance, there is the clear parallel in Scripture between marriage and Christ and the church. Similarly, the human family reflects God's relationship to his children. Throughout Scripture, God is referred to as Father, and we as his children. As Father, he not only demonstrates true love, but also acts as a model for how earthly parents are to treat their children. One place this is evident is in Luke 11:13, where Jesus says, "If you then, who are evil, know how to give good gifts to your children, how much more will the heavenly Father give the Holy Spirit to those who ask him?" Our heavenly Father both provides for his children and models what it means to parent children.

Second, the family is the setting for learning and correction. Throughout Scripture, parents are commanded to train up their children in the way they should go (Prov 22:6 ESV) and to teach them to follow the Lord (Deut 6:4–7). The family is the setting for this type of learning. Along those same lines, parents act as God's delegated authority; the family is the primary setting for discipline and correction, just as God's children are disciplined and corrected.

Additionally, the family provides a continual opportunity for disciple making. The Great Commission commands believers to go and make disciples of all nations (Matt 28:19–20), paralleled by the multiplication that we see in Acts 1:8. Paired with this, disciple making is a natural extension of the mandate to parents in Deuteronomy 6, to teach their children the ways of the Lord. By default, as parents teach their children, they are training up new disciples either in the way of the Lord or in ways contrary to it.

Finally, the family is an intimate, intensely personal community in which members learn clear and direct consequences for their actions. The family then provides the setting for members to know one another more deeply than anyone outside that community, and one in which they can practice biblical principles daily. It also gives opportunity to love one's immediate "neighbor" and learn how to interact with them.

Many of the struggles that counselors encounter with parents and children in many ways relate to a failure to either acknowledge or live out the theological principles above. For instance, when parents fail to discipline and teach the ways of the Lord, it naturally follows that (sinful) children will be disobedient and defiant. Or, when a parent is overly harsh, children may withdraw and isolate themselves emotionally from their family. It is essential, then, that parents not only understand the importance of the context they are providing for their children, but that they labor to live in accordance with what they teach. The following section in particular deals with living within the appropriate roles and guidelines for members of the family. These are conversations that might arise in a counseling context and might be useful for parents as they seek to lead their children.

Roles and Responsibilities within the Family

Parents

The primary responsibility of parents is to teach their children, an idea found in passages like Deut 6:4–7, among others. Specifically, it is the responsibility of parents to teach their children about the Lord and his commandments, talking about them often. Second, it is the role of parents to discipline their children, a concept that is drawn from passages like Prov 22:6 and 29:15. It is the place of parents to teach children right from wrong, providing correction to reinforce that teaching.

In a similar vein, parents are also responsible to act as authority figures, but a delegated authority, which is seen in Eph 6:1 and the example of Jesus. The obedience of children, as directed by their parents, is ultimately obedience to the Lord.

A fourth responsibility of parents, and one not typically focused on, is that parents are to treat children honorably. Specifically, Paul instructs fathers not to provoke children to anger. Essentially, discipline is not to frustrate or to anger; it is to teach and train up a child so that he does right before God. Parents are to view children as image bearers of God, just as they themselves are; this in itself requires honor, dignity, and respect.

Finally, parents are responsible to provide for their children, as we see in passages like 1 Tim 5:8. Not to be taken lightly, and not to be applied only in the literal, financial sense, parents are to provide for the needs of their children and provide an appropriate, biblical context for the children to grow up in.

Children

Children are not without roles and responsibilities within the family. Scripture speaks several places about children being a source of joy and pleasure to their parents; Ps 127:3, Luke 1:14, and John 16:21 support this idea. Children also have the responsibility to be obedient to their parents, a mandate that is repeated often throughout Scripture in both the Old and New Testaments. Finally, children are responsible to live at peace with one another. While the commandment to live at peace is universal (Rom 12:18), the Bible does relate this command specifically to siblings in Ps 133:1.

Struggles often arise from failing to fulfill one's role within the family. This seems to be the case for both parents and children, and sometimes multiple parties within the family are failing simultaneously. It is essential for counselors to understand Scripture's teachings on the responsibilities of both parents and children, so they are equipped to offer adequate biblical counsel on a given familial struggle.

Common Problems in Families

While space does not allow an in-depth discussion of all counseling issues that might present within families, the following are a few of the most common.

Family Conflict and Disobedience

Parents often come to counseling because of some sort of family conflict. It might be fights with siblings or parents, consistent disobedience, or a particular topic that seems to come up often, such as rules of the home. While the counselor will certainly want to explore the specifics of each situation, below are some general principles for counseling conflict within families.

Necessity of parents to model proper behavior/conflict resolution: The parents have particular roles within the home, one of which is to instruct their children clearly in the ways of the Lord. This includes modeling proper behavior; in this situation, specifically modeling conflict resolution. The parents should intentionally focus on the following areas:

- Speaking clearly in a way the child can understand (i.e., in a way that is developmentally appropriate)
- Clearly setting out consequences for actions
- Modeling self-control despite the conflict
- Maintaining proper authority as the one(s) setting the rules and following through on consequences

Walking a parent through some practical examples of what these points look like can resolve a great deal of the conflict. For instance, the counselor might encourage the parents to jointly write out a list of actions and their consequences. Then the counselor would encourage parents to share that list with the children, post the list in a common area, and be consistent in following through with consequences. Unity between parents is essential when setting out rules and corresponding discipline.

Sometimes, the parents fail to model proper behavior in conflict. This might be between the parents or between the parent and the child. In that case, the counselor should encourage the parent to apologize to whomever they have sinned against, adult or child/teen. This demonstrates to the child that the parent is a sinner in need of grace too, but in seeking forgiveness, they are showing humility and a willingness to submit to the Lord's directions. They are modeling proper behavior for their children.

Role of children to honor and obey: Most children do not need to be reminded that they should obey their parents; they know this is true. However, the reality is that almost no child (especially apart from the saving work of Christ) wants to obey all the time. They want to follow their own desires, and sometimes, because of developmental limitations, they might have a hard time exercising the self-control to do otherwise.

Nevertheless, children are responsible human persons. They are able to make choices and they do so often. Parents have a great deal of influence on this responsibility: they can discipline and correct, set clear rules, and reward or punish sinful behaviors. But ultimately, it is the child who makes the choice to obey or engage in conflict, knowing the consequences of their choice. Children are responsible.

A second reality that is often neglected, but was noted above, is that children apart from Christ are enslaved to their sin. By their very nature, they are sinners who will continue to sin (disobey, engage in conflict). Only by the saving work of Christ are they able to not sin. What this means, then, is that behavioral obedience is not the aim of counseling; a heart change is. While it is certainly more convenient for children to act rightly, ultimately it means nothing if they are separated from their Savior. Therefore, the aim of counselors and parents should be a change of heart toward Christ, a love for him over love for self, then love for others as an expression of their love for Christ.

Adjustment to Transitions

Childhood, especially from ages three through twelve, is often marked by numerous transitions that may bring struggles within the family. These might be things like:

- Changing schools
- Starting puberty
- Moving to a new place
- Changes within the family unit (death of a family member; divorce of parents)
- Creating new friend groups

In each of these, the child may experience feelings of confusion or fear, or a host of other emotions, and sometimes these feelings cause struggles or conflict between them and their parents. While transitions are a normal part of growing up, for a child, stability and predictability are important; these transitions will often disrupt that stability and predictability.

While the length of this text does not allow an in-depth discussion about each of these transitions individually, there are some overarching themes in counseling parents and children that may be helpful for the counselor.

Patience: the child going through any sort of transition might feel like she is in a state of confusion. What was predictable no longer is. There may be fears and worries associated with not knowing what is going to happen next. The counselor and the parents should exercise a great deal of patience with the counselee. Not only may it be difficult for the child to verbally express these emotions, but she might not even understand the emotions that she is feeling. Patience for the counselee goes far in these situations.

Normalizing without diminishing: As adults, we have all walked through seasons of transition; it is part of growing up. There is a careful balance to be had here, though, between normalizing (acknowledging that the child is not alone, their emotions are normal) and diminishing (leading the child to feel as if their struggle is not valid). The counselor may seek to normalize any worries or fears of both the parents and the children, perhaps through statements such as, "I remember feeling really overwhelmed before I started at a new school too," or, "I'm so sorry your grandmother passed. When I lost my grandmother, I was really sad too." This seeks to normalize their experience without conveying the message that they shouldn't be feeling a particular emotion. In using these phrases, the counselor is also modeling wise actions for the parents to replicate at home.

Listen and carefully address concerns: As counselors, part of our role is speaking truth in love to our counselees (Eph 4:15), including the children. Thus, we should listen and listen well. What are the concerns or fears of the parent and/or the child? How can we help bring clarity and understanding to the situation? As an example, consider a child who is fearful over her parents' upcoming divorce. She shares that she doesn't know what it will be like not having her mom and dad both around all the time or how she will know who will pick her up from school each day. This is leading her to worry and fear. The counselor in this case can affirm that this transition will likely be a bumpy one for some time, but the counselor can also talk through things like schedules, talking to the other parent before bed, and other logistical realities that may bring back some sense of predictability. These conversations can happen with the parents, the child, or both together. Additionally, the counselor can affirm spiritual realities such as God's continual care and concern for the entire family.

Crisis Situations or Traumatic Events

Unfortunately, it is not uncommon for people of all ages, including children and teens, to be subject to crisis or traumatic situations. When a crisis or trauma happens, the effects are felt by the entire family. These may include situations like:

- Becoming a victim of abuse
- Unexpectedly losing a loved one
- Unexpectedly changing living situation (possibly in conjunction with the loss of a loved one)

☙ Experiencing a car accident or witnessing a crime

In these situations, it will be helpful to read through the chapters on grief and trauma, to familiarize yourself with general principles in these situations. However, there are some specific things for counselors to remember as they seek to counsel parents and their children/teens through these sorts of events.

First, a child oftentimes cannot understand at the same level as adults. For instance, a child will have a much harder time understanding the permanence of a loved one dying. Developmentally, while much depends on the child's age and cognitive capacity, a child is still forming her understanding of the world around her and is constantly reforming that understanding based on events. For most children, this is all but automatic; unlike adults, most children are not consciously evaluating events as they form thoughts about how the world works. Rather, much of what happens, especially if consistent, becomes part of their "norm." Parents often have expectations about what their children or teens understand, or they might be confused about how to help their children work through these events. The counselor can give guidance based on the developmental abilities of the child or teen.

Second, it is useful to include a note on attachment and the importance of secure instead of insecure attachment. Most children develop a secure attachment to their parents or caregivers, and in this setting children learn things like empathy, compassion, worth, cooperation, and other important social skills. But children who do not develop this secure attachment, due to neglect, abuse, or traumatic events, often struggle with controlling their emotions and developing secure relationships later in life. Parents must be mindful of remaining available, supportive, and responsive to their children, especially during periods following a crisis or trauma situation.

Finally, the counselor should remind parents of the importance of pre-dictability. Children especially, but even teenagers, rely on consistency and predictability. Crisis events and traumatic experiences upend those two things, which may have implications for the child's expectations moving for-ward. They might become worrisome over seemingly minor things, or fear going too far from loved ones. They may also regress developmentally. These are typical responses for children during a crisis. The counselor can help parents tackle each of these things with patience and careful instruction.

Wayward Children

Sometimes, a woman (or couple) pursues counseling because she has a wayward child. This might be a teenager who has left home out of defiance, a young-adult child who has forsaken their faith or is living in continual sin, or an adult child who no longer has any contact with his or her parents. Such wayward children bring a myriad of emotions to their parents: grief, sadness, anger, fear, hopelessness, and others, most of which are understandable and appropriate.

In these circumstances, the counselor should lament alongside the grieving counselee. Such a situation is sad indeed, particularly if the child left out of anger or in the middle of a conflict. We should acknowledge the reality of the pain that is present; however, the counselor should also give hope to the counselee. While we cannot predict whether reconciliation will take place one day, we do know that our God changes hearts. He cares for that child and loves him or her deeply. While that child is living, hope remains.

However, we should be realistic; we cannot give false promises that the child will one day "come around" or reconcile. To do so is to give false hope. We should encourage the woman to pray and pray often, presenting this request to the God who does have the power to change her child's heart, despite her inability to do so. Counselors can also explore with the counselee if, when, and how it might be wise to engage the wayward child to demonstrate ongoing care and love.

Counseling Considerations and Homework Assignments

Though this chapter is primarily about counseling parents, with counseling children or teens as a secondary focus, the reality is that quite often, parents bring children or teens for counseling when they do not want to be there. In such cases, the counselor should be patient and work through the child's resistance, spending time building the relationship. During that time, the counselor can continue to work with the parent on their areas of struggle.

A second important consideration is the balance between helping the child directly and helping the parent to help the child. There is certainly a place for the counselor counseling the child or teen directly, but many counseling struggles between parents and children can be significantly impacted by helping the parents lead their children well. Of course, not all issues are resolved this way, but the Scriptures are clear that the primary teacher of children is their parents. As counselors, we want to equip parents to lead their children well, teach them God's ways, and model right living. We might work with them in that endeavor, but the responsibility is ultimately theirs.

It is also important to encourage unity and cooperation within the family. The family unit is meant to be a reflection of God and his family, his people. This means the family is to be unified, working together and cooperating to fulfill what God has called them to. The following exercises are helpful:

1. Encourage the family unit to spend quality time together, including in pairs of one parent and one child. This is especially the case when a child has been defiant, withdrawn, or struggling with problematic emotions like anxiety or depression. The quality time together is meant to build relationships and foster communication, and might include going for a walk, playing a game, or some other outing that both parent and child enjoy. Ideally this is also done with minimal distraction (i.e., phones/technology).

2. Help the family with practical communication skills they can practice at home. This might be allowing each party two minutes of uninterrupted speech, followed by reflective statements summarizing what was said. The counselor can help the family listen respectfully to hear and understand what the other person is communicating, rather than listening to respond.

3. Establish consistent rules and subsequent disciplinary consequences. If possible, these should be developed by both parents together, then clearly communicated (and upheld) to the children. The purpose is to establish order in the home, but also predictability and consistency under which children thrive.

4. Encourage family worship, including Sunday morning worship but also times of family worship throughout the week. Not only does this foster unity in the family, but it communicates the family's priorities. It should be the aim of the whole family to serve the Lord and serve others, both as a model to one another and to those outside of the family.

Conclusion

Counseling parents, and potentially their children or teens, can be as complex as the individuals who make up the family. A multitude of struggles may be presented. But God's Word gives us ample teaching on the roles of both parents and children and speaks at length about the various struggles that might be present. Ultimately, the aim of counseling parents is to help them lead their children toward Christlikeness, helping them live, think, and relate in ways that are honoring to the Lord and point others toward him.

Recommended Resources

Baker, Amy, *Caring for the Souls of Children: A Biblical Counselor's Manual* (Greensboro, NC: New Growth Press, 2020).

Fitzpatrick, Elyse, and Jim Newheiser, *When Good Kids Make Bad Choices: Help and Hope for Hurting Parents* (Irvine, CA: Harvest House, 2005).

Farley, William, *Gospel-Powered Parenting: How the Gospel Shapes and Transforms Parenting* (Phillipsburg, NJ: P&R, 2009).

Kellemen, Bob, *Gospel-Centered Family Counseling: An Equipping Guide for Pastors and Counselors* (Ada, MI: Baker, 2020).

Köstenberger, Andreas, and David Jones, *Marriage and the Family: Biblical Essentials* (Wheaton, IL: Crossway, 2012).

Lowe, Julie, *Child Proof: Parenting by Faith, Not Formula* (Greensboro, NC: New Growth Press, 2018).

Miller, C. John, and Barbara Miller Juliani, *Come Back, Barbara* (Phillipsburg, NJ: P&R, 1997).

Tripp, Paul David, *Parenting: 14 Gospel Principles That Can Radically Change Your Family* (Wheaton, IL: Crossway, 2016).

Tripp, Tedd, *Shepherding a Child's Heart* (Wapwallopen, PA: Shepherd Press, 2005).

20

Physical Ailments, Chronic Pain, and Medical Treatment

Mary comes to counseling discouraged and worn down. She shares that for the last four years, she has experienced chronic pain in most of her body; she has visited doctor after doctor, but none can find an explanation. Pain medicine barely helps and the side effects, Mary says, "almost aren't worth the little relief they bring." Though she seems to have learned to live with the actual pain, she is now feeling hopeless that she will ever find true relief; she is only thirty-eight, and the thought of this being her reality for the rest of her life is leading her toward despair. A friend recommended she come to counseling to work through these feelings of discouragement, to avoid falling into full-blown depression. Though Mary has not expressed a desire to harm herself, she did make statements like "I'm not sure how much longer I can take this," and "I don't know what I'll do if this never stops."

Most of us know what pain feels like: an unpleasant sensation that causes discomfort. It can be caused by a myriad of things: an illness, an injury, or even

233

psychosomatic distress. For many, pain becomes chronic and long-lasting. In fact, the CDC reported that, in 2016, an estimated 20.4 percent of adults in the United States experienced chronic pain and 8 percent of adults experienced "high-impact" chronic pain.[1] While chronic pain might not be a common counseling issue, it is a topic that most counselors will encounter at some point. It is quite likely that the chronic pain issue presents alongside another struggle that we have explored in this text. But physical ailments, pain, and sickness are real and they impact women, so we must be prepared to speak to these struggles biblically. We must also be ready to speak to the proper place of medical treatment for both physical and mental struggles.

From the very beginning, we must acknowledge that apart from sin, physical pain would not be a reality. It is a direct result of the fall (Gen 3:16), a curse on man and woman and part of the progression toward physical death. In today's world, that may present as a physical disease like cancer (and accompanying treatments), a sickness like fibromyalgia, an injury, physiological components of mental health struggles, or chronic muscle or nerve pain. Despite the relation to sin, we must also remember that sin is more than just volitional choice; pain more often comes from a broken and fallen body than it does one's own life choices. In a very real sense, physical pain is a form of suffering.

And yet, pain serves a purpose: it alerts us that something is wrong. Muscle pain, for instance, tells me I've used that muscle inappropriately and it is now injured; it needs to be cared for to heal. Even psychosomatic pain points to underlying heart (mental, spiritual) struggles—it clues us in to the fact that there is some form of distress that must be dealt with. Pain reminds us that our bodies are broken and in need of redemption. And ultimately, it points us to our Redeemer.

What Does the Bible Have to Say about Physical Ailments and Pain?

The Bible is clear that pain entered the world because of sin. It was part of the curse for both Adam and Eve; God's curse on Eve was pain in childbirth (Gen

3:16), and his curse on Adam was that work (harvesting food) was now pain-ful (Gen 3:17). That curse is now realized by each person (Rom 5:12–21) and pain is experienced by each person in some way. For many, that pain is chronic and ongoing, with little relief.

However, we see clearly a picture of God's design to relieve pain when Jesus came. As a picture of his kingdom that is to come, he healed many (Matt 4:24). Sometimes, this healing was for physical ailments, temporary and long-lasting, and other times healing came in the spiritual arena (exorcisms, spiritual awakening). Both were important to our Savior, and both remain so. Jesus was pointing forward to the promise we see in Rev 21:4 that one day, pain and sickness will be no more.

The Bible also gives us a bit of a clue about why pain and sickness come. At times, death or sickness was an act of divine judgment, like with Ananias and Sapphira (Acts 5:1–11), King Herod (Acts 12:22–24), and the believers in Corinth who failed to uphold the Lord's Supper properly and suffered sickness or death (1 Cor 11:30). Other times, and more importantly, sickness was used to reveal the works of God. We see this most clearly with the man born blind (John 9:1–12). When asked by his disciples if it was the man or his parents who had sinned, and therefore led to him being born blind, Jesus responded, "This came about so that God's works might be displayed in him" (John 9:3). Further, we see that Job's affliction was to test him and that Paul's thorn in the flesh drew him closer to the Lord.

In each of these examples (the blind man, Job, and Paul), God used their pain to accomplish his purposes. He tells us this in Jas 1:2–4, where James writes, "Consider it a great joy, my brothers and sisters, whenever you experience various trials, because you know that the testing of your faith produces endurance. And let endurance have its full effect, so that you may be mature and complete, lacking nothing." Our trials, including physical ailments, produce godliness and maturity in us when we respond properly. They also give us opportunities to comfort others in their affliction with the same comfort the Lord gives us (2 Cor 1:4).

Last, the Bible teaches us that physical pain serves as a reminder that it is the Lord who sustains us, even in pain and sickness. David wrote in Ps 41:3, "The LORD will sustain him on his sickbed; you will heal him on the bed where he lies." While the Lord does not promise to relieve our pain this side of heaven, here David is reminding his readers that it is the Lord alone who can sustain us. He and he alone can heal. In the midst of chronic pain, our hope must be in the Lord rather than any other savior.

How Can We Help Those Experiencing Physical Illness or Pain?

Most often, a counselee who is experiencing chronic illness or pain is actively involved in seeking medical treatment. Sometimes, the counselee has found a bit of relief, but other times, she has not. Each woman's experience of pain is different and impacts her differently. The following steps are helpful for us as counselors as we seek to minister to each woman in her unique situation:

1. **Listen and learn.** Before speaking to her pain or illness, listen and learn about her experience. Try to understand what led to her pain or illness and what that has been like for her. Ask her what her pain is like and how it impacts her everyday life. And find out how she is choosing to respond to her circumstances. As Jas 1:19 reminds us, we should be "quick to listen, slow to speak." Demonstrate care for her by listening and listening well.

2. **Empathize and grieve.** We should readily acknowledge the weight of her suffering, then grieve over the impact this has on her when or if it is appropriate. Her life has been affected significantly by persistent, unrelenting discomfort. As counselors, it is our role to bear those burdens with her (Gal 6:2), walking side by side with her. Just as Job's friends rightly grieved his suffering (Job 2:11–13), so should we grieve the suffering of our counselees.

3. **Assess for thoughts of suicide, self-harm, or addiction**, particularly if the pain is severe or has been long-lasting. Pain tends to demand one's mental energy and make it harder to be present. For many, this form of suffering can quickly lead to hopelessness or fear that things will never change (much like it did for Mary, above). Some women may find themselves tempted toward improper forms of relief, such as thoughts of suicide/self-harm or substance use. While we must not assume these to be present, we should be diligent to explore these areas and determine whether they are a struggle for our particular counselee.

4. **Ask the Lord to heal, but acknowledge that he may not.** We are told in Scripture that we can "approach the throne of grace with boldness, so that we may receive mercy and find grace to help us in time of need" (Heb 4:16). We can boldly ask for healing and trust that the Lord hears. And yet, he may choose not to heal, for reasons we might not understand. In either case, we are still responsible to respond rightly. We can pray with the counselee that the Lord would relieve her suffering but still encourage her to continue trusting the Lord and his goodness despite his answer.

5. **Recognize the true source of healing.** As counselors and part of our counselee's care team, it is right of us to encourage her to explore medical options. These are good things that the Lord has given us in his grace. But we should remind the counselee that, like Ps 41:3 says, it is the Lord who sustains and the Lord who heals. He may choose to use medicine to accomplish that healing, but ultimately the healing comes from the Lord.

6. **Encourage caring for her body.** With chronic pain, often the tendency is either to do as little activity as possible, in anticipation of more pain, or to push through the pain and try to do too much. A healthy balance is best. Counselors should encourage their counselee to exercise as possible and within wise limits set with input from her physician, and also to focus on healthy eating and sleeping. Our bodies are broken, but we also have been given the responsibility to

care for them. Proper physical treatment, including exercise, eating, sleeping, and medical treatment, are part of a woman's care for her body; they are stewarding what God has given us.

7. **Set doable goals.** Focus on the things the counselee can control, setting goals that she can accomplish that day. Small achievements build up to larger ones. They are also encouraging as she fights her daily battles. Along with this, the counselor can help her focus on enjoying the present moment rather than focusing too much on the past or the future.

8. **Explore her responses.** While a woman might not have much control over her physical ailments or sickness, she does have control (and responsibility) over her responses. How is she responding spiritually (mentally, emotionally) to her struggles? Is she hopeless, fearful, angry, or blaming herself or others? Is she wallowing in self-pity or feeling like a victim? If so, these are improper and sinful. The counselor should spend time exploring her heart responses to her struggles and evaluating whether they need to change. In areas that are found to be sinful, the counselor can help her repent and turn from these responses.

9. **Lead her toward a Christlike response.** For times when sinful responses to a counselee's physical struggles arise, the counselor should encourage her toward the following:

    a. Finding strength in the Lord (1 Pet 5:10): Help her see that her only hope is in her Creator, the sovereign God who gives strength to the weak (Isa 40:29).

    b. Seeing her pain as an opportunity to exalt the Lord (Job 6:10): He receives glory when we come to him and express our need for him.

    c. Looking toward future glory (Rom 8:18): Remind her that her suffering pales in comparison to the glory that is coming. Her perspective matters tremendously.

    d. Pointing others toward God (Matt 5:13–16): Others are watching how she responds to her pain. Encourage her to be mindful of how she is setting an example to those around her.

e.   Comforting others in their suffering (2 Cor 1:3–4): Paul tells us that we are comforted so we can comfort others. Help her find opportunities to encourage others.

10. **Remind her of her Savior.** As we look at the list immediately above in point nine, we are reminded that Jesus did each of these during the crucifixion and the events leading up to it. As Isaiah 53 details, he bore our sin and was afflicted on our behalf. And yet, he exalted the Lord (Luke 22:42), pointed toward his Father (John 19:11) and comforted others even amid his own pain (John 19:25–27). He is the example of how we are to suffer. But he is also our hope. Because of the cross and the resurrection, we can have hope that one day, he will relieve all pain and suffering (Rev 21:4). The gospel is of utmost importance to the woman who is suffering chronic illness and pain.

Helpful Homework Exercises

Several exercises may be used with those in chronic pain. First, encourage the counselee to read through the four passion narratives (Matt 26:30–27:66, Mark 14:26–15:47, Luke 22:39–23:56, and John 18:1–19:42), noting Jesus's response to his own physical suffering. The counselee can then make application to her own suffering, noting areas that she needs to better align herself with Jesus's response.

Second, though they stem from secular practice, mindfulness exercises, progressive muscle relaxation, and deep breathing have been found to be helpful in combating chronic pain. The counselee can focus on the biblical truths noted above during these activities. She can repeat statements like "The Lord sustains and restores" (Ps 41:3), "His grace is sufficient in weakness" (2 Cor 12:9), or "He is the Father of mercy and God of all comfort" (2 Cor 1:3). These remind her often yet simply that her hope is in the Lord, not in relief of her suffering.

Third, the counselee can be encouraged to write her own psalm modeled after Psalm 34, Psalm 13, or Psalm 121. The Lord desires that we call out to him, but he knows our hearts. Like the psalmist, we can acknowledge pain and discomfort and cry out to the Lord for relief, but we should also remind ourselves that he is good regardless of his response. He is accomplishing his purposes whether he chooses to provide relief or not.

Last, she can work toward creating realistic goals. She can make a list of things to do each day that are things she can reasonably accomplish, helping her experience little victories each day. These not only encourage setting further goals for the next day, but also keep her focused on the present moment and things she can feasibly control.

What about Medication to Treat Psychosomatic Pain?

For most of us, medical treatment for physical and mental ailments is barely a question; when we need relief, we seek out medication or medical treatment to provide that relief. And yet, there are situations where a counselee might be resistant to pursuing medical treatment. Perhaps she had a bad experience in the past, has others in her life telling her she doesn't need it, or has personal convictions against the use of medication. As counselors, we must be prepared to speak to the use of medication. However, we are not medical professionals; we are simply advisors who are part of her care team.

This discussion gets a bit less clear when psychosomatic pain is believed to be present. Ideally, as the underlying struggle is relieved, the pain is as well. But sometimes, the pain is a distraction and can be a hindrance to counseling. The counselee might struggle to focus and is slow in moving toward change simply because of the pain involved.

In such cases, should we consider medication to treat the psychosomatic pain; namely, to treat the underlying mental/spiritual struggles? Michael Emlet has a pertinent reminder for us as we seek to assess people's struggles—physical or spiritual—biblically: "We want biblical categories and themes to make sense of what we observe in others. Even then we need to remain humble, realizing that a complex array of factors that we may not fully understand could contribute to the person's struggle. The diagnostic task, whether

using biblical categories or secular ones, is never like following a simple rec-
ipe. Wisdom is key."[2] Counselors, in aiming to better understand the person
through the lens of Scripture, should fully recognize that women are complex,
including the ways that her brain and mind work. Counselors should also
recognize the multitude of contributing factors to the struggles of any given
counselee and move to treat accordingly.

So then, how can we best determine when to encourage a medical or
medicinal evaluation? When is it wise? The criteria below, while not exhaustive, may be helpful to consider.

Scriptural Teaching Has Been Thoroughly Addressed

The use of Scripture in counseling has typically been an area of strength for
biblical counselors. We are generally good at using the Bible to speak truth
into the lives of our counselees. In the consideration of the use of medication,
we cannot neglect to continue to do what we have done well. Ed Welch states
in *Blame It on the Brain* that most psychiatric problems are both spiritual
and physical, and he makes an appropriate statement on this matter when he
writes, "You will never find a psychiatric problem where biblical counsel—
counsel directed to the heart—is anything less than essential."[3] We cannot
divorce ourselves from ongoing counsel from God's Word, despite any evidence of a physical cause. Every problem encountered by women will have
at least some spiritual component to it that should continue to be addressed.

It Is Reasonable to Conclude There May Be a Physiological Component

While the application of Scripture has traditionally been an area of strength,
determining the possibility of a biological component is generally outside
of the biblical counselor's training and expertise. The biblical counselor can
recommend a general medical evaluation to rule out or point to a biological
concern, such as side effects from other medications, metabolic disorders,
infections, or other contributing factors. If these are present, the physician

can treat them. The treatment may very well impact any psychosomatic pain present as well.

Suicidal Thoughts Are Present

When suicidal thoughts, active or passive, are present, medications should be considered to stabilize thoughts or behaviors for the counselee's safety. In these cases, "that medicine may help calm her down, clear her thinking, or relax her so that she doesn't harm herself or others."[4] The medication has the potential to stabilize thought patterns and potentially reduce harmful behaviors. Note, though, that this is not a fail-safe; rather, suicidality simply leads us to expedite our consideration of medication.

Any Prior Experience with Medication Has Been Positive

An additional consideration for a referral for medication evaluation is any history of medication use. The counselor may choose to investigate this upon beginning counseling, and should certainly do so when considering a referral. The counselor should ask about past usage and the counselee's experience, if any. If medication has been used in the past, was it helpful? If so, there is a significant chance it may be helpful again.

Further, what were the counselee's reasons for using the medication in the past? While motivation will be addressed at greater length below, a history of those thoughts may be helpful here as well. Was the counselee resistant to using those medications? If so, why? The counselor can then use this information in determining any changes from past usage and any possible areas that need to be addressed before a referral is made.

Level of Functioning May Be Significantly Improved

Some counselees will experience a change in functioning because of their pain. This may present itself as difficulty in performing daily tasks like showering or cooking a meal, but it might be more severe in some cases, like an inability to keep a steady job. In those situations, it might be helpful to consider medication to restore functionality.

A comparison here that may be helpful is standard treatment for the common headache. For some, a headache does not lead to any change in functionality. Others, however, particularly those who experience migraines, may be debilitated because of the pain. They are unable to get out of bed or carry on a normal conversation. In those cases, treatment of the source of the pain allows the sufferer to function more normally.

The Counselee's Goal for Using Medication Is Appropriate and Heart Matters Have Been Addressed

Paired with the thorough use of Scripture above, the counselor should ensure that heart issues and motivation are being addressed, specifically related to medication to treat her ongoing pain. What is the counselee looking for in the medication, a quick fix or assistance in holistically addressing her presenting problems? Paired with this, the counselor should try to determine if the counselee's motivation to continue to work on heart issues will continue should the medication be helpful. Will she assume that her problem was purely biological and thus there is no more reason to continue addressing spiritual matters? Is she looking for an easy way to deal with her struggles? The counselor should evaluate these points and communicate with the counselee the need to continue addressing core issues, despite any relief provided by medication.

Suffering May Be Reduced or Eliminated

In counseling, many times we see counselees who are suffering tremendously from their struggles. Speaking to this suffering, Michael Emlet writes that "it is God's design to relieve the suffering that arose with the fall," and he points to numerous passages about Jesus's healing works as examples.[5] However, we must have a balanced approach to suffering. Speaking to this, Emlet writes that "while relieving suffering is a kingdom priority, seeking mere relief without a vision for God's transforming agenda in the midst of suffering may short-circuit all that God wants to do in the person's life."[6] The counselor, then, must evaluate the suffering experienced by the counselee and use that evaluation in her decision for or against a referral for medication. In many cases, a reduction of suffering may allow room for further efforts to identify and address core issues, but there may be times when the Lord is using that suffering to accomplish his purposes.

Upon Prayer and Consideration, It Appears a Wise Choice under the Direction of the Holy Spirit

The Holy Spirit is the third person in counseling. He is therefore necessary in the process of discerning when a referral for a medication evaluation is appropriate. He facilitates wisdom in the counselor and counselee, and it is one of his gifts. The Holy Spirit is called the Helper and Spirit of truth (John 14:15–17 ESV), the teacher of wisdom (1 Cor 2:13), and our aid in knowing about God (1 Cor 2:10), all of which are helpful for counselors.[7] The counselor considering a referral for medication evaluation must be diligent in prayer over the decision to refer and should actively be seeking the guidance of the Holy Spirit in each individual counseling situation and throughout the decision-making process. After inviting the Holy Spirit to lead, what seems most wise? This is not a final step in the evaluation process, rather an overarching part of the conversation.

Conclusion

Physical ailments and chronic pain are tough struggles to walk through; as counselors, we must be sensitive and patient as we walk shoulder to shoulder with women suffering in this way. We must be wise in exploring medical treatment, but always point her toward the hope she has in her Savior. As we do so, we can point her toward the future restoration that is to come and help her find rest in the Lord rather than in her search for relief. In our compassion, we can model Jesus for her and comfort her in her affliction, as we have been comforted in our own.

Recommended Resources

Bridges, Jerry, *Trusting God: Even When Life Hurts* (Colorado Springs: NavPress, 1988).

Carson, Donald A., *How Long, O Lord? Reflections on Suffering and Evil*, rev. ed. (Grand Rapids: Baker, 2006).

Eareckson Tada, Joni, and Steven Estes, *When God Weeps: Why Our Sufferings Matter to the Almighty* (Grand Rapids: Zondervan, 1997).

Emlet, Michael, *Descriptions and Prescriptions: A Biblical Perspective on Psychiatric Diagnoses and Medications* (Greensboro, NC: New Growth Press, 2017).

Piper, John, and Justin Taylor, eds., *Suffering and the Sovereignty of God* (Wheaton, IL: Crossway, 2006).

Powlison, David, *God's Grace in Your Suffering* (Wheaton, IL: Crossway, 2018).

Ramsey, K. J., and Kelly M. Kapic, *This Too Shall Last: Finding Grace When Suffering Lingers* (Grand Rapids: Zondervan, 2020).

Tripp, Paul David, *Suffering: Gospel Hope When Life Doesn't Make Sense* (Wheaton, IL: Crossway, 2018).

Welch, Edward T., *The Counselor's Guide to the Brain and Its Disorders*, 2nd ed. (Glenside, PA: Christian Counseling and Educational Foundation, 2015).

Conclusion

This text has sought to lay a foundation for counseling women and to walk through key principles for counseling women through various life struggles. Section 1 laid the groundwork for us by discussing who we are as women (chapter 1), the reality of sin (chapter 2), the context in which women live (chapter 3), the necessity of Scripture (chapter 4), how to help women well (chapter 5), and a woman's life stages (chapter 6). Each of these are essential in understanding how we might best counsel women through the various struggles they will inevitably encounter. Several of these issues were addressed in section 2, issues like depression, anxiety, grief, trauma, marriage and family, and others. While these are certainly not all the issues women may encounter, they are some of the most common.

Some Final Reminders

There are a few topics remaining that are pertinent for women as we seek to counsel our sisters, topics that have not fit well elsewhere. Despite this, they are important to consider.

Role of Women Counseling Women

Titus 2:1–5 says,

> But you are to proclaim things consistent with sound teaching. Older
> men are to be self-controlled, worthy of respect, sensible, and sound
> in faith, love, and endurance. In the same way, older women are to
> be reverent in behavior, not slanderers, not slaves to excessive drink-
> ing. They are to teach what is good, so that they may encourage the
> young women to love their husbands and to love their children, to
> be self-controlled, pure, workers at home, kind, and in submission to
> their husbands, so that God's word will not be slandered.

Here, Paul laid out some helpful guidelines for teaching within the church.[1]
First, he gave us the reminder that we are to "proclaim things consistent
with sound teaching." What we counsel should align with God's Word; it
should be sound teaching.[2] After a brief note to older men, which Paul would
come back to, he then encouraged older women to behave in certain ways.
Essentially, they are to have integrity. But this integrity has a purpose: so they
may encourage younger women. Their sound teaching and their example is
primarily directed at other women, namely those younger (either in age or
maturity). He gave a few examples as well of the sorts of things that young
women should be taught, many of which overlap the topics of this book.

In writing this section, Paul reminded older women of their responsibility to lead younger women. Women relate best to other women; we have
often been through similar circumstances and we hold the same roles within
the family and the church. We have much in common. Because of this, we
can relate to one another more directly. It only makes sense that the same is
true in counseling. This is not to say that a man cannot counsel a woman or
a woman cannot counsel a man—such a discussion is a wisdom issue—just
that it is generally helpful for women to lead and counsel other women.

Integrity of the Counselor

No one likes a hypocrite. We all know this, and yet it is easy for "little sins" to sneak into our lives as counselors. This might be failing to pray before sessions, missing our own quiet time in the Word, or exaggerating success in past counseling situations when talking to others. All these reflect sin in the heart of the counselor, and, particularly when she counsels toward right living, these sins make her a hypocrite.

You might read that paragraph and think, "Wow, those are harsh words." And they are. But recall the message in chapter 2: we can call out sin knowing that God's grace enables us to turn from it. God, by the power of his Spirit, enables us to live rightly as we counsel rightly. Paul echoed these sentiments in 1 Tim 4:16, where he told Timothy, "Pay close attention to your life and your teaching; persevere in these things, for in doing this you will save both yourself and your hearers." Our choices and behaviors matter; they impact us and our counselees.

What does it mean to have integrity as a counselor? On a basic level, it means that we must live what we teach. If we counsel others toward Christlikeness, it means we are pursuing it ourselves. We are spending time praying and searching God's Word for wisdom. It means that we are keeping the gospel central to our counsel and in our self-counsel. And it means that we uphold honesty in all our dealings with others.

Further, integrity as counselors means that we uphold counseling ethics. In short, we should aim to be competent, continually learning how we might help others well, and continually honing our counseling skills. We are honest about what we have been trained in and in what areas we are lacking, striving to learn more, particularly in those gap areas. It also means that we serve in an advisory capacity rather than an authoritative one, upholding client autonomy. Finally, it means that we always seek the good of our counselees, working toward what is in their best interest.

Self-Care and Avoidance of Burnout

Another pertinent reminder for us as counselors is the necessity of self-care as we seek to avoid burnout and compassion fatigue. When present, burnout and compassion fatigue reflect a failure to set boundaries and ensure that the counselor is maintaining her own physical, mental, and emotional health. She might start to feel complacent in her counseling, caring less about the struggles of the women she counsels, or she might feel physically fatigued or mentally sluggish. Such indicators tell her that she needs to slow down and care for her own needs, in order to care for others.

How might the counselor fight compassion fatigue and burnout? In part, she might set clear boundaries around when she counsels or what sorts of cases she takes on. Some types of counseling, like trauma therapy or working with child abuse cases, are emotionally draining. When doing this sort of work, she might take on fewer counselees or allow time between sessions to decompress. She might establish a schedule of counseling only three days a week instead of five, or commit to not answering texts or emails on the weekend.

Along with setting boundaries, it is wise to be proactive in preventing caregiver fatigue and burnout by practicing self-care. The counselor should intentionally find opportunities to do things she enjoys, spend time with others who can care for her, and take time away. Most importantly, she should spend time resting in God's Word, meditating on his care for her and his strength in her weakness. She cannot care for others apart from his help; acknowledging that reality and actively setting aside time to rest go far in preventing burnout.

The Role of the Church and Para-Church Organizations

A final reminder for the reader is connected to the last step of caring for women that we explored in chapter 5: leveraging support—namely, leveraging support for the counselor as she seeks to minister to her counselees. The local church is certainly the first place this support is found, but many para-church organizations exist to do the same thing. Some of those organizations are particular to one type of ministry (such as domestic violence or marital health), but others are counseling organizations that support counselors as they learn and grow as counselors. Organizations like the Christian Counseling and Education Foundation (CCEF), the American Association of Christian Counselors (AACC), and the Biblical Counseling Coalition (BCC), among others, exist to provide resources to counselors.

All these groups, whether they are church or para-church organizations, provide some essential things to counselors. First, they provide support and accountability. They encourage counselors to be trained and trained well, but quite often the leadership of these groups also hold counselors accountable to ethical standards and current practices. This may be formal or informal, but it is present. Second, both the church and many para-church organizations provide opportunities for learning. Larger churches in particular, along with the counseling organizations listed above, intentionally seek to train counselors, some even providing various levels of certification. Other organizations, like Bible colleges, universities, and seminaries, provide more formal education to those seeking to be counselors. The counselor should be mindful of the resources available to her through her church and para-church organizations; they can aid her in helping others.

Conclusion

I hope the reader finishes this book better prepared to both understand women and serve them. This text cannot be exhaustive, but it can provide a foundation for counselors as they go on to learn more about each individual topic. May the Lord receive the honor for the work of the reader as she leads others to him.

General Counseling Resources

The following texts are general counseling resources, or those not provided elsewhere, that are useful for further study (in alphabetical order):

Jerry Bridges, *Trusting God* (Colorado Springs: NavPress, 2018).

Timothy Clinton and George Ohlschlager, *Competent Christian Counseling*, vol. 1, *Foundations and Practice of Compassionate Soul Care* (Colorado Springs: WaterBrook Press, 2002).

Gary Collins, *Christian Counseling: A Comprehensive Guide*, 3rd ed. (Nashville: Thomas Nelson, 2007).

Michael R. Emlet, *CrossTalk: Where Life and Scripture Meet* (Greensboro, NC: New Growth Press, 2009).

Elyse Fitzpatrick, *Women Counseling Women: Biblical Answers for Life's Difficult Problems* (Eugene, OR: Harvest House, 2010).

Elyse Fitzpatrick and Dennis Johnson, *Counsel from the Cross: Connecting Broken People to the Love of Christ* (Wheaton, IL: Crossway, 2012).

Robert Jones, *Pursuing Peace: A Christian Guide to Handling Our Conflicts* (Wheaton, IL: Crossway, 2012).

Robert Jones, Kristin Kellen, and Rob Green, *The Gospel for Disordered Lives: An Introduction to Christ-Centered Biblical Counseling* (Nashville: B&H, 2021).

Bob Kellemen, *Gospel-Centered Counseling: How Christ Changes Lives* (Grand Rapids: Zondervan, 2014).

———, *Gospel Conversations: How to Care Like Christ* (Grand Rapids: Zondervan, 2015).

Bob Kellemen and Jeff Forrey, eds., *Scripture and Counseling: God's Word for Life in a Broken World* (Grand Rapids: Zondervan, 2014).

Bob Kellemen and Steve Viars, eds., *Christ-Centered Biblical Counseling: Changing Lives with God's Changeless Truth* (Eugene, OR: Harvest House, 2021).

Timothy S. Lane and Paul David Tripp, *How People Change* (Greensboro, NC: New Growth Press, 2008).

John MacArthur, *Counseling: How to Counsel Biblically* (Nashville: Thomas Nelson, 2005).

David Powlison, *Seeing with New Eyes: Counseling and the Human Condition through the Lens of Scripture* (Phillipsburg, NJ: P&R, 2003).

———, *Speaking the Truth in Love: Counsel in Community* (Greensboro, NC: New Growth Press, 2005).

Ken Sande, *The Peacemaker: A Biblical Guide to Resolving Personal Conflict* (Ada, MI: Baker, 2004).

Matthew S. Stanford, *Grace for the Afflicted: A Clinical and Biblical Perspective on Mental Illness* (Downers Grove, IL: InterVarsity Press, 2017).

Siang-Yang Tan and Eric T. Scalise, *Lay Counseling: Equipping Christians for a Helping Ministry* (Grand Rapids: Zondervan, 2016).

Paul Tripp, *Instruments in the Redeemer's Hands: People in Need of Change Helping People in Need of Change* (Phillipsburg, NJ: P&R, 2002).

Ed Welch, *Side by Side: Walking with Others in Wisdom and Love* (Wheaton, IL: Crossway, 2015).

Notes

Chapter 1

1. The word "man" here in Hebrew connotes human beings, not just males.

2. Roles as God established them in Scripture, not necessarily as culture defines.

3. Eccl 12:17; 2 Cor 4:16; Matt 10:28; Eccl 11:5; Ps 139:13–15; 1 Cor 9:27.

4. Luke 6:45.

Chapter 2

1. Though pain does not cause it. Hopelessness is still a volitional choice.

Chapter 3

1. Robert Jones, Kristin Kellen, and Rob Green, *The Gospel for Disordered Lives* (Nashville: B&H Academic, 2021), chap. 7.

2. Chuck Lawless and William Cook III, *Spiritual Warfare in the Storyline of Scripture* (Nashville: B&H Academic, 2019), 1.

3. As is evident in Genesis 3 and Job 1.

4. Lawless and Cook, *Spiritual Warfare*, 2.

5. Prov 22:6.

6. 1 Cor 10:13.

Chapter 5

1. Heath Lambert, *A Theology of Biblical Counseling: The Doctrinal Foundations of Counseling Ministry* (Grand Rapids: Zondervan, 2016), 13.

2. "The BCC Interview: Capitol Hill Baptist Church," Weekend Interview Series, Biblical Counseling Coalition, May 7, 2011, https://www.biblicalcounsel ingcoalition.org/2011/05/07/the-bcc-interview-capitol-hill-baptist-church/.

3. This might look different when counseling a believer versus a nonbeliever, but either way our aim is to ultimately point to Christ.

4. For similar approaches, see Robert Jones, Kristin Kellen, and Rob Green, *The Gospel for Disordered Lives* (Nashville: B&H Academic, 2021) and Paul David Tripp, *Instruments in the Redeemer's Hands* (Phillipsburg, NJ: P&R, 2002).

5. Much of what will be discussed below is referred to as counseling microskills. Several texts are useful for further study: Elisabeth A. Nesbit Sbanotto, Heather Davediuk Gingrich, and Fred C. Gingrich, *Skills for Effective Counseling: A Faith-Based Integration* (Downers Grove, IL: IVP Academic, 2016) and Allen E. Ivey, Mary Bradford Ivey, and Carlos P. Zalaquett, *Intentional Interviewing and Counseling: Facilitating Client Development in a Multicultural Society*, 9th ed. (Boston: Cengage Learning, 2017).

6. Some therapeutic approaches contend that when a counselee is heard and understood adequately, he or she has the power within themselves to find healing. Such approaches ignore the reality of a deceitful, sinful heart. In our own power, we are completely unable to find satisfaction of our true need, Jesus. We might feel better or suffer less, but this is for naught if it leaves us without a Savior.

Chapter 7

1. American Psychiatry Association, preface to *Diagnostic and Statistical Manual of Mental Disorders* (*DSM-5*), 5th ed. (Washington, DC: APA, 2013), xlii.

2. While an extensive discussion is not possible here, I do not necessarily endorse the use of the *DSM-5* for diagnostic purposes. Instead, any information drawn from this source is simply for demonstrative and information purposes, given as general information rather than necessary diagnostic criteria. See chapter 4 for a longer discussion of this topic.

3. *DSM-5*, 160–61.

4. See chapter 2 for a fuller discussion on this dynamic.

5. "What Causes Depression?: Onset of Depression More Complex than a Brain Chemical Imbalance," Harvard Health, updated June 24, 2019, https://www.health.harvard.edu/mind-and-mood/what-causes-depression. Also see David Healy, *Let Them Eat Prozac: The Unhealthy Relationship between the Pharmaceutical Industry and Depression* (New York: NYU Press, 2006), and Terry Lynch, *Depression Delusion*, vol. 1, *The Myth of the Chemical Imbalance* (Limerick, UK: Mental Health Publishing, 2015).

6. See Timothy S. Lane and Paul David Tripp, *How People Change* (Greensboro: New Growth Press, 2008).

7. See chapter 20.

8. It is unethical for a counselor to recommend medication or to counter directives given by a physician. The counselor acts simply in an advisory capacity, helping the woman think through pros and cons, realistic expectations, and when she might begin conversations about medication with her doctor.

Chapter 8

1. Some criteria are summarized or shortened for space; see the *DSM-5* for full criteria and discussion.

2. This is an important distinction for believers versus nonbelievers. While God certainly extends grace on the nonbeliever, she is an enemy of God. She does have much to fear. God remains sovereign, but she also remains opposed to him.

3. Space prohibits a lengthy discussion about panic attacks. However, we must recognize that the physical manifestation of anxiety through panic attacks is significant and can transition to panic attacks that seem to come without any evident trigger. When this is the case, referral to a physician for evaluation is encouraged.

4. This is a conversation not to be entered into lightly. For more about medication, see Michael Emlet, *Descriptions and Prescriptions: A Biblical Perspective on Psychiatric Diagnoses and Medications* (Greensboro, NC: New Growth Press, 2017), as well as chapter 20 of this book.

5. Again, space prohibits a lengthy discussion of intrusive thoughts or OCD. Research suggests that OCD may be related to a physiological problem in the

brain, though much is still unknown. For more, see Jeffery M. Schwarz, *Brain Lock* (New York: Harper Perennial, 2016).

6. While space does not allow for an extended discussion here, a proper understanding of the role of the brain and body is important. It is said, "neurons that fire together wire together"; pathways in the brain are created and strengthened as behavior and thought patterns are habituated. While not causative, they might increase a woman's temptation toward fear or anxiety simply because that has become her "norm." Old habits are hard to break, and the time needed to change a habit is in many ways proportional to the length of time the habit has been practiced. Much patience is warranted.

Chapter 9

1. For example, see Kristi Kanel, *A Guide to Crisis Intervention*, 6th ed. (Stamford, CT: Cengage Learning, 2018), or Gary Collins, *Christian Counseling: A Comprehensive Guide*, 3rd ed. (Nashville: Thomas Nelson, 2019).

2. Space does not allow for a lengthy discussion of stages of grief; for further information, see Bob Kelleman, *God's Healing for Life's Losses* (Winona Lake, IN: BNH Books, 2010) and Elizabeth Kübler-Ross, *On Death and Dying: What the Dying Have to Teach Doctors, Nurses, Clergy, and Their Own Families* (New York: Scribner Books, 2014).

3. A note here: Oftentimes expressions of grief are culturally directed. What is appropriate in one culture, such as public displays of mourning, may not be in another. The counselor should wisely investigate proper expressions of grief for the culture/subculture of the counselee.

Chapter 10

1. "Eating Disorders," Mental Health Information, National Institute of Mental Health, updated November 2017, https://www.nimh.nih.gov/health /statistics/eating-disorders.shtml.

2. "Eating Disorders," https://www.nimh.nih.gov/health/statistics/eating -disorders.shtml.

3. Ashley A. Hicks White, Keeley J. Pratt, and Casey Cottrill, "The Relationship between Trauma and Weight Status among Adolescents in Eating Disorder Treatment," *Appetite* 129 (October 2018): 62–69.

4. White, Pratt, and Cottrill, "Trauma and Weight Status."

5. Suzanne E. Mazzeo and Cynthia M. Bulik, "Environmental and Genetic Risk Factors for Eating Disorders: What the Clinician Needs to Know," *Child and Adolescent Psychiatric Clinics of North America* 18, no. 1 (January 2009): 67–82, US National Library of Medicine, National Institutes of Health, doi:10.1016/j. chc.2008.07.003.

Chapter 11

1. Though these feelings/attractions come from within us, they are ultimately driven by our sinful hearts. Therefore, we are not without personal responsibility. We choose how to respond to those feelings and attractions, adding another layer of volitional choice that must be taken into account.

2. The approach with an unbeliever struggling with SSA is going to be significantly different. Recall the earlier discussion that those apart from Christ are enslaved to their sin; we do not and cannot expect an unsaved woman to align herself with or submit to biblical teaching. We also cannot expect repentance apart from God's saving grace. When counseling an unbeliever with SSA, this means she needs the power of the Spirit within her to enable change. The gospel is of utmost importance. The same is true when counseling GD.

3. Mark A. Yarhouse, *Understanding Gender Dysphoria: Navigating Transgender Issues in a Changing Culture* (Downers Grove, IL: InterVarsity Press, 2015).

Chapter 12

1. "Suicide and Self-Harm Injury," FastStats, Centers for Disease Control and Prevention National Center for Health Statistics, last reviewed March 1, 2021, https://www.cdc.gov/nchs/fastats/suicide.htm.

2. "Suicide Statistics," Learn the Facts, American Foundation for Suicide Prevention, https://afsp.org/suicide-statistics.

3. Some counselors find it wise to convey to counselees that self-harm behavior that becomes dangerous (i.e., life-threatening) will be treated like suicidality, which includes an action plan as well as the potential for higher levels of care. Though this is a subjective assessment, this approach is generally effective for maintaining safety, ruling out behavior that is attention seeking, and allowing

root issues to surface (as the counselees, when not cutting, can experience and work through in counseling any emotions they faced when they chose not to retreat to the false refuge of cutting). In other words, in addition to increasing safety, using safety contracts for self-harm also helps to maintain focus on making progress in counseling.

Chapter 13

1. See, for example, B. Y. Park, G. Wilson, and A. P. Doan, "Is Internet Pornography Causing Sexual Dysfunctions? A Review with Clinical Reports," *Behavioral Sciences* 6, no. 3 (September 2016): 17.

2. Edward T. Welch, *Addictions: A Banquet in the Grave: Finding Hope in the Power of the Gospel* (Phillipsburg, NJ: P&R, 2001), 35, quoted in Robert D. Jones, Kristin L. Kellen, and Rob Green, *The Gospel for Disordered Lives: An Introduction to Christ-Centered Biblical Counseling* (Nashville: B&H, 2021), 339. I added the first clause, "Arising from our alienation from the Living God," from Welch's earlier book, cowritten with Gary Shogren, *Running in Circles: How to Find Freedom from Addictive Behavior* (Grand Rapids: Baker, 1995), 27.

3. See Jones, Kellen, and Green, *Gospel for Disordered Lives*, chap. 28.

4. While I would not give a blanket approval to every aspect of these organizations, they are tremendously helpful for providing accountability and community. Such things are essential in fighting addiction.

5. Some may legitimately question her role if she has withheld sexual relations or failed to show sexual interest in her husband. While she is responsible for loving her husband well in accordance with biblical teaching, he chose his response. Her lack of intimacy or pursuit of him is not an excuse. The counselor can carefully and wisely explore ways for her to lessen her temptation to assume responsibility, but the blame for his choice to use pornography should not be placed on her.

6. See Ken Sande, *The Peacemaker: A Biblical Guide to Resolving Personal Conflict* (Ada, MI: Baker Books, 2004).

7. Accountability partners are not primarily to provide a deterrent or consequences, but a safe space to disclose troubles and find help as she pursues godliness.

Chapter 14

1. United States Census Bureau, "Unmarried and Single Americans Week: Sept. 17–23, 2017," Facts for Features, news release no. CB17-TPS.62, August 14, 2017, https://www.census.gov/newsroom/facts-for-features/2017/single -americans-week.html.

2. These verses are not a prescription for believers to never marry. Paul went on to address this later, but here Paul was simply noting the preference toward singleness because of the advantages it brings (see more below).

3. The number of young women struggling with pornography is continuing to increase. For more on this topic, see chapter 13.

Chapter 15

1. While one could rightly argue that not all abuse is traumatic, the reality in counseling is a woman is not likely to seek counsel for nontraumatic abuse. Therefore, when "abuse" is used in this chapter, it is assumed the abuse is traumatic and significantly impacting the woman's life.

2. H. Norman Wright, *The Complete Guide to Crisis and Trauma Counseling: What to Do and Say When It Matters Most!*, rev. ed. (Minneapolis: Bethany House, 2011), 189.

3. It is incumbent upon any person who learns of an instance of child abuse to 1) determine the laws for their state, and 2) report accordingly. In many states, reporting is required for any *reasonable suspicion* of child abuse, even if it cannot be fully substantiated by the reporting party.

4. For consistency within this chapter and given that this is a text about counseling women, an abuser will be referred to as "he." This is not to say that a woman cannot be an abuser, but statistically men are more likely to abuse another person. Where "he" is written, it may be interpreted as "he or she."

5. This is not to alleviate personal responsibility. Rather, it demonstrates that the effects of trauma are more pervasive than we have historically believed. Treatment, then, must address the whole person rather than simply one's thought patterns or behavior.

6. Judith Lewis Herman, *Trauma and Recovery: The Aftermath of Violence— from Domestic Abuse to Political Terror* (New York: Basic Books, 1997; epilogue 2015), 96.

7. Bessel A. van der Kolk, *The Body Keeps the Score: Brain, Mind, and Body in the Healing of Trauma* (New York: Penguin Books, 2014), 21.

8. The use of the term "abnormal" here does not preclude a tendency toward sin. We can sin in our response to a traumatic event. Rather, calling a response "normal" indicates that it is common considering the situation.

9. Herman, *Trauma and Recovery*, 35.

10. Another important component of the counselor dealing with her own history of trauma, if present, is that the counselee will mirror the counselor's disposition, often without even recognizing it. For instance, if the counselor is anxious and fearful, the counselee's brain will pick up on those feelings and mirror them, even if not done consciously. Conversely, if the counselor is calm, even during tough conversations, the counselee is much more apt to mirror that calmness and sense that she is safe.

11. It may be useful for the counselor to educate herself on approaches like Narrative Exposure Therapy or other approaches to treating trauma. While I do not necessarily give a blanket recommendation for these approaches, many have high rates of effectiveness and aspects of each may be appropriate to incorporate into Christian counseling practice. Note, however, that some trauma approaches, like EMDR, are regulated in many states, so a referral would be required if the counselor has not been trained and certified.

Chapter 16

1. For the purposes of this chapter, we will assume that the husband is the perpetrator and the wife is the victim of the domestic violence and/or abuse. While a wife may certainly be an abuser, more often in counseling we will encounter women who are the victims. The principles below, however, can be applicable to either partner.

2. "Statistics," National Coalition Against Domestic Violence, *Statistics*, https://www.ncadv.org/statistics.

3. "Power and Control: Break Free from Abuse," National Domestic Violence Hotline, https://www.thehotline.org/is-this-abuse/abuse-defined/power-and-control-wheel-updated/.

4. "Behavioral Checklist," https://mensantiviolencecouncil.files.wordpress.com/2010/08/behavioral-checklist.pdf

5. Justin Holcomb and Lindsay Holcomb, *Is It My Fault? Hope and Healing for Those Suffering Domestic Violence* (Chicago, IL: Moody, 2014), 69.

6. Leslie Vernick, "What Does the Bible Say about Destructive and Abusive Relationships?," https://leslievernick.com/wp-content/uploads/newsletters/2018-10-9-What-Does-the-Bible-Say-About-Destructive-and-Abusive-Relationships.html.

7. This does not necessarily mean legal separation, but physical separation from one another. It is also sometimes wise to include legal counsel as it relates to separation agreements, protective orders, or organizations that can support her through this process.

Chapter 17

1. It is unwise for a counselor to advise divorce, but we must acknowledge that the counselee is autonomous (she can make her own choices). The Scriptures are clear about God's intentions for marriage (more to come below), but counselors serve in an advisory capacity, not an authoritative one. We cannot force her one way or the other.

2. David and Bathsheba, the adulterous woman in John 4, Judah with the Canaanite woman.

3. Some translations, like the ESV, use the word "whoredom." Essentially Hosea was to take a woman with a history of sexual immorality.

4. Most of these emotions/responses relate to the woman as the offended party.

Chapter 18

1. Carla Dugas and Valori H. Slane, "Miscarriage," *StatPearls*, last update January 29, 2021, https://www.ncbi.nlm.nih.gov/books/NBK532992/; "Infertility FAQs," Reproductive Health, Centers for Disease Control and Prevention website, accessed May 24, 2021, https://www.cdc.gov/reproductivehealth/infertility/index.htm#:~:text=Also%2C%20about%2012%25%20of%20women,women%20can%20contribute%20to%20infertility.

2. See passages like Luke 14:26 and Matt 19:29.

3. For more about this topic, see Jane Tooher, "Spiritual Motherhood," *Ministry, Leadership, and Training*, The Gospel Coalition Australia Edition, December 5, 2018, https://au.thegospelcoalition.org/article/spiritual-motherhood/.

Chapter 19

1. This chapter speaks broadly to parents, as ideally counseling involves both parents, not just mothers.

Chapter 20

1. James Dahlhamer et al., "Prevalence of Chronic Pain and High-Impact Chronic Pain among Adults—United States, 2016," *Morbidity and Mortality Weekly Report* (*MMWR*) 67 (September 14, 2018): 1001–6, Centers for Disease Control and Prevention, https://www.cdc.gov/mmwr/volumes/67/wr/mm6736a2.htm.

2. Michael Emlet, *Descriptions and Prescriptions* (Greensboro, NC: New Growth Press, 2017), 42.

3. Edward T. Welch, *Blame It on the Brain: Distinguishing Chemical Imbalances, Brain Disorders, and Disobedience* (Phillipsburg, NJ: P&R, 1998), 106.

4. Elyse Fitzpatrick and Laura Hendrickson, *Will Medicine Stop the Pain?: Finding God's Healing for Depression, Anxiety, and Other Troubling Emotions* (Chicago: Moody, 2006), 54–55.

5. Michael Emlet, "The Doctor Is In: Counseling and Physiology Class: Post 4" (blog post), Christian Counseling and Educational Foundation (CCEF), October 29, 2009, www.ccef.org/resources/blog/doctor-part-4.

6. Michael Emlet, "Listening to Prozac . . . and to the Scriptures," *Journal of Biblical Counseling* 26, no. 2 (2012): 17.

7. "And the Spirit of the Lord shall rest upon him, the Spirit of wisdom and understanding, the Spirit of counsel and might, the Spirit of knowledge and the fear of the Lord" (Isa 11:2 ESV).

Conclusion

1. This is not to say that these guidelines are directly applicable (i.e., prescriptive) for counseling outside of the church, or even to counseling in general, but they are helpful for us to consider as general principles.

2. See chapter 4 for more on this topic.

Scripture Index

Genesis

1 *14, 16, 123, 129*
1–2 *xiv, 3*
1:2 *11*
1–3 *6*
1:4 *10*
1:12 *10*
1:21 *10*
1:25 *10*
1:26 *4, 6*
1:26–27 *6, 165*
1:26–31 *4*
1:27 *7, 153*
1:28 *6–9*
1:29 *111*
1:31 *10*
2 *10–11, 14, 16*
2:7 *4, 7, 10–11*
2:15 *6, 12, 177*
2:15–17 *7*
2:16–17 *16*
2:18 *8, 12, 164, 166*
2:18–23 *7, 11*

2:19 *6*
2:20 *4, 8, 11*
2:23–24 *12*
2:23–25 *4*
2:24 *185, 197*
2:25 *7, 13, 185*
3 *xiv, 16–18*
3:1 *16*
3:2 *16*
3:4–5 *16*
3:6 *7, 16*
3:7 *17*
3:7–8 *13*
3:8 *7*
3:8–13 *17*
3:15 *17*
3:16 *234*
3:17 *235*
3:21 *17*
4:1–2 *7*
6:5–6 *100, 189*
9:3 *111*
9:6 *7, 37*

265